Enemies in the Plaza

THE MIDDLE AGES SERIES

Ruth Mazo Karras, Series Editor
Edward Peters, Founding Editor

A complete list of books in the series
is available from the publisher.

Enemies in the Plaza

Urban Spectacle and the End
of Spanish Frontier Culture,
1460–1492

Thomas Devaney

PENN

UNIVERSITY OF PENNSYLVANIA PRESS

PHILADELPHIA

Published by
University of Pennsylvania Press
Philadelphia, Pennsylvania 19104-4112
www.upenn.edu/pennpress

Printed in the United States of America on acid-free paper
1 3 5 7 9 10 8 6 4 2

Library of Congress Cataloging-in-Publication Data
ISBN 978-0-8122-4713-8

For Elizabeth, Ella, Julia, and Eoin

CONTENTS

List of Abbreviations   ix

Introduction   1

PART I

1. The Anatomy of a Spectacle: Sponsors, Critics, and Onlookers   27

2. The Meanings of Civic Space   52

PART II

3. Knights, Magi, and Muslims: Miguel Lucas de Iranzo and the People of Jaén   81

4. A "Chance Act": Córdoba in 1473   107

5. Murcia and the Body of Christ Triumphant   137

Conclusion   168

Notes   177
Glossary of Spanish Terms   213
Bibliography   215
Index   237
Acknowledgments   245

ABBREVIATIONS

AC	*Libros de Actas Capitulares*
ACC	Archivo de la Catedral de Córdoba
ACM	Archivo Catedralicio de Murcia
AMC	Archivo Municipal de Córdoba
AMJ	Archivo Municipal de Jaén
AMM	Archivo Municipal de Murcia
APC	Archivo Histórico Provincial de Córdoba
BAE	Biblioteca de Autores Españoles
BIEG	*Boletín del Instituto de Estudios Giennenses*
CCE	Colección de Crónicas Españolas
CHE	*Cuadernos de historia de España*
CR	Cartas reales
CSM	Alfonso X el Sabio, *Cantigas de Santa María*, ed. Walter Mettmann, 3 vols.
HID	*Historia. Instituciones. Documentos.*
MCV	*Mélanges de la Casa de Velásquez*
MHJ	*Medieval History Journal*
MMM	*Miscelánea medieval murciana*
Partidas	*Las Siete Partidas*, ed. Robert I. Burns, trans. Samuel Parsons Scott, 5 vols.
PCG	*Primera crónica general de España*, ed. Ramón Menéndez Pidal, 2 vols.

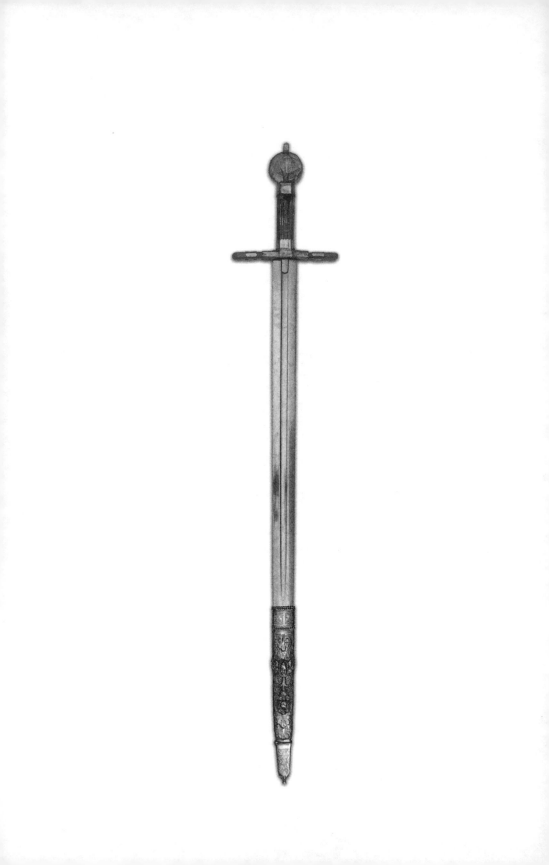

Introduction

Magical swords can be useful things. While preparing an invasion of Muslim-ruled Granada in 1407, the Castilian prince and regent Fernando "de Antequera" made his headquarters in the city of Seville. During his stay, he visited the cathedral of Santa María la Mayor and gazed on the funeral effigy of King Fernando III, a hero of the "reconquest" who had captured the city as well as much of the rest of Castilian Andalucía from the Muslims in the thirteenth century. A fourteenth-century description of this effigy noted that "in the right hand is a sword, said to be of great virtue, with which [Fernando III] conquered Seville. . . . And whoever desires protection from evil, let him place a kiss on the sword and he will be sheltered thereafter."[1] It was perhaps with this in mind that the later Fernando took the sword from the effigy's hand in a solemn ceremony viewed by many of his retainers. After private prayer before an image of the Virgin Mary, Fernando bore the sword in a mounted procession through Seville before taking it with him into battle. Over the next few years, he "borrowed" the sword several more times. Only after his campaigns culminated in the conquest of Antequera in 1410 did he finally return the sword to the cathedral once and for all.

According to the contemporary chronicler Fernán Pérez de Guzmán, none of this was Fernando's idea. Seville's *concejo*, or municipal council, had originally offered him the sword, and he decided to parade it about the city only after one of his nobles convinced him to do so.[2] Pérez de Guzmán's reasons for telling the story in this way are straightforward enough: he hoped to portray Fernando not as a grandstander who went about appropriating sacred weapons but as a pious man whose merit was recognized by others. It seems unlikely, however, that Fernando needed any prompting. He was

Opposite: FIGURE 1. Sword of Fernando III. Courtesy of the Excmo. Cabildo de la Catedral de Sevilla.

aware of the symbolic import of the sword and knew full well that taking it would encourage his soldiers and embellish his reputation.

To an extent, Fernando's audience consisted of the "knights, counts, and rich men" who joined him in the cathedral and on the procession.[3] They, like the regent, had been raised and educated in a chivalric culture that lionized fallen heroes; to truly excel and win fame, a knight must prove himself worthy of the past and of his lineage.[4] As warrior, king, and saint, Fernando III was a particularly powerful exemplar. His significance for fifteenth-century Castilian knights is perhaps best expressed in a chronicle written a few decades later and dedicated to another proponent of holy war, Rodrigo Ponce de León:

> Oh, what relief it would be to be counted among the most holy and illustrious kings of glorious memory and the very noble and virtuous knights, who shine before the order of God, having defended and held up the holy Catholic faith against the Muslims and infidels, enemies of the faith of Jesus Christ! Just as the magnificent king don Fernando, who took Seville on the day of San Clemente. On the evening before that feast day, Our Lady the Virgin Mary appeared to him and placed the keys to the city in his hand and took him inside [the walls of Seville]. And that holy king, having there knelt before her image with devoted prayers, forgot his sword upon his departure. The next morning, the Muslim king sent it to him, asking that he spare their lives by the mercy of Her Highness, because Her Highness had vowed to put them all to the sword.[5]

For Ponce de León, as for Fernando and his followers, the sword of the saintly king was more than a protective object; it encapsulated their personal and collective aspirations. By publicly but reverently co-opting this history, Fernando inspired his knights in a manner that engaged deeply held beliefs about themselves and their society. There is no reason to assume that his motives were cynical. Fernando's devotion to the Virgin Mary was lifelong and his crusading credentials were already established. A few years earlier, for instance, he had founded the chivalric Order of the Jar and the Griffin, dedicated to Mary's purity and the ultimate defeat of Granada.[6]

His own knights were not Fernando's only audience, however, and much of the population of Seville had little interest in chivalrous ambitions or the swords of dead kings. His plans for a campaign against Granada had earned a lukewarm response from the local nobility and populace. Despite rhetoric about unending hostilities between Christians and Muslims, war with Granada was hardly constant, and Seville's residents made effective use of a nearly uninterrupted series of truces from 1350 to 1450 to establish lucrative trading partnerships with their putative religious enemies across the border. The proximity to Granada that permitted this commerce, however, also meant that any renewal of fighting put the city and its environs in danger. Fernando's campaign was a response to a series of raids in central Andalucía, especially near Jaén and Baeza. Seville was not threatened, but that could change if its role as base for the regent's army made the city a target for Granadan reprisals. As happened often on the frontier, therefore, many people were disinclined to take decisive action. *Sevillanos* did not openly object to Fernando's plans. Many sincerely supported his plan for an invasion of Granada, in theory at least. But concerns about the practical and near-term implications of his ambitions meant that they did not actively or eagerly support him.

By taking up the sword, Fernando claimed its protective qualities and declared that he enjoyed the special attentions of the Virgin. By bearing it in procession through Seville, he extended that protection to encompass all those who lived there, thus relieving their anxiety about potential Granadan retaliation. Fernando's decision to take up the sword thus was a response to practical political concerns as much as anything, one meant to act in concert with other efforts to win over the people of Seville, such as the prominent role Fernando accorded to the banners of Seville and Saint Isidore in the vanguard of his army. Fernando's approach was not particularly innovative—rulers had long used pageantry and symbolic objects to their benefit and his great-grandfather Alfonso XI had employed Fernando III's memory in 1327—but it was fruitful.[7] He managed to bring a sustained campaign against Granada to a successful conclusion, a feat that had not been achieved for more than a century and would not be again until the 1480s. To do so, he had needed to appeal simultaneously to multiple constituencies. His claiming of Fernando III's sword, although not the sole reason for his victory, indicates his sensitivity to the Sevillan perspective and an understanding of the power of symbols.

* * *

Fernando's campaign illustrates several key aspects of politics in late medieval Castile. Leaders who hoped to wage war against Granada had to win a broad base of support. It was especially vital for them to ensure that noncombatants living near the frontier supported these military endeavors. Frontier dwellers bore the majority of the costs of holy war as well as the risks of retaliation. Frontier attitudes regarding putative religious enemies, moreover, were often more complex than those held by people who had little direct or regular contact with members of other religious groups. To effectively wage war against Muslims, elites had to adjust their public personae and messages in order to fit local sentiments. This was not only a question of Christian ideas about Islam; rather, the borderlands were marked by often contradictory sentiments about a range of religious communities, including Christians, Muslims, Jews, and recent converts. Ultimately, many Christians in Castile disagreed on the fundamental nature of their society: was it or should it be an exclusively Christian community? Or should non-Christians and converts play full and equal roles in a hybrid society? Such questions, combined with a constant sense of physical insecurity, caused a great deal of anxiety, one result of which was a turn to extreme and seemingly contradictory behaviors. These included unrestrained violence toward non-Christians as well as rejections of fixed religious identities; conversions to Islam, to give one example, were numerous. Such responses were often incomprehensible to those who lived away from the frontier, in places where they were free to consider issues of religion and identity in absolute terms and without the troubling presence of non-Christians.

In 1391, a few years before Fernando's sojourn in Seville, for instance, the city was the epicenter of a series of brutal assaults that decimated one of the most populous Jewish communities in Iberia. Several decades later, in 1449, plague broke out in Seville and local church authorities responded with penitential processions. Soon thereafter, or perhaps at the same time, Seville's Jews conducted their own procession, which apparently imitated a number of features of the Christian version. In place of the Bible, however, they bore the Torah aloft as they walked. The Jews did this with the permission of García Enriquez Osorio, archbishop of Seville, and their action occasioned little comment among the people and clergy of Seville. A notable exception was Antonio Ferrari, a cathedral canon, who remonstrated violently that Jews should not be allowed to emulate Christian practice and was excommunicated as a troublemaker. When he sought reinstatement from Rome, he was imprisoned. Word of these events soon reached the ear of Pope Nicholas V, who ordered an investigation into Ferrari's allegations of persecution. The pope contended that the canon had been correct to oppose the Jewish procession, presenting it as an attack on Christianity because it insinuated that God would prefer the pleas of Jews over those of Christians. Ferrari had attempted to prevent the Jews from acting "as if God did not hear the prayers of the faithful" and so should be completely indemnified, while those who excommunicated and imprisoned him should be punished for abuse of their powers.[8]

But convergences in religious practice, as Sevillan church authorities well knew, had long been common among Christians, Muslims, and Jews in Andalucía.[9] Their tolerance in this and several other cases stands in stark contrast to the brutality of 1391 and the more institutionalized persecution Seville's Jews would face later in the century. In order to further their own agendas or simply to keep order, leaders in frontier cities found it necessary to constantly address questions of religious conflict and coexistence. Public spectacle was one of their most effective tools, for spectacles are, by their nature, ambiguous. They can mean, to a degree, whatever a viewer wants them to mean. For this same reason, however, they can be subversive. Rulers cannot exert full control over their interpretation. Fernando's task was easy in one sense: as a sojourner on the frontier, he could focus on the short term and the attainment of clear, limited goals. Those who remained had to find ways to negotiate the physical insecurity and contradictory attitudes that conditioned frontier life.

Don Miguel Lucas de Iranzo was a prominent nobleman exiled from the royal court in the 1460s. Arriving in the frontier bastion of Jaén, he sought—like Fernando—to lead glorious campaigns into Granada. To do so, he too had to inspire a local population that was just as happy to trade with the Muslims as fight them. In response, Miguel Lucas spent the next decade conducting a dazzling and seemingly endless succession of elaborate tournaments, festivals, processions, and banquets. Oftentimes, these displays seem contradictory as the aspiring holy warrior dressed in Morisco attire, praised Islamic culture, or treated the issue of religious war in a jocular manner at odds with his serious purposes. Modern scholars have interpreted these events in any number of ways: as a cynical appropriation of popular motifs meant to solidify his rule, as "frontier fantasy" or "confirmatory magic," as military training exercises. In all these instances, historians have assumed that Miguel Lucas controlled the meaning of his spectacles, that he was able to impose a "frontier ideology" on the people.[10]

In fact, as we shall see, both the content and the interpretation of Miguel Lucas's spectacles were conditioned by the expectations of an audience that depended on predictable, if not wholly peaceable, relations with Granada.

Confronted with the ambivalence that his new subjects evinced toward their Muslim neighbors, he sought to reassure them that he would not seek an unrestrained war against Granada that might threaten their livelihoods and expel their trading partners. In effect, Miguel Lucas aimed to lower the stakes of holy war by suggesting that victory over Islam required the conversion of Muslims but not the destruction of Granadan culture and society. Through pageantry, therefore, Miguel Lucas attempted not to indoctrinate the people but to make his aggressive policies broadly palatable.

Only a few decades later, however, the conditions that required such a response had faded. There was a general hardening of attitudes toward religious minorities as influential groups in Castile sought to define their society as exclusively and ardently Christian. This transition can be seen through royal policies such as the Edict of Expulsion or the establishment of the Inquisition. But it is especially visible in civic pageants of the 1470s and 1480s that now presented Muslims, Jews, and recent converts either as imminent threats to society who must be neutralized or as unwelcome guests, irrelevant but still the focus of much attention. Like those of Miguel Lucas, these later performances have been described in dismissive or uncertain terms by both contemporary observers and modern scholars. And so a Marian procession that incited violence against converts in Córdoba was but a "chance act" and the particular roles accorded to Jews and Muslims in Murcia's presentation of Corpus Christi is a "puzzling mix of ecumenism and bigotry."[11]

Here again, close attention to the frontier and urban contexts of public performances can explain both their purpose and their significance. Spectacles reflected shifts in public sentiments toward religious minorities; in doing so, they accelerated the process. Like Fernando de Antequera and Miguel Lucas, most noble sponsors of spectacles had clear goals in mind. But, although they had a great deal of influence over the interpretation of performances, spectators did not mindlessly follow their lead. Indeed, the opposite seems to have been true. Elites constantly tried to "catch up" to what they perceived as popular sentiment. The perception of a growing popular intolerance for outsiders within "Christian" society encouraged rulers to craft performances that emphasized the foreignness of Muslims, Jews, and recent converts. The Christian populace, assured by these spectacles that religious minorities were no longer under the protection of the nobility, were then emboldened to act against them. The result was a semantic narrowing, as urban pageants that had previously been used to express a range of attitudes toward Jews, Muslims, and converts were now limited in practice to the rejection of those groups. By confirming and validating popular opinion, this shift fostered open intolerance across the social spectrum.

Immediate physical contexts played a significant role in this process. Sponsors understood that environments influenced how performances were experienced and received and made use of the connotations associated with particular urban locations in order to best present their own messages. These locations, of course, meant different things to different people, and so the connections between performance and context permitted multiple readings of the same display. Many spectacles were, therefore, deliberate efforts to transform those meanings by creating new cognitive or emotional connotations, to endow a prominent location with a significance understood by all and controlled by elites. Such moments are of particular interest in that they reveal contemporary understandings of how public *memoria* and social change were related.

Pageantry had long served as a means of negotiating and articulating the boundaries between religious communities. It was due to this tradition that Castilian elites, during a period in which traditional interfaith relations seemed to be less relevant, employed spectacle as a means of altering them. It also meant that these elites encountered receptive audiences familiar with the ability of performance to present social messages. By consistently turning to the theme of interfaith relations, they highlighted the importance of those relations and helped to transform the ambivalent attitudes about others that had characterized the borderlands. In the period with which this book is concerned, the result was an increasingly negative depiction of religious minorities. By the early 1490s, such festivities proclaimed a vision of a Castile that was triumphant and unabashedly Christian, a society in which Jews, Muslims, and recent converts might have a place, but only a tenuous one.

* * *

A great deal has been written about the so-called breakdown in religious tolerance in fifteenth-century Iberia. This is often presented as the transition from a golden age of *convivencia*, or peaceful coexistence, that was especially prominent in Muslim-ruled al-Andalus but also held, to varying degrees, through the initial period of Christian dominance from the thirteenth to mid-fifteenth centuries. The traditional account of what happened next has often been called the "Black Legend."[12] It depicts late medieval and early modern Spain as defined by a narrow religious bigotry in which the Inquisition, Edict of Expulsion, and conquistadors loom large. The Black Legend has now been thoroughly refuted by any number of scholars. In recent years, perhaps the most influential work has been that of David Nirenberg, who argues that medieval religious violence was not perpetrated by irrational masses who blindly adopted inherited ideologies and prejudices but by self-aware groups that carefully adapted discourses about others to serve a host of diverse needs.[13] In showing how religious violence could shape interfaith relations in often-constructive ways, moreover, Nirenberg suggests that we need to leave behind strict dichotomies like "tolerance" and "intolerance" when examining the medieval past. Other scholars, including Mark Meyerson, Barbara Fuchs, and Stuart Schwartz, have undermined the idea that conditions in the fifteenth and sixteenth centuries were wholly negative for members of religious minority groups.[14] In essence, the new view is that there was no dramatic break, that conditions in the earlier period were not as idyllic as had been imagined and they were not so dire in later centuries.

In revising what was indeed a flawed view of Spain's past, however, these authors may have gone too far in the other direction. They do not deny the significance of the Inquisition, the conquest of Granada, the expulsion of Jews and later Muslims from Iberia, or, in the New World, the harsh treatment of Native Americans. But they do contend that these innovations fail to reflect a broad social consensus about the place of non-Christians in Spanish society. Instead they cast them as imperfectly accepted policies whose impetus came from above. To some degree this is accurate. If there was a broad shift from a cultural paradigm of *convivencia* to one of a homogeneous Christian society, its progress was slow and uneven. Undoubtedly, many embraced the new emphasis on conformity and exclusion. It is equally certain, however, that others did not entirely or quickly reject their former neighbors, business partners, and friends. Ultimately, the crown cast out the Jews and later the Muslims, negating the potentially disruptive influence of religious minorities without the need to rely on the divided minds of its subjects.

During the period examined in this book, however, such sweeping and absolute solutions were not an option. The reigns of Juan II (1405–1454) and Enrique IV (1454–1474) were characterized by weak royal authority and unprecedented influence and power for the most prominent of the nobility. In frontier regions, local magnates such as Miguel Lucas in Jaén or Pedro Fajardo in Murcia acted with almost full autonomy, employing spectacles to build local consensus. Factional struggles among the nobility raised the stakes of these endeavors, leading to a golden age of sorts for public pageantry. After a decade-long period of civil war that led to Enrique's deposition, the Catholic Monarchs, Isabel I and Fernando II, had to deal with lingering challenges to their authority even while embroiled in wars with Portugal and then Granada. This meant that they required broad public support for their policies, especially those policies that threatened to destroy traditional modes of life on the frontier. Their efforts at centralization drastically reduced the independence of individual nobles but could not establish complete royal control. Municipal councils retained a good bit of power but had to wield it under the eyes of representatives of the central government. They too used spectacles to enhance their positions. Politics, thus, were always local but never divorced from broader trends.

By viewing the transition from late medieval to early modern Castilian understandings of Christian society through the twin lenses of frontier and urban spectacle, this book shows how the conditions that prevailed in cities close to the Granadan border fostered a dissonant outlook toward religious minorities, which I describe as an "amiable enmity." The resulting social anxieties left the populace vulnerable to attempts by elites to either deflect or exacerbate existing confessional tensions through public spectacle. Political transformation in the last decades of the fifteenth century—including the civil wars of Enrique's reign, the final war with Granada, and Fernando and Isabel's efforts to reestablish royal authority—brought frontier traditions and accommodations into dialogue with the rest of the realm and incited a broader reaction against religious minorities. But shifts in attitudes toward religious minorities were neither "top-down" nor "bottom-up." Instead I show how they evolved through public spectacles whose content reflected the interplay of noble and common perspectives about Muslims, Jews, and converts.

*   *   *

The concept of "frontier," so central to this book, deserves some explanation. For many modern Americans, the term conjures a variety of images. We speak of the frontiers of science and medicine, of new or unexpected frontiers in the farthest reaches of the globe, of space as the "final frontier." The word itself implies action: frontiers are to be crossed, conquered, pushed back, and made civilized. To be on the frontier is to be forward thinking, a pioneer at the forefront of a great and progressive endeavor; by implication, the alternative is stagnation, decline, complacency. These frontiers of our popular imagination are not so much physical locations as they are processes by which the unknown is made known and wilderness tamed, an understanding that owes much to the work of Frederick Jackson Turner and his influential 1893 paper "The Significance of the Frontier in American History."[15] Turner never offered a precise definition of "frontier," which he claimed was an "elastic" term. Rather, as the "outer edge of the wave—the meeting point between savagery and civilization," it was a set of conditions that challenged settlers, forcing them to leave behind European norms and establish a distinctly American way of life.

For medieval Castilians, frontier, or *frontera*, meant something quite different. There was never an encounter between civilization and wilderness. Rather, frontiers were arenas for interaction, both peaceful and hostile, between different cultures. Contact between Christianity and Islam in Iberia dates to at least 711, when Muslim armies from North Africa crossed the Strait of Gibraltar and swiftly conquered much of the peninsula. A Christian enclave survived in the northwest, however, forming the nucleus of what would become the kingdom of Asturias. Although there was no grand strategy of "reconquest" at this time, Muslim power in that region was weak and the Christians expanded slowly and unevenly for the next several centuries as Asturias was succeeded by the kingdoms of Castile-León, Navarre, and Aragón across northern Iberia.[16] Internal divisions and civil war, meanwhile, led to the breakup of the Caliphate of Córdoba and establishment of a number of small city-states or *taifa* kingdoms. Despite a number of setbacks, Christian rulers conquered nearly all these states between the eleventh and thirteenth centuries.

This process seemed to culminate in 1238, when Fernando III of Castile (the original owner of the famous sword) signed a treaty that made the Emirate of Granada, the last independent Muslim state, into a vassal. Fernando likely envisioned that the Christian reconquest of Iberia would soon be complete. In the preceding decades, after all, the Christians had won great victories and gained vast swaths of territory. The speedy dissolution of Granada was not to be, however. It instead remained independent for another 250 years and, as Map 1 shows, Christians coming to settle the newly conquered regions around Jaén, Córdoba, Murcia, and Seville found themselves in close proximity to Muslims, often trading together and sharing pastureland even while intermittent frontier warfare continued.

From the beginning, boundaries between the various Christian and Muslim states were porous; there were never effective barriers to contact. Even clearly delineated borderlines were vanishingly rare and it would be more

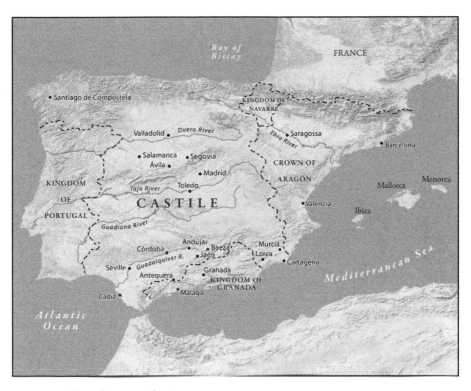

MAP 1. Fifteenth-century Iberia.

accurate to speak of zones in which authorities held varying degrees of control. People dwelling near the Granadan frontier—on both sides—encountered challenges and opportunities that differed markedly from those in more central regions. They lived in constant fear of physical attack and developed protective strategies ranging from militia forces to extensive fortification to frontier "institutions" meant to curtail private violence and mitigate the effects of general hostilities.[17] They were subject to influences from both their home culture and that of their neighbors. The dual dynamics of war and cultural exchange meant that the frontier was a place apart and was seen as such by contemporaries.

Although his arguments have been alternately adopted, adapted, and debunked in the century since they were first published, Turner's central contention—that frontiers *matter*—has remained tenaciously relevant. Historians have devoted much effort to understanding both the nature and the

significance of frontier communities, seeing them both as windows into myriad aspects of past societies and as engines of historical change. The Granadan
frontier has been a particularly popular subject for inquiry. It has been seen,
at one time or another, as a region of free land, an arena for the expansion of
Latin Christendom, a militarized border zone, or a site for cultural contact
and exchange.[18]

Early generations of historians hewed closely to Turner's original argument, contending that the freedoms and risks of the Granadan frontier
spurred the development of a particular set of Iberian cultural values quite
different from those of the rest of western Europe, even romanticizing it as a
"miniature wild west."[19] Later medievalists, while retaining an emphasis on
frontier-driven cultural change, linked the transformation to cultural contact
and exchange, noting the ways in which populations on either side of the
frontier intermingled to the point where they bore more similarities with
each other than their nominal home cultures. Acculturation, however, was
not an all-or-nothing proposition that led either to cultural immersion or
strictly controlled interactions. People living in contact with other societies
were able to adapt, borrow, or reject particular aspects of those societies as
they saw fit, leading to highly localized modes of cultural exchange.[20] More
recent scholarship has focused on the frontier as a "borderland," drawing on
theoretical work such as that of Homi Bhabha, who defines borderlands as a
"third space," or realm of negotiation, translation, and remaking. The third
space, for Bhabha, is not simply an amalgam of its two constituent cultural
groups but is instead a true hybrid, a new society that has the potential for
fresh understandings of each of its predecessors. From this perspective, frontiers were arenas for mostly friendly competition, with acculturation tri-
umphing over conflict.[21]

But the Granadan frontier does not fit easily into any broad definition.
It was a region that provided freedoms not readily available elsewhere, but
which exacted a heavy price in terms of taxes and military service. It was the
site of Christian settlement. But newcomers arrived in a land of long-standing
patterns of habitation into which they had to fit, at least initially. It was a
fortified boundary between two civilizations, but a boundary that was neither
defined nor linear. Nor, despite its many fortifications, was it closed; the
movement of people and ideas never ceased and even the religious identities
that defined it were not fixed. It was indeed a cultural melting pot, but one
over which religious intolerance proved ultimately dominant.

In this book, I understand the Granadan frontier as a borderland region in which multiple religious, linguistic, and cultural groups maintained close contacts.[22] It was not, however, simply a composite society. It was defined by insecurities, which stemmed both from the constant threat of physical attack and an awareness that there was a significant gap between ideologies of Christian dominance and the reality of acculturation. These anxieties effectively prevented the creation of what Bhabha calls a third space. A long-standing pattern of semibelligerency in which leaders had been unwilling to take decisive action regarding Granada, for either peace or war, created an equilibrium in which Muslims, Christians, and Jews could interact daily with each other but without true cultural hybridity. Many Christians living on the medieval frontier were caught between a sincere ideology of holy war against Islam and Christian dominance but also held an equally sincere respect and understanding not only for individual Muslims but also for many aspects of Islamic culture. This esteem went far beyond what Américo Castro called the "chance symbiosis of beliefs" and resulted in a conflicted attitude that we may best describe as an "amiable enmity."[23]

How could people reconcile ideas as contradictory as holy war and peaceful cooperation? Peter Linehan has offered one solution, pointing out that an either/or understanding of the frontier supposes a social homogeneity that we would not expect in our own times. As he puts it, "In *theory*, the very idea of frontier *convivencia* is inconceivable. Crusade and co-existence comprise a confessional oxymoron if ever there was one. But in *fact* people aren't like that."[24] Linehan goes on to suggest that this contradiction is unworthy of further discussion, as it was no more than a predictable outcome of human nature. But how did people cope with these all-too-human inconsistencies? For if, as the evidence suggests, there is no reason to suspect that medieval Castilians were unaware of the incongruities that lay at the core of their understanding of the world, the resulting tensions and general mood of uncertainty they created hold the key to understanding the medieval Granadan frontier.

Many of the songs and poems in the *Cantigas de Santa María*, a thirteenth-century collection gathered by or at the direction of Alfonso X, directly engaged such issues. *Cantiga* 185, for instance, described the great friendship between the Christian *alcaide*, or garrison commander, of Chincoya, a fortress near Jaén, and his Muslim counterpart in Bélmez.[25] The Muslim capitalized on their association by enticing his friend to leave the castle's safety. The ruse worked and he seized the hapless Christian, forcing him to reveal Chincoya's weaknesses. With this information in hand, a Muslim army soon attacked the castle. Fearing for their lives, Chincoya's defenders "took the statue of the Mother of the Savior which was in the chapel and put it . . . on the battlements, saying, 'If you are the Mother of God, defend this castle and us, who are your servants, and protect your chapel so that the infidel Moors will not capture it and burn your statue.' They left it there, saying: 'We shall see what you will do.'"[26]

The Muslims at once retreated, and three attackers who had managed to enter Chincoya were tossed from the walls, leading the king of Granada to confess that "I would consider myself foolish to go against Mary, who defends Her own."[27] This was no metaphorical protection; the illumination that accompanied this *cantiga* depicts Mary's image as physically mounted atop the castle and fitting neatly into the scheme of the battlements, almost as it were a natural extension of the stone walls.

The political content of this story is quite explicit. The whole sorry situation could have easily been avoided if only the *alcaide* of Chincoya had realized that true peace and friendship with Muslims was not possible, that the enemy saw such overtures merely as flaws to be exploited. As the *alcaide*'s squires warned, "the Moors are treacherous."[28] But Chincoya's commander trusted his Muslim counterpart anyway. Here we see the ideology of conquest confronting the realities of the frontier: fraternizing with the enemy was an unavoidable aspect of life. Yet the episode did not end in tragedy and this too is central to the political message. The Virgin Mary's defense of Chincoya left no doubt that this was a religious boundary, and that those on the other side were the enemies of God. Those tasked with defending the frontier must be always wary.

In reality, frontier Christians often found themselves in the *alcaide*'s shoes. They were told again and again that their religious duty was to view all Muslims and Jews with suspicion and to reject non-Christian religious practices. But these obligations were theoretical and could fade when confronted with living, breathing individuals, people whom they came to know and respect, even love. They found themselves unable to define clear boundaries between members of different religious groups and unable to take decisive action to alter the situation by abandoning either the goal of expelling infidels from Iberia or their regard for non-Christian acquaintances and culture. Nor did they want to be perceived as having "gone native" by their counterparts in more central areas. The interaction of competing social

FIGURE 2. Image of the Virgin defends the tower of Chincoya. Alfonso X el Sabio, *Cantigas de Santa María: Edición facsímil del Códice T.I.1 de la Biblioteca de San Lorenzo de El Escorial*, fol. 247r. In this detail from the illustration for *cantiga* 185, Granadan soldiers are retreating while the defenders of Chincoya Castle pray in the direction of the statue of the Virgin Mary, which appears almost as if it has become a part of the fortification.

realities—physical insecurity, ideological dissonance, and a sense of being on the periphery—defined late medieval frontier society in Iberia. There was always, despite real tolerance for other groups, a curb on how far frontier Christians were willing to adapt.

By the middle of the fifteenth century, the uneasy balance between acculturation and fear had reached a point of crisis. The victories of legendary kings like Fernando III were deep in the past and there had been very few sustained campaigns against Granada for two centuries. Long periods of truce (between 1350 and 1460, for instance, there were eighty-five years of truce and only twenty-five of declared war) and various forms of peaceful contact meant, in the words of one scholar, that "at times it would almost seem as if the frontier had in some ways ceased to exist." But for many frontier nobles, the ideal of expansion remained as strong as ever and they defined this ambition in religious terms. Despite centuries of close contact with Islam, they saw war against Muslims as a sacred duty. Truces with the enemy were ignoble devices that merely delayed the inevitable. Raised in a culture that cherished the mythology of holy war, these nobles sought to live up to the ideal of their ancestors and the great heroes of the past, especially Fernán González and the Cid.[29] To do so required that they insert themselves into the grand epic of Iberia's recovery from the Muslims.

Such aspirations were particularly appealing in a Castile whose political landscape was a morass of faction fighting and competing ambitions in which there was no strong ruler able to unite all in a holy purpose. And so the constable of Castile, Miguel Lucas de Iranzo, wrote to Pope Sixtus IV (1471–1484) on 15 October 1471 with both despair and hope: "Most blessed Father, to whom except your Holiness can we Christians, your most faithful children, appeal? To whom shall we go when my lord the king cannot come because of his labors and duties and when his knights are even less willing, with some of them more hostile to us than to the very enemies of Christ? No longer will Charlemagne, who used to [fight the Muslims], come, nor Godfrey de Bouillon who dared to, nor our most holy kings who won this land, for they are held by death."[30] The constable directed his appeal to the pope because, as he put it earlier in the letter, the fight against Islam was a holy exercise (*santo exerçiçio*), which required papal authority for success. Although Miguel Lucas and his followers were willing to offer "all our possessions, our wives, our children, our freedom, our homeland, and in the end, our lives," only a pope could offer the plenary indulgences that might inspire other Christians to join their struggle or at least make a small contribution (*un poco dinero*) to the cause.[31]

Rodrigo Ponce de León, marquis of Cádiz, petitioned a yet higher power, the Virgin Mary. In 1462, as a young man burning to prove himself in battle with Muslims, he prayed before an image of the Virgin each day until "Our Lady the Virgin Mary appeared visibly before him, and said to him, 'Oh good knight, my devout follower, know for certain that my beloved son Jesus Christ and I have received your prayers and, as they have been so constant and expressed such a pure and heartfelt desire, we promise that you will be victorious in any battles against the Moors in which you find yourself'."[32]

With talk of crusade indulgences and miraculous visitations, Miguel Lucas and Ponce de León evoked an imagined ethos of the past in which uncompromising faith had led to great victories. They brought to battle with Muslims a brutality born of righteousness. About a year before the constable's letter to the pope, for instance, a troop of his soldiers patrolling near Jaén came upon a smaller group of *almogávares* (Muslim raiders). After a brief scuffle in which two of the Muslims were killed and two captured, the Christian band returned to Jaén with their captives and the severed heads of the slain. They sent a report of the encounter, along with the heads, to Miguel Lucas, who was in the nearby town of Andújar. "And when he saw [the heads] and heard the tidings, he was pleased and ordered that each of them be impaled on a raised lance, and so they were borne into Andújar. There all the children of the town dragged them through the streets, and then they left them for the dogs to eat."[33]

Ponce de León showed similar disdain for the enemy in 1487. After defeating a Muslim force near Málaga, killing 320 enemies, his deputies executed all the wounded, about eighty in number, "because Don Diego [Rodrigo's brother] and Don Alonso [his cousin] had vowed that, should God grant them a victory, they would take no one alive." All four hundred bodies were then decapitated and the heads borne on lances for a triumphal entry into the royal camp where all "greatly enjoyed the sight."[34] Such mutilations were common, though rarely on so large a scale. Raiding parties would often return with severed heads or ears as grisly souvenirs of their successes. Indeed, the practice was even institutionalized at times. In the mid-1430s, for example, the *concejo* (or town council) of Murcia paid bounties of 100 *mrs.* each for the heads of Muslim raiders in the hope of inspiring vigilance against incursions.[35]

Despite complicity in such atrocities, Miguel Lucas and Ponce de León were no simple bigots with one-dimensional understandings of Islam. Both had extensive and personal dealings with Muslims, could respect them as noble and brave opponents, and even admired their culture. The ability to work with Granadans, moreover, was essential to military success on the frontier. The *almogávares* accosted by the constable's men accompanied a certain Juan, a "Moor who had converted to Christianity" (*vn cristiano tornadizo morisco*). This man, who had been residing in Miguel Lucas's home, was traveling to Granada in order to collect information under the pretense that he wanted to return home and again live as a Muslim.[36] Ponce de León, meanwhile, owed his 1487 victory to information brought to him by a

Muslim knight wishing to convert. Although initially suspicious, Ponce de León eventually concluded that the information must be reliable, as the Muslim who brought it was "such a strong knight" (*cauallero tan esforçado*).[37]

While one might dismiss such stories as *ruses de guerre* that imply no sincere rapport with Muslims, the point is not that these were the only times that Miguel Lucas or Ponce de León interacted with Muslims but rather that such contact was so customary that it played a role even in instances of savagery. The same Murcian *concejo* that paid bounties for Muslim heads in 1435 also conducted business with local Muslims that ranged from providing space within the city for their worship to contracting them as skilled masons and artisans to enforcing debts owed by Christians to Muslims.

All this took place in an atmosphere of continual physical insecurity. The Granadan frontier remained a dangerous place in the late fifteenth century. Although we know, with the benefit of hindsight, that the heavy lifting of the conquest of Iberia had been accomplished two centuries earlier and that Granada's final defeat lay only decades away, people are generally not conscious of living at the ends of eras. The many declared truces, moreover, gave little comfort to those who suffered at the hands of raiding parties who ignored them.

There was, in fact, no such thing as an effective truce.[38] To get a sense of how even periods of supposed peace were dominated by the fear of war, we might look at how the *concejo* of the frontier city of Jaén responded to news that Castile had signed a truce with Granada. This agreement, negotiated by Abū al-Hasan ʿAlī of Granada and Diego Fernández de Córdoba, Count of Cabra, was signed in March 1475 and meant to last for two years. At the time, however, the Catholic Monarchs faced serious opposition to their succession in Castile as well as war with Portugal. Hoping for an extended period of stability on their southern flank, they sought a new, more enduring pact. This was finalized on 11 January 1476 and added an additional four years to the terms of the original accord, or until March 1481.[39] The unusual duration of the truce seems to have raised expectations of stability, and the authorities in Jaén did their best to ensure that relations with Granada remained positive.

In that same month of January, for instance, the *concejo* agreed to pay restitution to the Muslims of nearby Cambil for an alleged theft of farm implements whose perpetrators could not be located.[40] A more serious threat to the peace emerged on 21 February when word reached Jaén that the town of Huelma, to the southeast, was besieged by local Muslims. The *concejo* reacted with a strongly worded letter to the ruler of Granada demanding both reparations and an end to hostilities. In response, the Granadans justified their actions by contending that Diego de Viedma, *alcaide* of Huelma, had instigated the fight, as he "had committed many crimes against the Moors of Guadix, having taken Muslims captive or ordered them taken as well as having stolen mules and mares during a time of peace."[41] An envoy was sent to Granada to sort things out and both sides agreed to withdraw their claims for restitution.

In May, rumors reached Jaén that Muley Hacén (as Abū al-Hasan was known in Castile) was approaching Cambil with a large force. In response, the *concejo* delayed a planned transfer of troops to the Portuguese front and discreetly placed watchers in the mountain passes "because we do not know what the Moors are up to."[42] Nothing happened for several months but on 8 August "came news that the king of Granada has mobilized and entered Christian lands to do evil and damage. Later the council ordered that the people of the city, both knights and infantry, be warned."[43]

Jaén itself appeared to be in no danger; the incursion was directed to the southwest, toward Priego de Córdoba and Alcalá la Real. Even so, the *concejo* continued to avoid provocations. They carefully facilitated trade, investigated crimes against Muslims, and punished offenders. Yet they also did everything possible to prepare for attack. They instituted regular watches on both the city walls and on towers guarding key roads and ordered that these fortifications be repaired. Most important, and most problematic, were Jaén's militia and cavalry forces. The *concejo* was perturbed to find that many of those legally required to provide military service were unprepared to do so. On 15 July, the *regidores*, or council members, reported that "the *caballeros de cuantía* [non-noble urban knights] of this city are much diminished and are not the *caballeros* they used to be, and from this situation comes great harm to the city and disservice to the monarchs, our lords."[44]

Notably, these preparations were not instigated by the credible threat of invasion but had been ongoing since at least the start of the year, with the first orders (on 3 January) coinciding with the beginning of the available records.[45] Nor did the vigilance end with the Granadan incursion. In 1479, the *concejo* maintained ten permanent night watchmen on the city gates as well as an unspecified number of others at the various towers around the city at a cost of ninety *mrs.* each per month. In that same year, *corregidor* Francisco de Bobadilla personally inspected each of the cavalry mounts and arranged numerous troop reviews to insure that the militia was ready to fight.[46] Despite their determination to rigidly observe its terms, local

authorities had scant confidence that the signing of a royal truce would
bring real stability. Indeed, stability was not in everyone's interests, as demonstrated by the case of Francisco Sánchez de Baeza. This man, a stonema-
son, was contracted in May 1476 to repair the parapets of Pegalajar, a key
point in Jaén's outer defenses that directly abutted the Muslim lands near
Cambil. But he never did the work and defended his inaction by pointing
out that he was unable to do it alone and his son Antonio, who was to have
assisted him, had instead left to pursue the more profitable business of
raiding the Muslims.[47]

Such constant anxiety could be creative and dynamic. In stirringly
romantic terms Juan de Mata Carriazo described how the risks and rewards
of frontier skirmishing brought people to action and led to "a singular eleva-
tion of individual virtues, a natural selection of frontier populations, with its
automatic elimination of the weak and its exaltation of the strong, the bold,
and the undaunted." The frontier provided opportunities for glory in abundance and here, in song and in deed, the Castilian knighthood found its
pinnacle of fame while the lawless and rebellious, welcome nowhere else,
sought atonement in "this unquiet and heroic world of the Granadan frontier." To his credit, Carriazo saw the other side of the coin as well, noting
that the frontier offered only peril and frustration for the peasantry on both
sides. Raiding stripped the land of its bounty, killed its keepers, and stymied
attempts to improve its productivity.[48]

And for what? Perhaps the most vexing aspect of the fifteenth-century
frontier was the continuity of organized violence despite a dearth of concrete
accomplishments. Neither of the most obvious motives for warfare—
financial gain or religious animosity—fit well with the pattern of conflict.
The economic repercussions included lost trade, burnt crops, ransoms for
captives, and the expense of maintaining standing armies, all of which far
outweighed the lucre brought in by raiding parties. Those adversely affected
included the wealthiest and most powerful members of society and so we
should expect to see their voices raised against actions that undermined their
interests. And indeed, it was Jaén's elites who ensured that the city did its
utmost to uphold the truces of 1475 and 1476. Yet the collective power of the
elite nearly always failed to prevent disruptive raiding in times of truce.

Part of the problem was the mountainous and underpopulated Andalucían terrain, difficult to police even under ideal circumstances. But much of
the marauding took place with the approval, or at least the benign indiffer-
ence, of frontier authorities. If this reluctance to enforce a true peace
stemmed from the idea that there should not be pacific relations with the

enemies of God, why did the fighting remain localized and limited? Only on rare occasions was conquest or conversion the goal (let alone the achievement) of an attack. With the exception of Fernando de Antequera's campaigns early in the century, attempts to reassert the crusading drive lacked sufficient support to accomplish much of anything. Holy war was no longer a unifying message and would not be so again until well into the reign of the Catholic Monarchs.

It was the interaction of competing realities—an ideology of holy war, a tradition of *convivencia*, and a lack of physical security—that defined the amiable enmity so prominent in what we might call the frontier mentality. The fundamental characteristic of this mind-set was not, as Carriazo would have it, a creative tension or a drive to heroism. Rather it was indecision that prevented the elite from pushing too vigorously for stability while also confounding the ambitions of those who sought a return to general warfare. Holy war was central to the self-image of many Castilians and especially the frontier nobility, offering purpose and rationalization as well as dreams of glory. But the realization of its objective, the expulsion of Muslims from Iberia, posed a very real danger to their raison d'être. And so the raids continued, judges, ransomers, and city councils kept a modicum of order, knights made their reputations in savage battle, and kings negotiated truce after truce. All the while, the farmers, herders, and merchants on both sides endured, working shared lands, trading when they could, smuggling when they could not, and engaging daily in a thousand little interactions with their "enemies."

My purpose is, in part, to describe how fifteenth-century frontier Christians coped with the anxieties resulting from the gap between ideology and reality. Unrestrained violence against members of certain religious groups served as one form of release. The rejection of fixed religious identities was another. But these were both modes of extreme behavior, which, if left unchecked, bore the risk of even greater insecurity. More successful were the urban spectacles that offered a means of publicly addressing the contradictions inherent in intricate ideas of conflict and coexistence. That the dialectic between urban spectacle and attitudes toward members of different religious communities took place in *frontier* cities is therefore relevant. It is ironic, then, that this tradition of pageantry ultimately contributed to the rejection of frontier compromises and to the redefinition of Castilian society as exclusively Christian.

*   *   *

This book is divided into two parts. The first of these outlines the various contexts for late medieval Castilian frontier spectacles to clarify their presentation, reception, and functions. These performances often built on familiar and ritualized forms, such as those of a tournament or a religious procession, while overtly or subtly manipulating their content. Interpreting these events presents multiple difficulties. We only know of medieval spectacles through written representations that generally offer only the perspectives of the elites who sponsored the events. Even this is retrospective and highly mediated, reflecting not only the personal biases of the author but often also a conscious attempt to control the spectacle's meaning.[49] In interpreting these pageants, I therefore focus extensively on their social, political, and physical contexts, arguing that ritualized performances bear multiple and situated meanings that only become clear when considered in this manner.[50] Chapter 1 therefore explores the relations between enacted performances and written descriptions in order both to permit multiple readings of a pageant and, when possible, to best identify the perceived intent behind a particular presentation.

Spectacles could succeed only through the complicity and participation of audiences. This was especially true of political theater, a point I demonstrate using the 1465 "Farce of Ávila" as an example. Without the audience's perspective, we can have only a warped understanding of what a particular event meant. Spectators, however, generally did not record their experiences or responses. I therefore examine the discourses current in Castilian society about the nature and character of public performances, highlighting the disparate perspectives of the nobility, the clergy, and the commoners. This allows us to move beyond the mediated presentation of the goals of elite sponsors and offers a range within which the responses of most spectators were likely limited.

In Chapter 2, I argue that civic spaces bore meanings to local residents that could contribute to or define the overall experience of a spectacle. Siting, decoration, size, and even the choice of materials for buildings were often consciously chosen to convey a message or establish a mood. The particular conditions of the Iberian frontier had long provided rulers with both the need for effective modes of expressing their readings of social, political, and religious issues and an abundance of themes with which to do so, making the region a crucible of "rhetorical architecture."[51] In exploring the various physical contexts for spectacle, I pay particular attention to ephemeral architecture, temporary structures tailor made for specific events. These could range from viewing stands and barricades to whimsical wooden castles and palaces. All served to repurpose quotidian spaces, transforming them in various ways. As with the spectacles themselves, however, civic spaces could have multiple meanings and could be understood in ways unanticipated by rulers.

Part II substantiates the framework established in the initial chapters by looking at specific performances from Jaén, Córdoba, and Murcia. Through these examples, I trace evolving understandings of Christian society and the place of Muslims and Jews within it from the 1460s to the 1490s, a period when well-established traditions of frontier life were challenged by a growing intolerance and a renewed push for holy war. Chapter 3 tells the story of Miguel Lucas de Iranzo, the frontier magnate who, hoping to reap material rewards and fame, rallied a reluctant populace to support his plans for intensified frontier warfare in the 1460s. Appreciating the importance of strong commercial and personal ties between Andalucía and Granada, he did so with vivid theatrics that pointed to the benefits of Christian victory while ensuring the people that such a triumph would not destroy those transfrontier relationships. This was, at best, an uncertain vision of *convivencia*, one that required Christian victory and Muslim submission, but it did acknowledge the cultural contributions of non-Christians. The enemy was to be converted and embraced, not expelled or eradicated.

But Muslims were not the only minority religious community in Andalucían cities. Jews and recent converts were also alternately, or even simultaneously, viewed with welcome and suspicion. When a wave of anticonvert riots swept through Andalucía in 1473, the catalyst was a Marian procession in Córdoba interrupted by inadvertent insult to the Virgin by a young convert girl. In the ensuing riot, the Passion story was dramatically retold through the death of a blacksmith who called on all to avenge his death at the hands of the converts. Chapter 4 places these events in the context of noble factional politics, arguing that the procession and ensuing violence were a deliberate provocation meant to release previously suppressed popular resentment of converts' social and economic success. By linking anticonvert sentiment to the Virgin Mary and the Passion story, the procession and the blacksmith's stylized death released a wave of violence that far surpassed the expectations of both nobles and commoners.

War with Granada, which had previously consisted primarily of frontier skirmishing, began in earnest soon after Fernando and Isabel took the throne in 1474. This newly confident and aggressive pose toward the Muslims of Granada inspired fresh approaches to representing ideal relations between members of different religious groups. Muslims and Jews were no longer seen as economically relevant groups. Instead, they were remnants of the past and symbols of the defeated. They were unwelcome but yet not enemies. Irrelevant but still the focus of much attention. Chapter 5 examines how this diminished social role was dramatized in Murcia through triumphal renditions of the city's Corpus Christi celebration organized to commemorate the conquests of Málaga and Granada. Forced to wear their finest clothes and participate in the Christians' triumph, Murcian Jews and Muslims were relegated to the rear of the processions, a position often occupied by prisoners of war. There were no incitements to violence, no overt rejections. Instead the revelries expressed that non-Christians were no longer part of society. Instead, they were defeated enemies, reminders to all of Christian triumph. With the end of the frontier would come an end to frontier accommodations.

I close the book by briefly considering the long-term implications of the disintegration of traditional modes of frontier life, touching upon the expulsions of Jews and later Muslims from Iberia, the Inquisition, and the transference of particular attitudes toward religious others to the New World. I also place the events in fifteenth-century Castilian history in the context of the broader Mediterranean encounter between Christians and Muslims and of continuing uncertainties about the role of Muslims and Jews in Iberian history.

PART I

CHAPTER I

The Anatomy of a Spectacle:
Sponsors, Critics, and Onlookers

On 5 June 1465, about sixty years after Fernando de Antequera took up his holy sword, a group of rebellious nobles ritually deposed an effigy of King Enrique IV and crowned his half brother Alfonso king. As with the earlier event, the so-called Farce of Ávila was consciously intended to make a political statement by invoking symbolic powers and was meant to be seen by as many people as possible. The conspirators took great care to conduct it in an accessible location and to ensure that the stage was visible from every angle. The essential elements of the ritual were straightforward. Having placed a dummy adorned with the symbols of monarchy (including crown, sword, and scepter) on a stage, they read out a series of accusations against Enrique and proclaimed their sentence of dethronement. The rebels then removed the emblems of kingship and cast the effigy to the ground with a shouted curse. As described in contemporary chronicles, the effigy's fall to the ground was the ritual's central moment, leading to a great cry of lamentation from the massed spectators. Moments later, with the king symbolically dethroned, Alfonso strode on stage, took up the royal accouterments, and was acclaimed king by all present.[1]

Spectators at this event were not, it seems, expected to remain passive or silent. Their reactions were important enough, in fact, that they were worth recording. And that tells us that these responses were also significant to the organizers of the spectacle, significant enough, perhaps, that it led them to present their performance in a manner calculated to achieve precisely that result. The ways the crowd's behavior was recorded, however, suggest that everyone watching acted unanimously, raising several questions. How did people of the time experience an event like this or, for that matter, a tournament, a procession, or a festival? Were they seen as simple entertainments without deeper meaning or were they understood to be social or political statements? Did people view them from an innocent or a cynical perspective? Most important, how can we, several centuries later, even attempt to answer such questions when there are relatively few contemporary records that address them?

These questions matter because, as we will see, the success of the Farce of Ávila depended on the responses of the audience. People watching the event were more than onlookers, they played a role as important as those on stage. In this regard, the Farce was akin to most other urban spectacles. Processions, festivals, tournaments, political theater—all were moments that brought together people from all social classes to engage in dialogues, sometimes overt but more often subtle, about the nature of society and its priorities and values. Access to the necessary financing, expertise, and social capital permitted municipal councils, cathedral chapters, and nobles to determine the content of most public performances. Their control, however, was not absolute. Other privileged members of the community, such as merchants and artisans, sought and often obtained influence over civic spectacles, particularly annual events such as Corpus Christi. More generally, elites had to present messages that the urban population would accept; spectacles that failed to accord with popular expectations or sentiments were worse than useless, creating unrest or leaving the sponsor open to public ridicule.

This was especially relevant in frontier cities where powerful and contradictory impulses meant that a wrong step could have severe repercussions. Elites there had to tread carefully indeed if they wanted to direct public sentiment, especially regarding religious minorities, in particular directions.

Audience participation was a common feature of public pageants that permitted spectators to directly and immediately signal their approval or displeasure. The meanings of spectacles were therefore created by both sponsors and audiences. Each group or social class, even each individual, brought a set of expectations and values to a performance and created an ensemble of associations through which to interpret it. But spectacles were not, as some have suggested, blank tapestries on which the viewer could inscribe what he or she wished.[2] Most spectacles bore dominant meanings intended by their sponsors to produce conditioned responses from both participants and observers. This meant that there was a relatively limited range of probable reactions.

To consider one common spectacle in which many of us have participated in one way or another, a graduation ceremony can bear different connotations for each participant and spectator. For one person, the event may
inspire feelings of nostalgia for milestones past. Another observer may feel
reminded that commencements are one of the very few occasions on which
the entire educational community comes together. Degree recipients will
likely focus on their own accomplishments, but they might also be thinking
of unrelated issues or be planning a subversive statement. All the while, the
speaker might be thinking of nothing more profound than not flubbing a
name. Even given these potentially divergent responses, however, it would be
the inattentive spectator indeed who lost sight of a commencement's central
purpose in recognizing the achievements of a graduating class.

This chapter outlines the complex relationship between a performance's
intended meanings and its reception by various audiences. Given the lack of
contemporary evidence, many scholars have generalized what can be considered universal aspects of public spectacle, such as the presence of cues meant
to help spectators understand the purpose and structure of a performance.
Such cues are, and were, often meant to inform the audience of their proper
roles: where to direct their attention, what to wear, when to stand, applaud,
or be silent. Yet audiences do not always do what they are told. They might be
disruptive, apathetic, or overly enthusiastic. And even when they do behave as
intended, we cannot assume that this demonstrates their agreement with the
performance. The spectators' lament and acclamation at the Farce of Ávila,
for instance, has been taken as evidence of their complicity. In fact, these acts
reveal little of their actual reactions to the event.

The crowd's behavior instead points to a central problem in the interpretation of medieval spectacles: eyewitnesses did not typically record their personal experiences, leaving us to reconstruct them through accounts from
other sources. These include subjective descriptions penned by (usually) elite
authors as well as legal codes and ordinances. Attempts to legislate proper
behavior at public performances, to give one example, might indicate the
kinds of disorderly conduct organizers expected to encounter. Since the
sources offer limited insight at best, many scholars have dismissed audiences,
considering them only when particularly strong reactions were recorded.
Spectator responses, however, were rarely unanimous and usually fell some-
where between blatant complicity and opposition.

To understand the experience of the crowd, we therefore must look
beyond contemporary accounts to approach what one scholar has called the

"culture of the spectator."[3] Spectators were both free and constrained in their reactions as a host of individual factors (such as class, gender, and religion) interacted with both community solidarity and fragmenting social tensions. Individual spectator responses were influenced by these divergent pressures, by the staging and enactment of the spectacle, and by the physical surroundings. They were therefore unpredictable. At the same time, the reactions of surrounding members of the audience can have a powerful influence on the individual, channeling his or her latent reactions into a few particular directions. This ultimately limited the potential for destabilizing or subversive outbursts.

Multiple influences, thus, acted simultaneously to regulate the range of potential audience responses. Prominent among them were widely held opinions about certain subjects. In this chapter, I consider debates regarding knightly tournaments, one of the most popular and most controversial forms of spectacle at the time. By considering in turn each of the three orders of medieval society as understood at the time—the nobility, the church, and the populace—we can see how each produced independent strands of discourse. The many arguments made to rationalize or condemn festive military exercises as well as the ways in which these strands intersected and overlapped created a network of competing alliances and perspectives. Although these did not strictly curtail an individual's potential responses, they did set limits within which onlooker experiences were likely to fall.

Although the focus is on tournaments, there were no absolute divisions between types of spectacle at this time. Fifteenth-century tournaments often included dramatic performances and popular festivities. Sometimes they even coincided with religious processions. This merging of genres resulted in part from a repurposing of tournaments, which previously had been limited to courtly settings. They were now presented in urban contexts to mixed audiences, leading sponsors to integrate popular and ecclesiastic elements in order to enhance their appeal. The pressures of the frontier, moreover, had created new social networks and alliances. Physical and ideological uncertainty undermined, or perhaps transcended, the traditional "three orders of society." We must be careful, therefore, about lumping frontier spectacles into a general category of urban performances.

Such an analysis, moreover, is based in part on modern observations of crowd behavior, raising the question of the degree to which we can fruitfully draw comparisons between modern and medieval spectacles. Most references to twentieth- and twenty-first-century mass culture made by historians of medieval Castile are impressionistic, intended to clarify concepts through comparison to a familiar phenomenon or to lament enduring inequalities. This approach permits the reader to visualize the events more fully but raises epistemological questions. Do modern renditions of public spectacles, often enacted at least in part for tourist audiences, bear anything in common with their medieval antecedents? Or do such comparisons ultimately delude us into thinking that we can understand experiences that have been irretrievably lost?

Book layouts can help to explain how modern analogies might apply to medieval public spectacle. A modern scholarly text includes a number of features that help readers orient themselves and access critical information, including a table of contents, footnotes, page numbers, and indexes. Such tools are relatively specific, requiring a basic level of cultural literacy for easy use. The location and format of these finding aids vary widely and we would not expect to see the same layout for a novel, for instance, as for a scientific textbook. Similarly, the *mise-en-page* of a medieval manuscript contains helpful features, including the organization of the page into columns that accommodated glosses and commentaries and the use of incipits and initials, all of which permit the experienced reader to move quickly and easily about the text. Both the modern printed book and the medieval manuscript offer solutions to the universal challenge of efficiently navigating a long text. Both, moreover, are part of the same centuries-long tradition. Thus, although far from identical, they bear enough commonalities that meaningful comparisons can be drawn between them. To put it another way, book layouts that mark different stages of the same process of development can be said to be written in the same language.

Public performances contain similar cues meant to help the audience navigate the event's content and meaning. These range from overt messages clear to everyone present to subtle signals meant for only a few. As with books, some measure of cultural literacy is required to make sense of them. Such prompts are often visual, with particular combinations of color or symbols expressing complex messages about the nature of the spectacle.[4] But they can also be verbal, with explicit statements or the tone of a speaker's voice pointing the audience in the desired direction. Styles of dress, written signs, verbal hints, the layout of the venue: these cues act in concert to inform spectators of the type of event presented, its structure, its message, and their role. The audience can also add its own prompts, whether invited to do so or not. As these can materially affect the unfolding of the spectacle, the boundary between actors and audience is often murky.

At times, spectators play an invited, supportive role in a spectacle. Fans at modern sporting events create banners, perform synchronized gestures, engage in chants. The applause at a concert or play is an expected response that not only signals the audience's approval but also acts as a ritualized conclusion to the performance. But audience responses do not always fit with the intended aims of a spectacle. Public spectacles always bore the possibility that some groups would take advantage of the assembled masses to advance unofficial agendas.

*   *   *

The interpretation of crowd reactions is often difficult. Even when we know what audience members did or said in response to a particular event, it is not always clear whether they acted to bolster or challenge its intended meaning. The response of the crowd to the Farce of Ávila is a case in point. Angus MacKay has argued that the rebel leaders sought to overcome a challenge inherent in replacing a reigning monarch: there could not be two living kings in the same land.[5] Although he rejects the idea that the conspirators believed the effigy actually became Enrique IV in some magical way, MacKay contends it did represent the death of the king and the passing of kingship from Enrique to Alfonso.[6] In doing so, he relies on a pair of related ideas: the Castilian understanding that kings depended on noble election and popular acclamation for their legitimacy and the more general medieval notion of the king's two bodies, the separation of the physical person of the king and the *dignitas* of the crown.[7] For the conspirators, Enrique did not die at Ávila, but *King* Enrique did perish when symbolically stripped of his emblems and thrown to the ground. From this perspective, the crowd's lament was a necessary step in the ritual sequence needed to depose one king and crown another. Alfonso could take the stage to be crowned only after the people's cries had confirmed that the effigy was dead and the throne vacant. And he could only truly be king once they had acclaimed him.[8]

Scholars have generally assumed that the lament was pro forma, an imitation of the ritual cryings (*llantos*) that took place at a royal funeral and preceded the acclamation of a king's successor. But, if this was indeed the case, the language used by the chroniclers is curious. Alfonso de Palencia, although an ardent polemicist who rarely missed an opportunity to heap invective on Enrique, noted that the effigy fell to the ground "amid the sobs of those present who seemed to be crying because of the unfortunate [*desastrada*] death of the deposed."[9] If the lament was a necessary element in the ritual, why did Palencia choose to describe it as a spontaneous outpouring of grief and not explicitly as a *llanto*? At the funeral rites conducted in Ávila upon Enrique's actual death in 1474, the laments not only are unambiguously referred to in the sources as *llantos* but bear a markedly formal character. In this case, the funeral procession stopped at four different locations on its way to the cathedral. At each of these, a black shield was shattered to the cry of "¡A por buen rey é buen Señor!"[10]

The idea of a ritual lament also implies that Enrique was presented as a *real* king deserving of the proper protocols of respect. The conspirators, in planning the event, had decided that the best means of discrediting Enrique was to accuse him of tyranny and weakness, characterizing their rebellion as a response to "the swift and sudden oppression of a tyrant who had in his favor neither mental energy, nor talent, nor capacity, nor any other gifts." This reasoning supposes that Enrique, lacking the perquisite qualities, had never truly been a legitimate king. A ritual crying was therefore unnecessary and a potential distraction from the central message that Enrique was "king in name only."[11] Furthermore, a formal lament required either that the crowd had been advised in advance to cry out at the predetermined time or that they were so well versed in royal funereal customs as to know precisely the correct moment for the lament. The latter was no mean feat. The effigy had been dressed in mourning (as if already dead) throughout the deposition but only symbolically lost its kingship upon hitting the ground. The former seems equally unlikely, as Palencia noted that the construction of the stage was the only means of publicity used to attract the people of Ávila. While the crowd could well have been "seeded" with sympathizers prepared to lead the crowd at the right time, they would have needed to be convincing indeed to entice all those present to go along. These difficulties and Palencia's choice of words indicate that the crowd's wailing was not anticipated, but potentially signaled that the show did not altogether please the crowd, that Enrique enjoyed at least some support in Ávila and the people felt genuine sorrow at the harsh treatment given to him in effigy.

Yet Palencia reported that this same audience erupted a short time later into the popular acclamation symbolically necessary for Alfonso to become king.[12] This seems more like the intended and perhaps planned response that MacKay suggests and challenges the idea that their prior lament for Enrique was a display of contrary emotion. So what really happened? In all likelihood, some spectators expressed genuine grief, some understood that the *llanto* was needed to depose Enrique properly, some followed the lead of those around them, and others remained silent. In this sense, the crowd was typical, demonstrating the difficulty of characterizing the actions, emotions, or thoughts of an assembly as if it was a unified entity. Even if medieval people conceived their identities in corporate terms, their thoughts remained their own. It does not follow that they were necessarily subsumed in the collective identity presented in a spectacle. Some at Ávila may indeed have comprehended and embraced the deeper meanings of the Farce, but we should view with skepticism the claim that all did.

When historians write about popular contexts to political propaganda, they are, in essence, describing elite efforts to sway the populace rather than directly addressing the popular reception of such propaganda. Insofar as elites of the time knew popular mind-sets better than we can, studies of how they expected (or hoped) the people would react do indeed shed light on the crowd's responses. But there is a tendency to assume that elite agendas were realized, that the crowd understood spectacles to mean just what was intended by those who presented them.

This same set of issues holds true for spectacles conducted in frontier cities; indeed the twin stressors of amiable enmity and physical insecurity meant that both the tendency for a multiplicity of responses and the pressure on spectators to conform to those around them may have been even more intense than elsewhere. There too, however, scholars have tended to limit themselves to recreating elite perspectives. Miguel Lucas de Iranzo's program of spectacles in 1460s Jaén is known chiefly through the contemporary *Hechos del condestable*, whose author was not only an intimate of Miguel Lucas, the constable of Castile, but likely participated in many of the events described. This chronicle, which revolves around detailed descriptions of the numerous feasts, pageants, and rituals that Miguel Lucas organized to commemorate nearly every significant day on the calendar, explicitly presented him as a latter-day Cid, recounting the constable's struggles with his rivals, his daring feats against Granada, and his careful governance of Jaén. The chronicler's emphasis on Miguel Lucas's persona reveals the intent of his theatrical productions in ways that a more journalistic approach may not. But it also presents a perspective shared primarily by the town's elites, telling us little about how the majority of people in Jaén experienced and understood the festivities.

Modern scholars are well aware of this problem and have focused on the intended political utility of Miguel Lucas's theatrics to argue convincingly that he used spectacles to augment his own status and to diffuse social tensions by directing lower-class unrest toward external enemies.[13] This approach does not seek nonelite perspectives for Jaén's festivals, instead giving voice to the oppressed by exposing the strategies of the powerful. But, in limiting the gaze to those on stage, those scholars casually contend that the "entire urban population" of Jaén lent their support to these festivals, cheerfully absorbing not only the playacting but also the political content, and implies widespread complicity in Miguel Lucas's agenda.[14] The conclusion here, as in MacKay's study of the Farce of Ávila, is that the common people bought into the propaganda presented to them. In both cases, the crowd's role is reduced to a single voice, a unified roar of support. Certainly Palencia and the author of the *Hechos* wanted their audiences to think so, but can we trust them?

So how can historians represent enacted performances and oral popular culture known solely through such texts? Even leaving aside the question of authorial bias, the symbolic gestures in any performance are inherently ambiguous and thus capable of bearing multiple meanings in a sense that words can never be. Language can be thought of as sequential, with each word modified by the next to ultimately create meaning, while visual depictions present multiple images simultaneously, which must be read together for proper interpretation. Such multivalence is an essential aspect of a spectacle's relevance to its audiences, for it allows meanings to be indeterminate, endlessly modifiable.

A written description of a spectacle can therefore never include all the various potential meanings because an author must emphasize one while minimizing others. Still less can the written word capture the divergent responses of engaged and participatory audiences to those multiple meanings. To return briefly to a textual metaphor, it is as if the ambiguous character of both the symbolic elements of the spectacle itself and of the crowd's response are the marginalia on the page of a manuscript, the commentaries that offer insight into the significance found in a static text by its various readers. The chroniclers who transcribed the event offer us not the complete, annotated version but a formal, modern edition that carries only a single "authentic" version in which viewpoints apart from the dominant one have been submerged. Modern parallels offer a possible means of recovering these lost glosses, but with the danger of unintentionally introducing anachronistic concepts. But there are other options. By identifying various contemporary discourses on the social functions of spectacle, we can apply an insight gained through modern spectacle—that spectator responses are individual but constrained—while ensuring that these are confirmed by medieval sources.

Contemporary controversies over the nature and presentation of medieval pageants offer several points of view through which they were interpreted, which are roughly analogous to the "three orders" of medieval society: the rulers (e.g., the king, nobility, and knights), the church, and the people. Such a division is laid out in Alfonso X's thirteenth-century legal code, which noted:

> There are three kinds of festivals, the first, those which the Holy Church orders to be observed in honor of God and the saints; as, for instance, Sundays, the birthday of Our Lord Jesus Christ, and those of Holy Mary, of the Apostles, and of the other male and female saints. The second are those which emperors and kings order to be observed in honor of themselves; as, for instance, the days on which they are born; those of their sons who expect to reign, or the days of which they have been successful in great battles with the enemies of the Faith by conquering them, and such other days as they order to be observed in honor of themselves, which are treated in the Title on Citations. The third kind, called *Ferias*, are instituted for the common benefit of men, as, for instance, days upon which fruits are gathered.[15]

Members of each group not only participated in each kind of spectacle in different ways but also were able to draw upon a set of shared experiences and associations that conditioned their responses when they were in the audience. If we describe the interplay between cues, symbols, and associations that organized spectacles as a language, then each of these groups could be said to share a distinct dialect through which they filled in the symbolic images presented to them with the specifics of their own perspectives. This is not, of course, to say that membership in a social group imposed absolute limits on an individual's possible reactions or that a certain performance would appeal to only one such group and no other. There was, in fact, a great deal of overlap. Many medieval religious festivals had secular aspects; at the same time, most secular festivals also had a strong religious component. Audiences were often diverse. Penitential processions, burlesque tournaments, royal entrances, spontaneous revelries—all these drew spectators and participants across social, economic, gender, and even religious boundaries.

All types of urban spectacles drew on this language to evoke particular intended responses, and each type inspired a range of corporate responses. A popular celebration such as Carnival might be broadly supported by the people, viewed with suspicion by nobles and civic authorities watchful for signs of trouble, and roundly condemned by the church on moral grounds. The perspectives characteristic of each group, however, did not constrain individuals: we do not have to look hard to find carousing priests, moralizing knights, or nervous townsfolk. But, as we shift the focus from the intent behind public spectacles to their popular reception, the interactions between these dominant strands of discourse become central. A number of critics have construed the individual as strong in the face of cultural pressures and have emphasized the ability of spectators to remake meanings to their own specifications. But these critics tend to minimize the multiplicity of influences that shape the experience and perception of performances.[16] We cannot reduce audience response to a dichotomy of conformity or resistance. Nor can we say that individuals freely created their own responses. Instead there was a limited spectrum of possibilities established by ingrained cultural patterns. The sponsors of urban performances may not have been able to put a name to these processes, but they were aware of them. What they presented to the public, therefore, took into account their perceptions of likely reactions. Audiences may not have had a visible or the decisive role in determining the content of a performance, but their influence was profound and ubiquitous.

* * *

A full consideration of the range of responses to all the myriad forms of spectacle in fifteenth-century Castile would be unwieldy. A detailed reading, however, of the ways in which the nobility and the church rationalized and critiqued the knightly tournament can serve to illustrate the interplay of multiple perspectives and their influence on audience responses. Tournaments were one of the most common urban spectacles. As such, they spawned an outpouring of rhetoric that often invoked issues directly related to the frontier.

Fifteenth-century Castilian tournaments took place within the context of significant changes in the position of the aristocracy. To understand what nobles thought of their tournaments, therefore, it is necessary to first consider these contexts. On the one hand, a succession of weak kings accorded the greatest nobles unprecedented influence and power, while the Granadan frontier offered autonomy and glory, leading Castilian chivalry to the pinnacle of its fame. On the other, competition from the *caballeros de cuantía* (non-noble mounted warriors) and *letrados* (university graduates trained in canon or civil law) undermined the aristocracy's traditional military and political roles. At the same time, nobles increasingly lived in cities where they often had to understand and address the needs of urban constituencies. These social and economic changes inspired passionate discussions on the functions of chivalry, nobility, and monarchy. Among the nobles, these took place through literary debates that explored the comparative values of arms and letters or of birth and personal achievement.[17] In order to appeal to the populace, however, they adapted tournaments and dramatic skits previously limited to courtly audiences.

While the Farce of Ávila was unusual in its direct political significance, it drew on the relatively recent practice of presenting courtly exhibitions as public entertainments. This trend had gained momentum in the fifteenth century as nearly every extraordinary event or holy day was taken as an excuse for recreation or as the object of a ceremony. The range of spectacles enacted on the streets and plazas of Castilian cities is seemingly endless: processions, tournaments, mime shows, dramas, and bullfights. These marked occasions including royal visits, religious events (such as Corpus Christi, Christmas, and Epiphany), the anniversaries of key dates in civic history, noble weddings, funerals, and births, and so on. Local fêtes were often the liveliest, but external events, especially royal deaths and coronations, were publicly commemorated throughout the realm. The Farce of Ávila, for instance, was understood to make Alfonso king in Ávila only. For his crowning to be meaningful, nobles elsewhere needed to accept his claim and enact similar public rituals in their towns.[18] By conspicuously sponsoring a variety of events and by controlling their content, urban nobles sought to maintain or extend their influence at the expense of their rivals.

Long-term frontier fighting and political instability exacerbated the situation. Because of the military requirements of war against the Muslims, specifically the need for large numbers of horsemen, the nobility lacked the monopoly over the role and accoutrements of the mounted warrior enjoyed by their counterparts in France and England. Members of urban militias, the *caballeros de cuantía* (or *de premia*), could claim at least some of the honors and obligations of knighthood, even though they lacked titles, and even some merchant associations adopted the trappings of chivalry.[19] Political innovations dating to the mid-fourteenth-century accession of the Trastámara dynasty provided other rivals. The first of the Trastámaras, Enrique II (1369–1379) had overthrown his predecessor in a lengthy civil war. Because his hold on the throne was insecure, he rewarded his followers with privileges and extensive grants of lands. The result was a transformation of the high aristocracy, as families prominent since the eleventh and twelfth centuries made way for the "new" nobility, which consisted mostly of formerly minor branches of the great old noble houses.[20] To balance the power of the new nobles, Enrique turned to the *letrados*, giving them control of the *audiencia*, the king's own court of law with jurisdiction in cases involving the nobility.

While challenged by *caballeros de cuantía* and *letrados*, nobles could not even take solace in their ancient and storied lineages. Most, even those of the highest rank, traced their privileges and titles only as far back as the Trastámara accession, highlighting the contingent nature of their position. Just as they had replaced the old nobility, so too could they be replaced. So, in order to defend their privileges, the nobility had to identify those qualities that distinguished them and made their class socially relevant.[21] It was not wealth (merchants had that, after all) or land (many noble lands remained, in theory, the property of the royal fisc) nor horse and armor (knights and urban militias fought with the same equipment and in the same manner) nor influence (which was shared with the *letrados*).

Ultimately, many chose to argue that true nobility derived from personal virtue. Authors like Diego de Valera and Rodrigo Sánchez de Arévalo emphasized that nobles and knights should earn their social status through lifelong service and an unremitting dedication to honor and prudence. These authors never lost sight of the nobility's principal vocation of fighting, which differentiated them from the *caballeros de cuantía*, whose distaste for their military duties was notorious. For the true knight, lack of a civilian calling made possible the regular attention to military training necessary to his proper station: "Those who have been made knights and given very noble horses and arms suitable for mounted battle are enjoined to exercise these weapons in peacetime, so they will be the more ready whenever war looms."[22]

These authors consciously wrote of the world as it should be, not as it was, setting a high standard. Arévalo, for instance, concluded his *Suma de la política* with a list of the qualities possessed by a good knight, including the admonition that "every knight should be well armed and poorly dressed," a piece of advice no doubt disconcerting for the knights and lords whose lush attire is minutely described in many chronicles.[23] But they dressed in this manner not solely from personal conceit. The bright clothes, gorgeous trappings, and general pomp that suffused their public exhibitions of military training—for such was the rationale behind their many tournaments, jousts, mêlées, and hunts—were different means of confirming their rank and place in the social hierarchy.

Armed with learned treatises that elevated their training exercises to an act of virtue, nobles throughout Castile missed no opportunity for displaying both their martial skills and their talents for putting on a good show. Johan Huizinga has argued that the knightly ideal was, at its heart, more an aesthetic than a moral code, one that presented honor in combination with egoism and audacity.[24] Civic spectacles, especially those with a military theme, were the ideal venue for displaying all these to the whole of society. The esteem these events supplied to those who hosted and engaged in them is incalculable. And this prestige was not only presented to their peers but displayed "above all before the eyes of the people who, just as they acclaimed monarchical power during royal *entradas*, were dazzled by the power, valor, and skill of the aristocracy."[25]

Although elusive, the virtuous ideal of those like Valera and Arévalo was not wholly ignored. It endured as a source of inspiration, a goal to be forever sought, even if only rarely attained. Nor were these authors the sole arbiters of what it meant to be noble. Though unwilling to cast aside their finery, many nobles and knights did spend their careers and often their lives in pursuit of what they saw as the epitome of knighthood: military success. During times of war, there were occasions aplenty for the bold to win glory and fame. But during peacetime, such opportunities were in short supply. This inspired a powerful disgust for kings who signed truces with Granada. It meant the frontier nobles with an urge to wage war on their own initiative were never without a supply of willing volunteers.

For many, however, the only routes to martial renown were tournaments and jousts, bitterly contested sports that at times carried a real threat of serious injury or death and therefore served as a proxy for the battlefield. For Arévalo, it was this danger, the fact that it was more than playacting, that made tournaments a worthy sport: "Particularly admirable is the joust, more so than target practice and other games of chance, because it is difficult and brings one into danger, instilling the virtue of fortitude. Moreover, the tournament is a sport even more noble than the joust, because it more closely resembles war, and is more pronounced in its danger and test of strength."[26] Putting on these contests was obligatory for all aristocrats with social aspirations and there was never a shortage of participants. Many young and often penniless *hidalgos*, or hereditary nobles, traveled from competition to competition throughout Castile and even beyond in search of fame and advancement.[27] Balancing these little-known contestants were senior nobles, famous men whose presence raised the profile of a tournament. The chroniclers described the most dazzling contests as more than entertainments or diversions, as events significant in their own right, moments when love or honor or fame was won and lost.[28]

The romances and poetry of the fifteenth century, in singing the praises of knights errant who risked their lives for the respect of their peers and the adoration of eligible women, bring their readers into a highly charged atmosphere of rivalries, real fighting, maimed contestants, and the brilliant play of sound and color.[29] The dramatic and romantic aspects of the knightly tournament were deliberate, an integral part of the action rather than a distraction or a backdrop. The challenges, oaths, and love interests that often organized these events reveal a blurring of the distinction between reality and fiction, as *caballeros* built episodes from the great romances into their own life stories.[30] In doing so, they gave to these sports narrative dimensions, a plot and protagonist. A tournament was rarely just a test of skills between two or more combatants, but a pivotal moment in their lives in which they sought to put into practice and on display their love, virtue, and fidelity. As such, it filled the social need for the enactment of dramatic and erotic stories that the theater, at this point still focused on biblical themes, would later appease.[31] Even the scenery could be deliberately designed to invoke the romances, as in the tournament at Valladolid in 1428, whose sets created an imagined world that included a mock castle complete with twenty-seven towers, a belfry, and a great arch.[32]

The dramatic and ornamental features of the tournament predominated at times, especially when kings or prominent nobles were involved, muting its warlike aspects and, in the eyes of those like Arévalo, its virtues. Lances tipped with coronals reduced the number of casualties and elaborate, ceremonial *arnés real* replaced the authentic and more dangerous *arnés de guerra*.[33] In losing its purely military focus, the tournament became a festive event for courtiers, with dancing, music, banquets, *entremeses* (brief plays, usually performed during the natural interludes between tournament events), poetry, and *invenciones* (word games and riddles). Such was the tournament that Alvaro de Luna, constable for Juan II, organized in honor of the royal family on 1 May 1436: "this festival was very well ordered with daytime jousts involving practice lances in a clearing and later with real weapons by torchlight in the palace. Many knights competed in the jousts, and the King, Queen, and prince dined richly in the constable's palace and they composed skits and danced the night away."[34] Luna was a master organizer of these multivalent spectacles; his biographer claimed that "he was very creative and much given to presenting *invenciones* and putting on *entremeses* in festivals or jousts or in mock battles, in which his *invenciones* always meant just what he intended."[35]

The *entremeses* and dramas were often comic, even burlesque, but they were never seditious. On the contrary, they served the same end as the tournaments themselves, to confirm the rank and privilege of those involved and to honor, even exalt, the monarchy. The closing ceremonies of a huge tournament held at Valladolid in 1434 neatly combined the literary, military, playful, and propagandistic aspects of knightly spectacle. After the jousts had been completed, the royals and contestants retired for dinner and dancing along with a number of nobles, ladies, and churchmen. Following dinner, the tournament judges rose and, dressed as the deities Eros and Mars, gave their verdicts, pronouncing Juan II as champion "because of his excellence as much as for the virtue of his magnificent royal person" and awarding him a fine horse while Alvaro de Luna, as host, received a feathered crest.[36]

Far bolder was Juan II's appearance at a 1428 tournament in Valladolid: "and the King left the *tela* with a dozen knights, he dressed as God the Father, and the others, all wearing crowns and each with the title of a Saint, carrying a sign of a martyr who had passed to our Lord God."[37] Yet here too the overt political significance of the monarch publicly identifying himself with God was leavened with a sense of play. Even so, Juan's decision to play God, so to speak, was a reminder to himself and to the crowd of the high expectations of a monarch. As God's regent on earth, he was above worldly reproach but was subject to divine judgment for his actions. The theme of humility and the quest for virtue, subtle though it often was, is a constant in fifteenth-century Castilian tournaments. While publicly proclaiming their status and power through wealth, literary diversions, and military proficiency, the nobility returned time and again to the values of their order, to the integrity of past heroes, to their holy mission.

From a cynical perspective, this is unsurprising. After all, knights owed their social station to their supposed ideals of piety, generosity, and asceticism. They could do no less than pay lip service to this standard for the benefit of the people, while they were bedecked in rich apparel and prancing about on fine chargers as a prelude to long nights of playacting, dancing, and drink. But the very pervasiveness of the theme points to a real insecurity; nobles knew what was expected of them, sincerely admired the heroes of the past, and did not delude themselves into thinking that the Cid or Fernán González would have behaved so. If they devoted themselves to wholly realizing one aspect of the model, that of physical courage, they did not reject its other facets but took pains to remind themselves, even in moments of revelry, of what true knighthood meant. In subordinating but not abandoning these lofty aspirations, the *caballería* kept alive the hope—in themselves as well as in the people—that they would someday be worthy of them.

Huizinga and others have condemned fifteenth-century knights for propping up an outdated ideal with the same tired scenes to the point where the repetition stripped the spectacles of their original beauty.[38] Perhaps, however, the endurance of a few dominant motifs is evidence of their lasting utility rather than of an inability or unwillingness to move forward. The themes of the tournament were archetypal—war, love, and virtue—and their sensory expression through sound and color was compelling. Even today, the glittering knights and bright banners of the joust are evocative images of the Middle Ages. Because they were based on fundamental ideas, their meanings were malleable. Knightly spectacles were adapted to each moment, each new set of circumstances.[39] The Farce of Ávila, though drawing on the same set of social understandings and staged in a similar manner, has little in common with the joyful larks of Juan II's court. Neither bears much resemblance to the ideal of knightly virtue advocated by Valera and Arévalo.

The frontier gave added resonance to the debates over the meaning and propriety of knightly tournaments. In one sense, it struck some observers as odd, even offensive, that knights would play at war while their "real" enemies lay just over the horizon. In another, just as jousts permitted nobles to symbolically define themselves and justify their place in society, the frontier was the one place in Castile where their redemption could be achieved in actuality: here play fighting and savage battle went hand in hand. The marriage of tournament and drama that evolved over the course of the fifteenth century was perhaps most fully realized on the frontier. Amiable enmity and physical insecurity provided a rich source of themes with which to play as well as a pressing need for magnates to engage with local populations. In Jaén, for instance, Miguel Lucas used tournaments and public displays of military skill as real training tools, his knights might compete against each other one day and raid Granada the next. But he also arranged complex theatrical performances to complement those tournaments, with mêlées and skirmishes often held on or near major holidays. In these productions, there was only a fine line between the political and social functions of the spectacle and the pure diversion of the *entremeses*. In all of his pageants, Iranzo made full use of visual elements—colorful costumes, coats of arms, and sumptuous embellishments—and constant music in order to heighten the audience's sense of unreality and to create a fantastic and diverting environment in which quotidian cares could be forgotten. From productions such as this, in which the dramatic element sometimes overshadowed the military training, it was only a small step to pure drama, to transforming the *entremeses* from sideshow into main event, as at Ávila.

*   *   *

The defense of and theoretical justification for military exercises and contests were, in part, responses to steady but, by the fifteenth century, generally passive clerical condemnation of tournaments and spectacles that dated back centuries. In the twelfth century, church luminaries such as Bernard of Clair-vaux as well as multiple popes harshly condemned the frivolity and vanity of knights, leading to a ban on tournaments. In the later Middle Ages, however, as more worldly clerics came to dominate the church, there was a shift in emphasis and in tone as the proper conduct of secular knights, and not their very existence, became the central issue. Didactic exhortations replaced, for the most part, the severity of Bernard and his ilk.[40]

In fifteenth-century Castile, the prominent bishop of Burgos, Alfonso de Cartagena, saw tournaments as an analogy for the faction fighting and civil wars that had plagued the country. Arguing that two unworthy activities dominated nobles' time, "the one is in conflicts of the kingdom, the other is in games of arms," Cartagena devoted an entire section of his mid-1440s *Doctrinal de los caballeros*, a compilation of Castilian laws relating to chivalry, to an impassioned plea that such games be banned.[41] He was particularly opposed to the fanciful and idealistic notions of knighthood presented in romances such as *Amadís* or the Arthurian legends, which he dismissed as reading material "of no useful value." Instead he espoused a concept of nobil-ity akin to Valera's, with an emphasis on knightly obligations and ideals.[42]

For Cartagena, a knight could earn prestige and honor only through the defense of the realm and holy war, never through success at tournaments. But too many knights saw the games as an end in themselves, a way to make a living, a reputation, and even an advantageous marriage. Their focus on play not only led to injuries and to death but also fomented noble rivalries and thus delayed the prosecution of war with Granada.[43] The tournament was not even a useful form of military training, for it lacked the true risk to life and limb that permitted a man to test his own mettle. As such, the honors and fame granted to champions were hollow. And so he lamented:

> But what can we tell ourselves, when we see a land full of money and of arms, and at peace with Granada? Should the nobles fidgeting to exercise their arms pit their armies against relatives and those who should be friends, or in jousts and tournaments, of which the one is loathsome and abominable and a thing which brings dishonor and destruction, and the other a game or test only, not the principal activity of a knight? For which reason, the philosopher [Aristotle] said that one cannot determine who is strong through tournaments and tests of arms. For true fortitude can only be known through terrible and life-endangering acts done for the common good. And an ancient proverb says that sometimes the successful tournament knight is the timid and cowardly one in battle.[44]

The prevalence of tournaments was, for Cartagena, an urgent problem. The knights of Castile guarded the frontiers of Christendom, but, as he stressed in the *Doctrinal*, the "recovery" of formerly Christian lands had not significantly advanced since 1264 because of infighting and distractions. The heroes of the past had triumphed because of their unity and because of Muslim complacency, but also because of their piety and gratitude for divine aid. Invoking Santiago's appearance at Clavijo, for instance, Cartagena held up King Ramiro I as a suitable model.[45] But now it was the Christians who had become complacent. Their failure to expel Islam from Iberia posed real dangers now that a new Muslim power, the Ottoman Turks, had arisen at the other end of the Mediterranean. Fearing a "pincer movement" in which Granadan and Turkish Muslims joined against them, Cartagena reminded *caballeros* of their obligations. Knights in France or England could play at their games and squabble among themselves; those in Castile needed to end their frivolous rivalries and engage the real enemy.[46] Noting that "jousts were banned in France at one time because it was understood that they obstructed the war in *Outremer*," he explicitly compared the twelfth- and fifteenth-century situations to present the reconquest of Iberia as a holy war equal to the Crusades in its importance.[47]

But Cartagena was also a pragmatist. He realized that his appeals were unlikely to end tournaments, given that papal bans had failed to do so. He therefore proposed a compromise: if knights must have their tournaments and jousts, they should do so within a strict set of rules. He specifically had in mind the code of the Order of the Band, a secular military order founded in the early fourteenth century by Alfonso XI.[48] For Cartagena, the order offered a number of advantages, foremost of which was order itself. It would join in brotherhood the young, ambitious, and competitive knights most likely to participate in tournaments. Its emphasis on piety and obedience would return knights' attention to their duties. Jousting would be a pastime only and tournaments held under the order's auspices would be both safer than in unregulated events (blunt weapons only would be permitted) and stripped of their playful and theatrical aspects. In short, Cartagena hoped that the Order of the Band would make the joust and melee what he thought they should be, military training exercises conducted in a spirit of collegiality rather than dangerous spectacles that sparked destructive rivalries and vendettas.[49]

Rodrigo Sánchez de Arévalo, who was Cartagena's student, presented a far sunnier perspective. A *letrado* theorist and bishop of Palencia who spent much of his life in Rome, Arévalo agreed with Valera on the link between virtue and military training, describing the practice of arms in the most glowing terms. In his *Vergel de los príncipes*, written in the mid-1450s, Arévalo described the importance for rulers and nobles of "honest sports and commendable exercises."[50] He began by arguing for the restorative value of such pursuits, observing that "continuous mental effort overtaxes and weakens not only the body, but also the human heart and its powers." In need of respite from their intellectual duties, a ruler should turn to physical activity instead of passive relaxation, because, in addition to offering their own rewards, "these sports and delights are the same as comfort and repose."[51] So which kinds of physical activities were the most virtuous and necessary? Foremost was "generous and noble exercise of arms, through which not only are kingdoms and lands defended but also expanded and improved." Second was hunting on horseback, and third was playing and composing of music.[52] For each of these noble pursuits, he described twelve *excellencias*, or qualities.

He summarized the benefits of martial sports in the eighth *excellencia*, listing the many noble virtues it might foster: obedience, patience, perseverance, fortitude, magnanimity, liberty, openness, justice, and temperance. The exercise of arms also destroyed vices and evils, including injustice, pugnacity, avarice, pride, and arrogance. The ultimate goal of all this military preparation, as revealed in the twelfth *excellencia*, was no less than the redemption of the world and the triumph of good over evil. For "through such noble exercises and temporal deeds of arms, men are prepared and trained for the spiritual war which we have with our invisible enemies, that is to say, with the devil, and with the world and with vices."[53] For Arévalo, this spiritual war was inherently unending and required eternal vigilance. And so the ruler "should not cease the acts and exercises and preludes which are the image of war," for such training not only kept Christian warriors fit for battle but, by improving their moral character, were themselves significant victories in the struggle against evil.[54]

Church observers may have been divided on the merits of martial sports but they had no such difficulties with nonmilitary spectacles. Clerics of all stations were regular participants in any number of organized performances, both secular (coronations, royal entrances, noble weddings, births, and funerals) and religious (the liturgy, processions honoring local saints, and sermons). Public spectacles were the central means by which the Church communicated with the masses and, like the organizers of tournaments, they intentionally evoked emotional responses through clothing, decoration, and formalized speech. Such displays could be as elaborate and expensive as any knightly creation. Feast day processions, for instance, often required ad hoc taxes to defray the costs of splendid decorations, troops of musicians, and sumptuous feasts. Another type of major event was public preaching. Although local priests generally gave Sunday sermons, municipal *concejos* or guilds would contract mendicants for holidays, when a big crowd might be expected.

Successful preachers were master performers, unafraid to give their lessons a theatrical character. They could move from invective to tears in a few moments and the emotional absorption of both preacher and flock could be so complete as to disturb those unfamiliar with the experience, like the later French traveler Barthélemy Joly, who commented that, "in their preaching, they make use of an impressive vehemence. . . . On this topic, two things disturb me in the Spanish sermons: the extreme, almost turbulent, impetuousness of the preacher and the continual sighs of the women, so loud and forceful that they completely disrupt one's attention."[55]

Saint Vincent Ferrer's well-documented tour through Murcia in 1411–1412, while unusual in its scale, exemplifies the importance accorded to public preaching. Ferrer, who came to Murcia at the invitation of Pablo de Santa

María, bishop of Cartagena (and father of Alfonso de Cartagena), brought a retinue of three hundred, all of whom had to be fed and lodged, a task that fell to the local Dominican prior.[56] Additional preparations included the construction of a pulpit and arrangement of space for the substantial crowds who came to hear the famous preacher. Efforts were likely taken to ensure that the audience was orderly, even to the extent of forbidding mothers to bring young children "because their crying distracts the preacher," as happened in 1435 and again in 1472.[57]

In return for their efforts and expenditures, the municipal authorities hoped for dramatic social repercussions and in this they were largely gratified. Ferrer effectively called Murcianos to greater moral fervor, permitting the *concejo* to pass a series of new laws against collective sins such as gambling.[58] At the same time, the amiable enmity of the frontier meant that visiting preachers had to tread carefully when commenting on interfaith concerns. Ferrer, for instance, made an impassioned appeal for strict segregation between the various religious communities in the city, and particularly for the removal of Jews from much of civic life. But, although they were very much open to these ideas, the *concejo* was chiefly concerned with local antiseignorial movements and the broader problem of urban violence. Their hope for Ferrer's visit was that, "through the words he preaches to many people, he may move Christians as well as Jews and Muslims to voluntarily pardon the deaths of their fathers and mothers, siblings and other relatives as well as other offenses and injuries" and thus put an end to reciprocal violence and ongoing feuds.[59]

Although they could be comfortable on stage, clerics tended to remain on the margins of more playful public events. The idea that they should spend their leisure time in service to God was well established, as were priestly obligations to serve as moral exemplars. The expectations for their public and private comportment were explicitly laid out not only in ecclesiastic law but also in the civil code, as the *Partidas* decreed that "prelates should pay careful attention to their conduct as men whose example others follow, as above stated; and for that reason, they should not witness exhibitions, as, for instance, lance throwing, tilting or fights with bulls or other wild beasts, or visit those who take part in them. Moreover, they should not throw dice, or play draughts, or ball, or quoits, or any games like those which tend to interfere with their composure, nor should they remain to witness them, or be familiar with those who play them."[60]

The documentary record for the actual behavior of ecclesiastics is scattered and frequently unreliable. This is due partly to the paucity of official church records, which understandably glossed over this issue, and partly to the nature of chronicle and literary descriptions, which often presented highly subjective views of the clergy. The minutes, however, of a number of synods held in fifteenth-century Castile detail attempts to legislate clerical behavior, while reports from diocesan inspectors describe the failings of the parish priests.[61] From these sources, it appears that efforts to proscribe playful activities were less than effective, leaving the councils repeatedly obliged to ratify formal bans on any number of private or semiprivate diversions. These ranged from drinking in taverns, consorting with women, and playing at cards and dice to attending bullfights or public dances and musical performances to participating in burlesque dramas.

But church authorities sought to improve not only the morality of the clergy, but also that of society as a whole. Both Cartagena and Arévalo, although they disagreed sharply in their views of *caballero* tournaments, emphasized the moral influence of these spectacles. Although Cartagena's objections were frequently echoed by others, knightly jousts and melees did not receive much overt church scrutiny. This lack of reaction may in part be explained by the frequent presence of high ecclesiastic officials at the more lavish events, where they mingled with their temporal peers. What really drew their ire were the *entremeses* and theatrics that frequently accompanied these games, especially those that mocked, or seemed to them to mock, holy rituals. Most efforts to suppress *entremeses*, however, focused on popular festivals. While these had much in common with noble tournaments, their relative lack of powerful sponsors made them more attractive targets for suppression.

Such events were performed in all Castilian cities but seem to have been more popular and prevalent—or at least better documented—in some places. On the frontier, Murcia, for instance, possessed a particularly vibrant festive culture that led to a number of ecclesiastic and civil attempts to curb its ardor.[62] These festive activities took a number of forms, from spontaneous celebrations and games to formal dramatic presentations. The most elaborate tended to fall near major church holidays, including Carnival immediately before Lent or the festival of the *reyes pájares* on 27 December.[63] This timing incensed the clergy, who especially despised games of ridicule (*juegos de escarnio*), in which sacred rites were given a comic or burlesque treatment.[64] They therefore tried to abolish popular events that coincided with religious observances but lacked a strictly liturgical character. In 1473, for instance, the Council of Aranda prohibited playful spectacles during the festivals of Christmas, Saint Stephen, Saint John, and the Holy Innocents, referring specifically to "staged games, performances with masks or monsters, spectacles and other diverse fictions . . . clumsy poems and burlesque speeches."[65]

How does this discourse relate to ecclesiastic reception of noble spectacles and tournaments? Whether or not Church authorities considered sporting events to be moral threats for secular participants and spectators, they deemed clerical involvement in almost any aspect of those occasions as unacceptable. Moreover, they would likely have deemed the majority of the plays and skits presented during breaks as *juegos de escarnio*. Nevertheless, the church's purview was not wholly spiritual, and political considerations made direct criticisms of *caballero* spectacle relatively rare. That positive relations with influential nobles outweighed the moral dangers of irreverent theater is attested to by the presence of often-senior churchmen at these games. Several prominent bishops and archbishops, to give just one example, attended the closing banquet for the 1434 tournament in Valladolid in which Roman gods handed out the trophies.[66] It is unlikely that they openly decried any pagan or burlesque elements in a skit honoring the king himself. Politics aside, such acts were *fun*. Church officials high and low attended them, participated in them, and tacitly condoned them for just that reason; they were a guilty pleasure that many no doubt rationalized as less heinous than other available forms of entertainment.

*   *   *

The onlookers who gathered at knightly tournaments to enjoy the sports as well as the skits and *entremeses* were perfectly aware that the nobility presented such shows to confirm their social status, to parade their wealth, fidelity, and courage before their peers, and to demonstrate both their generosity and their monopoly on the use of force. They were also fully cognizant that the church nominally condemned these shows but that this disapproval was insufficient to prevent all but the most zealous prelates from attending. Commoners lacked a voice both in the content of these performances and in the dominant mode of analyzing them. They did not record in writing their experiences of the tournament and, when they appear in chroniclers' accounts, it is collectively, as the large crowd whose presence confirmed the prominence of the organizers or the appeal of the message.

However, audiences need not have consented to the perceptions of reality shown to them. In practice, spectator priorities acted in concert with noble and church messages to create meaning. Although popular concerns varied from time to time and place to place, and it is misleading to make broad generalizations, there were several structural issues that nearly always influenced popular perceptions of power in fifteenth-century Castile. Chief among these were economic stresses related to the degradation of the currency and particularly the price of grain. The structure of urban society and the concentration of power in noble hands rankled many of the nascent merchant class who not only resented high taxes and their lack of influence but also aspired to the very trappings of nobility and knighthood flaunted in the tournaments. Religious as well as social boundaries divided urban populations, with ambivalence toward religious minorities a constant undercurrent.[67] There was a growing desire among the populace for their own public statements of civic identity and religious devotion, expressions that may have competed with noble tournaments but also drew inspiration from them.[68] Finally, the role of diversion should not be ignored; festivals were enjoyable, regardless of their sponsorship, and even the bluntest propaganda represented a bit of excitement and a break in the workday.

Elites were aware of all this. For them, it was imperative that their spectacles would result in the desired audience reactions. To do otherwise would be to open themselves to ridicule, to inadvertently promote undesired ideas, or to risk the crowd getting out of control. This meant that they were forced to adjust their messages to fit the expectations of spectators or, rather, to fit their own perceptions of what those expectations might be. In order to achieve their own purposes, Fernando de Antequera, the conspirators at Ávila, Miguel Lucas, and others had to meet their audiences, composed primarily of commoners, halfway. This could take a number of forms: they might deliberately employ familiar themes and turn these in new directions, they could pander to the crowd by telling them what (elites thought) they wanted to hear, or they softened a message by presenting it in ambivalent terms. What they could not do was explicitly tell the crowd what to think; spectators had to reach their own conclusions. They did so by weighing the ideas presented to them through their personal experiences and through the dominant discourses in Castilian society.

CHAPTER 2

The Meanings of Civic Space

For Miguel Lucas de Iranzo, the birth of his son and heir was a momentous occasion, one that he marked with a flurry of celebrations, both public and private, that lasted several days.[1] He began by formally presenting baby Luis to the people of Jaén. Well-wishers were admitted to his palace in strict order (nobles and officials, then noblewomen and their maids, merchants, artisans, peasants, and finally common women). Miguel Lucas then emerged to the shouted congratulations of the crowd and, hoisted on the shoulders of two knights, joined an impromptu parade to the church of Santa María Magdalena. There he asked nuns to join him as he prayed for his son. Next on his crowded itinerary was a lunch with high-ranking officials at the palace, followed by jousts in the afternoon and public banquets at all the parish plazas in the evening. The next day began with more banquets, now in the parish cemeteries, and further popular entertainments. *Regidor* Fernándo de Berrio led a live wolf through the streets with hunting dogs and horns while mummer shows, dances, and skits ensured that a range of diversions were available.

Six days later, on 18 April, Luis was baptized in the cathedral. The journeys to the cathedral and back to the palace were in formal procession, but Miguel Lucas then walked with the people to a bullfight at the Plaza del Arrabal, outside the city walls. There he, as was his custom, "with the *regidores* and other knights and squires, ascended a viewing stand (*mirador*) of the kind made for such events. This was very finely adorned with the best French tapestries and others made of silk."[2] The day ended with a private banquet at the palace, while those outside were treated to a free meal and the various performances in the streets and plazas continued unabated. Castilian nobles often marked key events in their lives—births, deaths, marriages—

with public displays of munificence, the usual intent of which was to confirm their own social standing. Miguel Lucas was nothing if not thorough, however. In fêting his son, he aimed not only to enhance his reputation by appealing to all his many constituencies but also to unify and transform civic topography.

Some of his displays deliberately inverted customary uses of particular spaces (a wild animal in the streets, banquets in the cemeteries) and were meant to fix the day in public memory. Others (sporting events and free meals) exhibited the constable's generosity, while his ostentatious prayers in the cloister and cathedral proved his piety. The egalitarian processions to the Magdalena and the Arrabal, moreover, demonstrated his affinity for the masses and singled out particular neighborhoods for his attention. No parish failed to receive at least some notice, as smaller banquets and entertainments were offered in each. Miguel Lucas thus transformed the birth of Luis de Iranzo from a notable event within the city's ruling family into a celebration of Jaén itself in all its guises—as a unified entity, as Christian, as a collection of barrios, as both sacred and profane, as a highly stratified society and an egalitarian brotherhood. In other words, he portrayed Jaén as an authentic community, but also emphasized it was a community centered on himself.[3]

The civic community Miguel Lucas proclaimed and the displays through which he proclaimed it were indelibly linked. The tournaments and theatrics that proliferated in fifteenth-century Castile were urban phenomena, requiring the physical environments, artisanal skills, financial resources, and organizational expertise cities fostered. Only in cities, moreover, were there crowds sufficient to make the effort worthwhile. But urban settings did more than provide the logistical capacity to conduct mass spectacles. As the physical and social stage on which such performances were conducted, cities had an indelible impact on their content and reception.

A civic spectacle was more than a village event writ large. Living in a city, according to fifteenth-century authors, was transformative; the urban environment had powerful and lasting effects on one's personality and character. But its effect was not necessarily positive. Someone daily stimulated by positive, temperate sights and sounds would be energetic and creative. But that same person would fall prey to lassitude and degenerate behavior if regularly oppressed by an unforgiving climate or crime or decrepit buildings. It was not only the physical milieu that mattered, however. To fully realize their personal potential, citizens required opportunities to cultivate their minds and bodies, including access to parks, musicians, teachers, and a close-knit, supportive society and the leisure time to make use of all of these. Public spectacles, from this perspective, were integral to a city's proper functioning, allowing the community moments to withdraw from quotidian cares and to come together as a unified body social. Jean-Charles Payen has argued that, without cities, "le théâtre ne peut exister."[4] In fifteenth-century Castile, the reverse was also true.

The commentaries that expressed such opinions centered on philosophical descriptions of ideal cities, but they were not wholly theoretical. Fifteenth-century accounts of Seville and Córdoba, for instance, applauded them for actually creating model environments. Neither of their authors, however, succeeded in considering the cities in their totality. They focused instead on those districts with which they were most familiar and that best fit their agendas. This reveals a central feature of medieval Castilian cities: their division into neighborhoods or quarters with distinct characters. The fragmentary quality of cities had a number of consequences for the experience of public spectacles. It defined potential audiences, for instance, as individuals tended to move within limited areas of their city, frequenting the same streets and markets while staying close to familiar people and sights. For all but the most anticipated or publicized events, the composition of the crowd largely reflected the demographics of its immediate surroundings. By determining the collective influences on members of the audience, the location of an event thus predicted, to some degree, its reception.

Strong neighborhood allegiances also influenced individual identities. While a person might describe oneself as a native of Jaén and take great pride in this heritage, professions of parish affiliation and occupation that qualified the general statement of Jiennense birth were more meaningful because they explained *which* Jaén one hailed from. Those presenting spectacles to the public had to navigate sentiments of both unity and divisiveness, leading them to promote a myth of civic solidarity while confirming existing social divisions and hierarchies.

Public spectacles were a primary means through which civic elites communicated with those under their authority. Rulers like Miguel Lucas did this by making use of the ways in which people emotionally and cognitively navigated their urban environments. They employed specific civic spaces—public buildings, markets, plazas, streets, and landmarks—to define, clarify, or augment the messages expressed in their spectacles. In some cases, this was a simple association of a pageant with a location whose meaning was well defined. Those meanings, however, could be and often were mutable. At times, rulers were able to shift or transform them to better suit the purposes of their spectacles. Works of ephemeral architecture, or structures built for a particular event, were a favored means of doing so. By constructing barriers and viewing platforms, elites underlined the stratified nature of civic society by assigning a spatial hierarchy to formerly egalitarian spaces. But not all ephemeral structures were overt attempts to confirm the social order. Fanciful wooden palaces, castles, or arches, for instance, could turn a market square into a scene from a romance or a cathedral plaza into a frontier citadel that must be defended from infidels. Regardless of their specific form, the purpose of all such edifices was the same: to make spectators more amenable to the message behind a performance. This strategy was based on contemporary understandings of what a city was and what it meant to live in one. While it was not limited to cities on the frontier, of course, the use of spectacle and of the mutable meanings of urban spaces was of particular importance to the rulers of borderlands cities. Amiable enmity and physical anxiety meant that elites often had to address important issues obliquely. Their need for effective modes of expressing their readings of social and religious issues combined with an abundance of themes with which to do so, making the region a crucible of political pageantry.

*   *   *

For fifteenth-century thinkers, cities were more than mere aggregations of people and buildings; they were natural and artificial environments that profoundly influenced the character of those who dwelled in them. In this they differed from the thirteenth-century *Partidas*, which described the city as "a place surrounded by walls" and a "communal gathering of men—the old, those of middling age, and the young."[5] Drawing upon a body of work that included classical authors such as Aristotle and Strabo as well as more recent travel literature including the *Mirabilis urbis Romae* and humanist descriptions of other Italian cities, several Castilian authors commented on how an agreeable setting benefited human temperament. Among them was Rodrigo Sánchez de Arévalo, who stressed the importance of situating a city in an advantageous location, particularly one with a temperate climate.[6]

He also devoted significant attention to issues relevant to the frontier and perhaps inspired by it. Although he did not refer specifically to the amiable enmity of the border with Granada, Arévalo argued that too much contact with foreigners undermined the social structure of a city "because people are

naturally eager to try new customs and things, from which great inconvenience and harm comes to the city and which is the beginning of corruption
within it."[7] Instead, he proposed that commerce with foreigners take place
in smaller towns and villages located on the water (or on the frontier), a
solution that kept outsiders segregated from the general population and
allowed the city to remain free of possible contagion.

On military matters, Arévalo decreed that leaders should ensure that
their cities be well prepared for war, with a unified citizenry and extensive
stockpiles of provisions and weapons. The most significant of these preparations was the fostering of a disciplined and well-prepared standing cavalry
militia. By describing in detail the attributes of such horsemen and the training required to develop their potential, Arévalo underscored their central and
indispensable role in his idealized city. They were not only to provide physical security to the populace but also to defend municipal honor and morality.
Arévalo would brook no attempts to water down these holy duties: "Although the *caballeros* nowadays do not swear specifically to these things, they
swear to them silently in accepting the knighthood, and they are no less
hypocritical than if they were to do something contrary to what they expressly
vowed."[8] The city, as conceived here, revolved around knights; if they failed
to uphold their venerable traditions, the social structure would inevitably fall.

As we have already seen, Arévalo saw public military training as an essential component in the creation of an urban militia that was both morally
sound and effective in combat. But he did not limit the benefits of public
displays to the martial. He took a classical understanding of leisure time
(*otium cum dignitate*) as the opportunity to withdraw from daily affairs in
order to cultivate one's intellectual or spiritual aspects and ultimately achieve
virtue. Leisure was also an opportunity for people to invigorate themselves,
cast off the worries of the world, refresh their social bonds, and take joy in
life. Certain types of public spectacles facilitated all this, and so Arévalo
advised rulers to guarantee "that certain representations and public games are
presented on special days for the joy and consolation of the inhabitants of
the city."[9]

If such a city—situated in a beneficial location and free from foreign
influences, shielded by a dedicated order of *caballeros*, governed by the wise,
and peopled by thoughtful citizens who came together on occasion for public
acts of catharsis—was the ideal as seen through fifteenth-century eyes, how
did real cities measure up? Arévalo did not comment at length about any
particular city. In fact, only a few fifteenth-century Castilian authors offered

extended descriptions of contemporary cities, a marked contrast to the popularity of the genre in later centuries.[10] In those that portrayed frontier cities,
we can see agreement with Arévalo on the links between the human spirit
and its environment but also important differences, particularly on the role
of foreign influences.

Don Jerónimo of Córdoba, a canon of the Real Colegiata de San Hipólito
during the reign of Enrique IV, likely wrote his *Descriptio cordubae* sometime
before taking up this position and while away from the city. In his prologue,
he described himself as an exile and referred to wide-ranging travels: to the
Holy Land, Italy, Greece, and Muslim countries.[11] These journeys and his
experiences abroad made a deep impression on him. Nevertheless, he retained
a fond memory of his native land's soft beauty, noting its ideal combination of
rivers, fields, and hills, a landscape that evoked images of the Garden of Eden.
In terms akin to those of Arévalo, he opined that "a sweltering climate generates
plagues but also inventive people. A cold climate brings forth slow, fraudulent,
and ignorant minds. Only a temperate climate brings together positive qualities
in the customs of the people. This is what was said about ancient Athens, the
seat of wisdom, because the clarity of the air there brought about clarity of the
senses and prepared people for the contemplation of wisdom."[12]

Alfonso de Palencia, in an undated letter composed at roughly the same
time as Jerónimo's *Descriptio*, praised Seville to the archdeacon of Carrión, a
friend who had left that city to live in Palencia, as a means of comforting him
in his exile. Palencia similarly commented on the beneficial climate and the
natural bounty of the city's hinterlands, but in an altogether more practical
sense. For Palencia, the advantages of the natural environment lay in its contributions to civic wealth and physical vigor.[13] In cataloging Seville's wealth in
wheat, fish, olive oil, and livestock, he noted its self-sufficiency and its ability
to outproduce any three Italian cities. In describing the temperate climate, he
made the familiar comparisons to regions that are too cold or too hot but
emphasized its health benefits rather than its ability to foster a particular character: "For here a person does not endure the numbing cold which makes one's
limbs lifeless, nor can we compare it to the tropics when the summer sun is
most intense. There never lacks a breeze strong enough to refresh the young,
breathe vigor and life into the old, and comfort and succour the infirm . . . it
seems as if people here only rarely die of illness before the age of eighty."[14]

Palencia did not contest the notion that one's surroundings have a profound influence on his or her character; rather, he deemed the most relevant
physical features in the urban environment to be those made by man. Nature,

or more properly God, "that supreme artisan and architect," had provided
Seville most generously with the raw materials of prosperity and virtue.[15] It
was only in the hands of a noble and talented people, however, that such
gifts could be made to flower. Palencia's perspective on this had been shaped
by his time in Italy and particularly by the impressive reworking of Florence
that took place over the course of the fifteenth century. In *De perfectione
militaris triumphi*, a treatise written in the late 1450s, Palencia has Exercitum
(an allegorical figure representing military discipline) marvel at the links
between noble people and noble surroundings: "He did not leave before
seeing all parts of the great city and delighting in visiting the beautifully
arranged temples and in considering the public buildings, much more refined
than the pen can describe, on whose façades were written letters that praised
the deeds of its citizens in peace and in war . . . and the men on the streets
seemed like consuls or patricians, not unlike their ancient Roman ancestors."[16] To this flowering of human potential, Palencia contrasted Rome
itself, whose magnificent ancient buildings had fallen into ruin and destroyed
the harmonious ambiance that once had been. Now, "this ugly landscape
wounds the soul through the windows of the eyes" and the Romans "for this
reason have turned their native intelligence to interpretations of the law and
other bureaucratic obligations." Meanwhile they had been outstripped by
their Florentine neighbors, who were ingenious and eloquent "because they
daily contemplate with joyful eyes their well-ordered world and contemplate
a city flowering in more than just name."[17]

So how did the people of Seville build their world? According to Palencia, it was with elegant simplicity and pragmatic industry. His discussion
of why Seville had developed into such an entrepôt neatly encapsulated his
understanding of natural and artificial environments. Here too the city possessed a number of natural benefits that human hands had harnessed and
improved. "The river," for instance, "accommodates great ships and protects
them from all storms. These ships are propelled by wind or oars until they
reach the city's bridge, which, because of the water's great depth and the
sandy bottom, was constructed upon small boats."[18] Further, the city's general layout was circular, with high walls designed to act in concert with the
river to provide a secure defensive system. Within the walls was a dense
network of streets, public buildings, and housing that provided for the needs
of a large population while simultaneously displaying the civic pride and
architectural skills of the citizens, "between the walls are sacred temples and

incredible buildings constructed through the arts of Daedalus [that is, with great skill] that house 150,000 inhabitants."[19]

Although it would seem thus far that he was in accord with Arévalo (with whom he likely studied in the household of Alfonso de Cartagena), Palencia emphasized throughout that the source of Seville's wealth was the trade to which much of the populace was devoted. He had no fear of foreign influences and commented a number of times on the close relationships between Seville and the Italian cities whose merchants thronged the markets of the city. It was not only the Italians who came to buy and sell. In a passage that recalls the cosmopolitan Seville of the thirteenth-century *Primera crónica general*, Palencia noted with pride that "here there is such a great gathering of merchants that, if you consider only the languages, it truly seems like another Babel."[20]

It was the moral virtue of its citizens and specifically their ability to not be overcome with greed, however, that enabled Seville to maintain and expand its trade. In *De perfectione militaris triumphi*, Palencia praised the citizens of Barcelona for their self-criticism, which enabled them to avoid complacency and arrogance, while also commenting on the beauty and size of the exchange in which they gathered to transact business. He later claimed that Barcelona's leaders succumbed to these very sins in the 1460s, to the detriment of their city.[21] He saw no danger of the same happening in Seville, for its inhabitants could live comfortably enough while still devoting themselves to cultural activities, which they knew to be more wholesome than the pursuit of ever-greater wealth: "They possess great domestic comforts and would have even more if it were not that surfeit leads to sloth. For those are not wanton, the benefits of dwelling under the sun here in our homeland are life and light and joy; one does not have to labor unduly, and is appropriately recompensed for his work."[22] For Palencia, as for Arévalo, leisure well spent was a hallmark of civic society. Seville's achievement was that its wealth permitted such repose even as its harmonious architecture inspired the people to engage in cultural activity.

The modernity of the built environment was nearly as important to Palencia as its appearance. He allowed that ancient edifices could be as sublime and as capable of rousing the spirit as anything built in the fifteenth century, but, as demonstrated by the example of Rome, these usually retained but a shadow of their former glory, having fallen into disuse or been plundered for building materials. And so his exemplars were invariably modern:

the Florentine customs and architecture he praised were quattrocento innovations and the exchange in Barcelona was built at the end of the fourteenth century. He did not, however, devote much ink to the monuments of Seville, choosing to focus instead on its utilitarian marvels.[23]

If Seville's virtue lay in forbearance, Córdoba could boast the courage of its residents. Its very name—which Jerónimo understood to mean "it raises up the heart"—referenced this quality, as did the outline of the city walls, which he described as resembling the shape of a lion. This layout was no happenstance for him, but a symbol of the city's valiant defense of the frontier: "like a lion tears apart the beasts, just so this city of courageous people frequently suffered the insults of its pernicious enemies and attacked them with a mighty hand."[24] The constant vigilance implied by this comparison carried over into civic life, which revolved around its public spaces. The most notable such area in Córdoba was not an imposing, modern marketplace thronged with Italian merchants, but its "large and spacious open-air theater in which the judges meet to hold court and rule on civil cases and the young men learn their military skills through games." That such events were public is clear from his account, as he referred to the training exercises as "spectacles," describing their intricacies in detail.[25] Córdoba's most prized product was not one destined for export and trade. Instead, the locally bred horses were renowned for their agility and strength, qualities necessary for complex military maneuvers that challenged their riders and protected the citizens.

Jerónimo gave some attention to other significant civic landmarks, including the Alcázar and its extensive gardens, but he reserved his most lavish praise for the "glory of Spain and Córdoba's signal distinction of honor, the illustrious seat of its bishop, and a monument that honors its kings," the Cathedral of Santa María, the former Great Mosque of Córdoba.[26] In a fulsome description of a building that he claimed outshone all the seven wonders of the ancient world, Jerónimo seemed not to care that its twelve doors, its arcades, and its fountains were all products of Islamicate culture and a testament to the vibrant civilization of those "pernicious enemies" displaced by Córdoba's Christian inhabitants. He even commented on the beauty of the minaret: "Standing there is a famous tower built of stone, inscribed with geometric patterns and decorated with marble latticework, whose cornice terminates in a bronze pinnacle. One climbs it by the two interior staircases where it seems that the architect truly outdid himself."[27] Here is Arévalo's fear of foreign contagion imbued with a frontier flavor: in a city where preparations for war against Islam were constant, a city whose shape and name alluded to this overriding purpose, one could still wander a mostly intact mosque and take pleasure in the elegant design of the "throne made for a certain king Almanzor, decorated with ivory tracings and set under a coffered ceiling."[28]

*   *   *

Palencia's and Jerónimo's accounts of their respective cities bear several features—a wholesome climate, impressive buildings, an active citizenry—in common with each other as well as with Arévalo's ideal metropolis. Can these parallels, however, be said to reflect a broad consensus about perceptions of urban life in Castilian society? Certainly none of these authors was typical, nor did any have a popular audience in mind. Palencia and Jerónimo wrote in Latin while making generous use of literary and biblical allusions to display their erudition, limiting potential readers to scholars and clergy. Although *Suma de la política* was one of two works that Arévalo composed in Castilian as opposed to Latin (*Vergel de los príncipes* was the other), a circumstance that implies a desire to reach a wider audience, his extensive reliance on classical philosophy and his subject matter would only have added intellectually inclined aristocrats to this readership.[29]

Nor were their experiences representative of Castilian city dwellers, even among the literati. It is surely no coincidence that all three spent significant amounts of time in Italy or that all their writings allude to exile.[30] In one sense, this is to be expected. Few people devote much time to reflecting on familiar surroundings; how many of us have given serious thought to the spaces in which we spend our daily lives? It is only when we have left our regular haunts that we contemplate their comforts and personal significance. Their travels also exposed these authors to a broad range of urban conditions, permitting them to view their native lands from a comparative perspective. It is certainly true, as Robert Brian Tate notes, that "a trip to Italy does not mean that one necessarily returns as a humanist." But Italy *did* have this effect on Palencia, whose work bore many of the hallmarks of the humanists with whom he studied and who was particularly clear about his reactions to different Italian cities, seeing in Florence the epitome of urban life while using Rome as a cautionary tale about resting on the laurels of the past.[31] But the label of humanist fits only moderately well on Arévalo and not at all on Jerónimo. Yet even their more traditional outlooks had been developed through extended exposure to many of the most cosmopolitan cities in the

Mediterranean world and to the literary debates raging within them; even
the most parochial of Jerónimo's arguments reflects the influence of these
experiences.

Humanist aspirations were not the norm in Castilian society but neither
were they unknown or limited to a select group of scholars. To a degree, the
culture of the court and the high nobility was a combination of medieval
mores with Italian humanist principles.[32] But even if Palencia and Jerónimo's
impressions of urban space were familiar to some magnates, we would still
have little reason to suspect that they reflected popular understandings.

We do not—alas!—know of any displaced Andalucían artisans or laborers who, pining away in Italy, penned an account of how they recalled their
native city, its personal significance, or its ideal features. We can, however,
turn to the fictional experiences of Francisco Delicado's heroine Lozana, an
Iberian expatriate in Rome lavishly described in the novel *Retrato de la
Lozana andaluza*.[33] Drawing historical conclusions from any work of fiction
entails the risk of mistaking artistic license for reality. The dangers are minimal in this case, however, as Delicado has been widely applauded for his
faithful portrait of the lives of lower-class Andalucían women in Spain and
in Rome at the time, with one commentator going so far as to describe the
"photographic naturalism" of the work. Delicado himself wrote of his efforts
to base events on real life and paid much attention to linguistic details, composing *La Lozana* in the common tongue of Andalucía and revealing a familiarity with "the culture of the street."[34]

La Lozana begins in Córdoba, where the protagonist Lozana (also called
Aldonza) was born into a poor *converso* family around 1490. After her parents
died, she traveled throughout the western Mediterranean world before set-
tling in Rome in 1513. Although much of the action therefore takes place in
the Pozzo Bianco, an Andalucían quarter of Rome, the novel includes a number of invaluable references to Córdoba that provide a counterpoint to Jerónimo's idealized presentation of a city distinguished by its favorable climate,
natural beauty, and imposing monuments. Lozana instead defined Córdoba
through personal relationships, local allegiances, and notable events, a perspective that highlights several Cordoban landmarks not mentioned at all by
Jerónimo while casting others in a new light.

Early in the work, for instance, Lozana offers an impassioned defense of
her culinary talents, concluding that "all the cloth merchants in the Calle de
la Feria wanted to try [my cooking]."[35] The Calle de la Feria, shown in Map

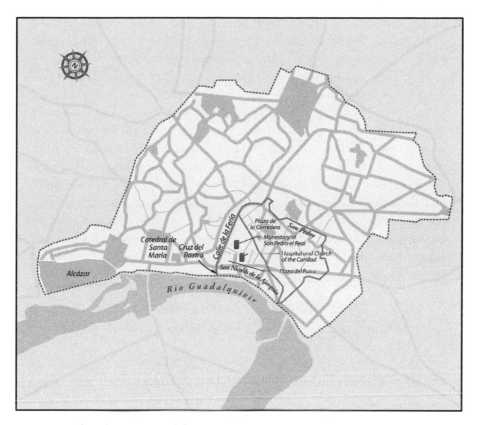

MAP 2. Fifteenth-century Córdoba.

2, played a central role in Cordoban life, both as a physical divide (between the older walled Medina area to the west and the eastern and more industrial Ajerquía) and as the heart of the city's commerce.

In addition to housing numerous shops and workshops, this street was, as its name indicates, the site for regular market fairs specializing in woolen cloth and luxuries.[36] Lozana's talk of cooking blurred the line between private and communal spaces, explicitly linking the domestic duty of preparing food for family to the public role of selling such food in the marketplace. But the differences between relations, neighbors, and acquaintances could be blurry. Later in life, comparing her current situation and poverty to her past in Córdoba, she noted that her cooking had pleased "not only my father, but all my relatives." This loosely defined group seems to have included those cloth merchants on the Feria, for she went on to lament that "then I spent my time pleasing my own people, now I please only strangers."[37]

Delicado again invoked this sense of neighborhood solidarity when describing Lozana's first days in Rome, when she was trying to find a means of earning a living and a place to stay. Her plan was simple: she would seek out Spanish expatriates and then claim that she had relations in their hometowns to ingratiate herself. "If she met someone from Alcalá la Real, then there she had a cousin, and another in Baena, and relatives from Luque and in Peña de Martos. She met people from Arjona, Arjonilla, and Montoro, and had relatives and cousins in all these places."[38] Central to the ruse's success, of course, was the ubiquity of such widespread families and a culture of hospitality that extended to even the relatives of neighbors. As it happened, Lozana soon came upon an authentic connection when a woman from Seville spotted her walking along the street and called out to her:

My lady, are you Spanish? What are you looking for?
LOZANA: Madam, even though I'm dressed as a Genovese woman, I am Spanish and from Córdoba.
SEVILLAN WOMAN: From Córdoba? By your life, all of us have relatives there! In what part of Córdoba did you live?
LOZANA: Madam, in the Tannery [*Curtiduría*].
SEVILLAN WOMAN: By your life, a cousin of mine married a rich tanner there! So relax here, I want to send for my cousin Teresa de Córdoba so she can see you![39]

The Tannery of Córdoba was located just to the north of the Guadalquivir River in the parish (*collación*) of San Nicolás de la Ajerquía. Tanning, which involved a great deal of pollution, had a deleterious effect on those living nearby and was often associated with Jews or *conversos*. It is therefore no surprise that the neighborhood was known for its *converso* character.[40]

The same parish also housed many of Córdoba's brothels, which were centered around the Plaza del Potro; their attendant crime combined with the stench of the tanneries made for an unsavory environment. The area was famous at the time and even Cervantes, who briefly lived in Córdoba, reportedly modeled the inn featured in *Don Quixote* on the Mesón del Potro.[41] It was, in short, just the sort of place that Jerónimo would neglect to mention in his tribute to Córdoba but whose dangers and *converso* population would have fostered close ties among moderately respectable families such as Lozana's.

The differences between Jerónimo's Córdoba and the grittier city remembered in *La Lozana* are best clarified by comparing their treatments of an identical location. Jerónimo's spacious open-air "theater" is the still extant (although much modified) Plaza de la Corredera, an area originally set aside as open space in which to exercise horses.[42] By the fifteenth century, the Corredera, in San Pedro parish directly to the north of San Nicolás de la Ajerquía, had become one of the central gathering places in the city, so busy that the municipal authorities made their public announcements there. The judges Jerónimo mentioned were the *alcaldes ordinarios*, who settled cases from a public bench on the east end of the plaza, near the Hospital de la Santísima Trinidad y San Pedro.[43] The equestrian military exercises Jerónimo extolled were still common in the fifteenth century, but were only one of a host of sporting events and festivities. These were so popular that property owners who rented homes along the plaza reserved for themselves the rights to use their buildings for views of the bullfights, festivities, and other events.[44]

Like the Calle de la Feria, the Corredera was a commercial center. Whereas the former hosted major semiannual events centered on wholesale textiles, the Corredera's trade was more inclusive. Markets were held each Thursday, with quotidian wares ranging from the ubiquitous woolen cloth to fresh or salted fish.[45] It was in this sense that Delicado referred to the plaza. As Lozana and her beau Rampín walked through Rome, he told her of the wonderful markets held in the Piazza Navona each Wednesday, where everything "born on land or in the sea" could be bought. His description sparked a rare mood of nostalgia in Lozana, who responded:

> Then I want you to show me that. In Córdoba, they do this on
> Thursdays, if I remember correctly:
> > *Thursday, it was Thursday,*
> > *market day*
> > *that Fernando invited*
> > *the Commanders.*
> Oh, if only I had died when I heard that lament![46]

The verses Lozana quoted were from the popular *Cantar de los Comendadores de Córdoba*, which related the tragic deaths of brothers Jorge and Fernando Alonso Córdoba y Solier, both commanders (*comendadores*) in the

Order of Calatrava.[47] Their story was well known in Córdoba and through-out Castile. In 1448, Fernando Alonso de Córdoba, *veinticuatro* (council-member) of the city and lord of Belmonte, suspected that his wife, Beatriz de Hinestrosa, was romantically involved with one of the brothers and invited both *comendadores* to join him on a hunt. They declined, complaining of urgent duties in the city, and Belmonte pretended to depart, leaving them free to act as they would. He then returned home suddenly to catch them in flagrante delicto, Jorge with Beatriz and Fernando Alonso with her niece. The offended husband murdered all four, as well as several servants in the house who had known about his cuckolding. He then fled to the court of Juan II, who offered him a pardon but sent him to fight against Granada on the frontier.[48] The Plaza de la Corredera reminded Jerónimo of order and chivalry, with its judges and martial youths. The image that struck Lozana so forcefully when thinking of it was one of bustling commerce and of violence, of word passing through a crowd of a horrific crime.

Like other commoners, of course, Lozana herself would have had little to do with such families. Direct interactions in public between disparate social groups were rare; one saw the great and noble from a distance, if at all. That there was mutual disdain between the elite and the masses is taken for granted in *La Lozana*. Indeed Delicado depicted elites as so removed from the populace that they seem like foreigners, completely alien in dress and manners. While walking with Rampín down the Via dell'Orso near Piazza Navona, Lozana spotted a peculiarly dressed individual.

LOZANA: Who is that? Is it the bishop of Córdoba?
RAMPÍN: If only my father lived as well! It is one of those outland-ish bishops from Asia Minor.
LOZANA: A Mamluk always has to be in charge.
RAMPÍN: The cardinals here are just like the Mamluks.
LOZANA: They are to be worshipped.
RAMPÍN: And the Mamluks too.
LOZANA: Cardinals are so arrogant.[49]

That Lozana could mistake an Anatolian prelate for one from her own home city points to social and physical divides in Córdoba. Not only had she never attended any services over which the bishop of Córdoba had presided, which is perhaps to be expected, but she had also apparently never even seen a Castilian bishop or cardinal and could only assume that such a person would dress in an "outlandish" fashion. Certainly, Juan Rodríguez de Fonseca, bishop of Córdoba when Delicado lived there, was a courtier and bureaucrat often absent from his seat.[50] He was, however, a tireless self-promoter and, like his predecessors and successors, was a visible presence in the city when resident there, taking part in the numerous processions conducted in and around the cathedral districts. Thus, Lozana's complete lack of familiarity with episcopal trappings implies that she had never, or only rarely, crossed the Calle de la Feria to walk about the Medina.

Despite her exile, Lozana, like Jerónimo, remembered Córdoba fondly and was fiercely proud of her birthplace, proclaiming that "I gave many thanks to God that he made me in Córdoba rather than in any other land, and that he made me a wise woman and not a beast, of the Spanish nation and not of any other."[51] This statement expresses a quality of the medieval city that all these authors would agree upon: it was a source of identity, leaving an indelible mark on its natives. Throughout his world travels, Jerónimo reflected at length on Córdoba. Similarly, Lozana defined herself as Cordoban throughout the novel, even though most of her life experiences occurred elsewhere.

* * *

The spatial organization of Córdoba that so conditioned the accounts of both Lozana and Jerónimo merits further comment, as it was a source of communal identities inextricably linked to how urban spectacles were presented and experienced. For Jerónimo and Lozana, Córdoba was less a panorama of an entire city and more a series of snapshots that tracked their former lives, in each case encompassing only a small section of the city. Therefore, it is not surprising that they had different perspectives on the city. When Lozana remembered her life in Córdoba, she actually referred to the Ajerquía, an area economically and socially distinct from Jerónimo's Medina neighborhood. The Calle de la Feria was not an absolute barrier, and we can find *converso* leatherworkers, for instance, to either side of it. It was, however, a metaphorical divide between different, and generally exclusive, social networks.

Boundaries were common features of medieval and early modern cities. Access to some spaces was explicitly limited. Some of these served political or military purposes, such as barracks and training grounds or the open-air courts of which Jerónimo wrote. Most significant among forms of "official" spaces were markets, which were defined in part through law. Full access to some markets was available only to certain people and only for certain purposes, restrictions that regularized trade in vital goods to ensure their availability and quality. Even so, markets were not wholly separate from the rest of the city. Much of a city's trade took place outside these privileged zones while noneconomic activities—festivals, social interaction, political pageantry—penetrated the marketplace.[52] Despite the explicit branding of a space for particular purposes, it could not be kept isolated from activity around it. Sacred spaces acted in a similar manner; although theoretically apart from "profane" quotidian space, worship nonetheless spilled into the streets through festivals, processions, and acts of popular piety, and secular business often entered the precincts of cathedrals, churches, and monasteries.

The Calle de la Feria and other "soft" boundaries that divided cities into quarters defined by their occupational, ethnic, or religious character were of a different kind from those delineating markets or churches. They were unwritten, unregulated, and even more open to transgression. They were also at odds with official efforts to present cities as unified, "public" entities.

And yet, although these boundaries were rarely officially enforced, custom and social approbation generally prevented one from frequenting areas of a different social rank than one's own. A tanner, for instance, might draw the attention of the town watch if loitering along the Calle de los Plateros at night; by day, he was unlikely to garner more than disapproving stares. At the same time, civic ceremonies, confraternal and guild processions, and festivals deliberately eroded these boundaries by linking diverse locations and creating legitimate reasons for people to move about the city. The torturous routes often followed by such processions, in fact, were explicitly meant to express the idea of a uniform civic space.

Residents, of course, were well aware of the various boundaries, both official and informal, within their city. To use the terminology developed by Kevin Lynch in his seminal *Image of the City*, people navigate cities by means of emotional and cognitive responses to their surroundings. There are, moreover, just a few common types of location, defined by Lynch as "paths," "edges," "nodes," "districts," and "landmarks."[53] Understood from this perspective, the Calle de la Feria was a central location in Córdoba that functioned in multiple ways. It was simultaneously a "path" linking disparate areas of the city and an "edge" that acted as a symbolic barrier between the distinct districts of Santa María and San Nicolás de la Ajerquía. But it was not defined solely by its navigational attributes. The shops and fairs dedicated to cloth provided the Calle de la Feria with its own distinctive character and atmosphere, making it a district in its own right that drew residents from other parts of the city. Finally, the Cruz del Rastro at the river end of the street was a convergence of paths or a "node," both a point of congregation for local residents and a space in which residents from all parts of the city passed through on a regular basis. Lynch calls attention to such nodes as places of particular significance that often dominate the local urban landscape. But his work also reveals that longtime residents of an area pay most attention to small landmarks. Nearly any physical feature, therefore, could serve as a focal point for personal and communal associations and could play a role in one's assessment of a spectacle that included or passed by that feature.

How were such associations created and how did they become established in collective memory? We have seen several examples already. Jerónimo and Palencia created connections between their physical surroundings and classical or biblical allusions. Their writings, no doubt, passed these associations to some of their readers. Likewise, a tragic event and its commemoration in song created indelible meanings for Lozana. Processions and festivals, however, were deliberate efforts to define spaces to serve particular agendas. While such references usually acted subconsciously, elites occasionally made overt efforts to endow certain sites with clear associations. These moments are of particular interest in that they reveal contemporary understandings of how specific landmarks came to acquire diverse meanings in the public mind.

One such instance for which we have a detailed account is Miguel Lucas's 1470 attempt to fix permanently Jaén's contested boundary with the neighboring town of Andújar.[54] As discussions had failed to resolve the issue, representatives from both Jaén and Andújar requested that Miguel Lucas, whose position as constable of Castile made him (in theory) an unbiased judge, adjudicate the dispute. He took the request seriously, studying all available documents and personally walking the countryside in order to reach a solution. On 7 May, he gathered all the interested parties to hear his judgment and mark the agreed-upon boundaries in a version of ceremonies sometimes used to "beat the bounds" of a parish. The group was a large one, including the dean and prior of Jaén's cathedral and the head of the local Franciscan house, as well as knights, squires, and commoners from both towns. Miguel Lucas also invited a large band of children and youths from the towns and the surrounding countryside "so that they might see it [the boundary line] and retain the memory for all time."[55]

He led this group on a tour of his proposed boundary line, conducting various activities at each of several landmarks, or *mojones*. At the first, Iranzo

threw a lance into a small well, then instructed one of the accompanying
youths to jump in fully clothed. After the boy had been pulled out, the
constable then invited all the children to engage in a water fight. From the
well, the party moved along a line marked by small cairns until they reached
a nearby hill, where they built a much larger pile of stones. To celebrate its
completion, the younger members of the excursion enjoyed a game of "mares
in the field."[56]

The third marker was constructed of earth and consecrated with the
sacrifice of a ram, whose head was placed in its center. Some of those present
then suggested that this marker should be named "The Ram" (El Carnero).
Miguel Lucas, however, appeased the clerics present by announcing that it
would be more appropriate to christen it "The Lamb" (El Cordero). The
priests declared themselves well satisfied.[57] The seemingly tireless leader led
his group through the construction of several more markers before reaching
the conclusion of his trek, where again a great pile of earth was raised into a
landmark. Here, to ensure that it would be remembered (*por memoria*), the
constable's knights conducted a bullfight, inviting the residents of the nearby
villages of Cazalilla and Villanueva de la Reina. They quickly erected a make-
shift corral and had their sport, dispatching the bull with sharpened spears
(*cañas*). Afterward, Miguel Lucas had the bull butchered and the meat distributed to local paupers.[58]

Miguel Lucas employed any number of tactics in order to establish a
boundary that would long be remembered. By including a large number of
young people, he ensured that the events would long remain in living memory. The wide array of different elements, ranging from comic activities to
generosity to religious allusions to landmarks and cairns, were calculated to
appeal to each of the diverse groups in the crowd: the children would recall
the water fight and dunking at the well, the pious christening of a marker
mollified the clerics, and the bullfight was enjoyable not only for the knights
who participated but also for the rural dwellers who rarely had the opportunity to watch such a spectacle.

Such directed content, and the care with which he made certain that the
events were distributed among the various markers so that no single *mojón*
bore too many or conflicting associations, reveals the constable's sophisticated
understanding of both his audience and the ways in which public *memoria*
can be created. By making himself personally available to his subjects, Miguel
Lucas made the day yet more noteworthy while burnishing his personal reputation as a compassionate and munificent ruler. No doubt many of the

children present related the story of the wild doings with the great man to their grandchildren, just as he had intended. Finally, Miguel Lucas took care not to rely solely on communal memory. Just as he employed both written records and oral testimony to ensure that the boundary be laid out "just as it always had been" and to give his verdict the proper *auctoritas*, he arranged that a precise and detailed written record of the layout of the boundary be compiled.[59]

Just as with Miguel Lucas's boundary marking, though on a less overt level, civic spectacles attempted to create cognitive or emotional significance for physical features of the city. Some structures, of course, had their social meanings built into their architecture. City walls, for instance, needed no ritual associations to convey their purpose nor could the primary roles of a church or palace be mistaken for anything else. But architectural forms could be employed in subtler and more complex ways that went beyond the function of a particular structure. Siting, decoration, size, and even the choice of materials for buildings were often consciously chosen to convey a message or establish a mood, meanings that played a central role in the overall experience of a spectacle conducted in or near them. The particular conditions of the Iberian frontier had long provided rulers with both the need for effective modes of expressing their readings of social, political, and religious issues and an abundance of themes with which to do so, making the region a crucible of what we might call "rhetorical architecture." Fifteenth-century architects and patrons, especially in frontier cities, built on this legacy.

San Pedro at Loarre, for instance, was a monumental and lavishly decorated church housed within a major frontier castle and within sight of towns remaining in Muslim hands. It was erected under the patronage of King Sancho Ramírez of Aragón in the 1070s and 1080s, a moment when Christian control of newly acquired territories was tenuous.[60] The complex's combination of military and ecclesiastic features acted to remind viewers both of the ruler's legitimate and divinely authorized rule and of the differences between themselves and their Muslim neighbors. Its Romanesque style marked a break from earlier Mozarabic churches, signaling both a change in the ownership of the land and the idea that all Christians sprang from a common background.

This expression of a cohesive and self-assured Christianity was heightened by the decorative scheme. Through carved portrayals of biblical victories and God's wrath against his enemies, the church emphasized the role of faith in war against the Muslims. Even the disposition of the church sent a powerful message. Situated at the most vulnerable point in the complex, it was the

only means of ingress to the castle available to enemies and thus protected
the fortifications, rather than the other way around. Attackers would have to
navigate its narrow spaces and confront the visual depictions of God's might
that defined Loarre as a bastion of spiritual as well as physical strength.[61]
Given the historical and political contexts in which San Pedro and other
similarly organized church-fortress complexes were built, Janice Mann has
proposed that the Aragonese rulers employed architecture as a weapon of
psychological or spiritual warfare, meant to rally the faithful and overawe
the enemy. In 1067, for instance, Sancho Ramírez described the purpose
of a tower near Alquézar as "to exhort the Christians and confound the
Muslims."[62]

While some of the conditions that prompted these innovative uses of
architecture were particular to eleventh-century Aragón, others remained relevant for far longer. Kings and nobles continued to struggle with their inability to project effective power on the periphery and the perceived need to
remind frontier Christians that their beliefs were opposed to those of nearby
Muslims. To these problems, later rulers responded as had Sancho Ramírez,
with monuments that emphasized their divine right to rule while encouraging
Christians to reclaim Iberia from Islam. Yet the real victories of the intervening centuries permitted a degree of triumphalism that led architects such as
Juan Guas and Simon de Colónia to incorporate Muslim motifs into their
masterpieces. Perhaps the best-known example of this approach is the Franciscan monastery church of San Juan de los Reyes in Toledo, which brought
together Italian, Gothic, and Mudéjar elements in a fusion known as the
Isabelline style. The church, commissioned by Isabel and Fernando in 1477
to commemorate their victory over Portugal in the 1476 Battle of Toro that
effectively ended the Castilian succession crisis, was intended to be the royal
burial site. Its decorative themes combined elements that recalled the Mezquita of Córdoba, and thus paid homage to the work of Muslim architects,
with explicit reminders of the Catholic Monarchs' success in war against
Granada, most notably the chains of Christian captives freed during the conquest of Málaga in 1487 that adorned the church's exterior walls.[63]

Spectacles conducted within or near such buildings augmented, adapted,
and expanded their messages, sometimes even turning older structures toward
new meanings. Occasions in which rulers conducted spectacles involving
buildings they had personally commissioned, however, permit us to consider
the purposeful integration of the symbolic content of spectacle and of architecture. Miguel Lucas again offers a useful example, as his palace played a

role in nearly every public or semipublic spectacle he sponsored during his time in Jaén.[64] While he made use of other buildings, notably the cathedral, the visual language of his palace was deliberately meant to complement his theatrical productions.

He began to use the palace, and especially its *sala baja*, or main hall, for public events soon after his arrival in Jaén, beginning with the reception honoring his wedding to Teresa de Torres. After the ceremony, held in the cathedral, the couple joined a number of local notables at the palace, where "they went directly to the large main salon, decorated with rich and new French wall hangings portraying King Nebuchadnezzar. At one end was a high wooden platform with steps, all covered with tapestries. On this was the hosts' table; at their backs was an expensive canopy of rich brocade."[65] This and other gatherings in the *sala* followed a predictable course: first dinner with the constable and his wife presiding at the high table, then dancing to tunes played by professional musicians. The dancing might last for hours, with breaks for participatory singing, poetry, and *invenciones*. The *sala* was also the site for theatrical performances, *entremeses* as well as set pieces involving complex costumes and props. The festivities often continued to the small hours of the morning.

This was an intimate space. The *sala*'s dimensions, roughly fifty by fifteen feet, meant that gatherings, which often included upward of fifty people, were closely packed.[66] It was also a public space; Miguel Lucas's guests included not only his circle of friends and family but also church officials, members of the city *concejo*, and prominent nobles from throughout the region. As such, its decorative scheme was meant to portray the constable in a particular light, to impress strangers and acquaintances alike with his lineage, generosity, courtly manners, and social standings. Thus the rich brocade, à la mode tapestries, and raised dais worked in concert with the heraldic carvings, the ranks of servants, musicians, and attendants lining the walls, and the bountiful feasts and rivers of wine. Somewhat at odds with this vision, however, are the room's Mudéjar embellishments, notably an ornate ceiling akin to that of San Juan de los Reyes.

While both ceilings expressed a confidence in Christian culture and ultimate victory strong enough to permit the adoption of the enemy's artistic forms, the constable's palace was built just as noble resentment over Enrique IV's supposed maurophiliac tendencies was gathering force. So although Miguel Lucas's palace demonstrated an unfashionable loyalty to the king, his public lifestyle was full of positive references to Moorish culture that reflected his grasp of the contradictory views of Islam fostered by frontier life.[67] The Muslims were dangerous and nearby enemies of the faith, to be treated accordingly and not to be lightly provoked. At the same time, they were trading partners, vital to Jaén's economic well-being and to the fortunes of those influential residents invited to the *sala*. Finally, the Muslims were also neighbors, whom many Christians in Jaén had come to know and respect as individuals. The Mudéjar accoutrements in Miguel Lucas's palace appeared nowhere in the private quarters, indicating that they were a public display, designed to reassure local officials that the constable could view Muslims as more than religious enemies.

Performances and diversions in the constable's *sala* were public in the sense that they included people with whom he had no strong personal attachments. They were not, however, open to the community as a whole. In fact, he ended his public wedding festivities by inviting Jaén's elite to the palace after open-air processions specifically intended for popular enjoyment. This set a pattern to which he generally adhered. Pageants began in the private spaces of the palace, from which Miguel Lucas and a select few would emerge to join a procession of knights and officials that then marched to the focal point for the day's festivities, usually a tournament, bullfight, or banquet open to all. After the main event, the constable and his retinue returned to the palace for revelries. Meanwhile, outside the palace, food, drink, and popular amusements—mummers, trumpeters, and short theatrical skits—were provided for the public.

The difference in the type of entertainments offered was not accidental, but reflected perceptions about the intended audiences. Courtly pageantry, notably the hierarchical processions whose protocol was strictly enforced, marked the spatial transition from private to public while ribald and carnivalesque themes featured prominently in events open to the commoners. Upon the return to the palace and subsequent exclusion of the masses, courtly manners reappeared: formal dining, elegant music, and refined dances.[68]

These patterns of inclusion and exclusion illustrate how spatial hierarchies were central to fifteenth-century civic spectacle. Restrictions to access were, and are, a central aspect of power relationships.[69] Both indoor and outdoor spaces could be hierarchical. Marketplaces, as have been mentioned, were freely accessible only by some, and that access denoted one's full membership in civic society. Populations who lacked this visible badge of citizenship—religious minorities, outsiders, paupers, and especially women—were thus marginalized in a spatial, as well as economic and social, sense.

Strategies employed to control entry and create spatial distinctions during public spectacles included temporary shifts that transformed previously public locations (a corner of a plaza or a stretch of roadside, for instance) into areas accessible only to the elite.

Miguel Lucas's ability to grasp the city of Jaén on so many levels, as illustrated by the fêting of his son's birth, is particularly impressive when we consider the fractured nature of other accounts. In a single series of spectacles, he reached out to perspectives as diverse as the religious idealism of Jerónimo, the civic humanism of Palencia, and the local networks essential to Lozana. All this would, he likely hoped, convince the people to consider his good fortune as their own and to celebrate the occasion as a genuine triumph for Jaén rather than a mere opportunity to enjoy noble largesse.

Such measures were necessary at a time when the relatively novel presence of nobles in cities created new social dynamics. In order to affirm their status, Miguel Lucas and his peers recast traditional relationships in a manner appropriate to urban constituencies. When conducted in municipal plazas rather than in castles or palaces, spectacles drew large numbers of spectators with widely variant perspectives. Unable to insulate their productions from what one scholar has described as a "process of democratization," urban elites nevertheless sought to rigidly define the content of festivals and to limit popular improvisation. They emphasized their military might, displayed emblems of judicial authority, and referred to their intrinsic superiority. Processions of knights in tight ranks, tournaments, mace-bearers, and banners adorned with heraldic devices or symbolic color schemes were all calculated to demonstrate the continued preeminence of the nobility.[70]

The organization of the audience along hierarchical lines was a central feature of this statement of noble hegemony. Elites typically viewed events from the comforts of raised and shaded viewing platforms (*cadalhalsos, catafalcos*, or *miradores*) while the common folk had to scramble for advantageous spots and endure the elements. Miguel Lucas was particularly fastidious with his personal arrangements when appearing before the people. On nearly every occasion, he was not only dressed to perfection but also situated in an elevated and visible location, an honor he customarily extended to guests, prominent knights, and civic officials. During his wedding celebrations, for instance, he and some nobles "mounted and went to the *mirador* that the *concejo* had made in the Plaza de Arrabal. This platform was carefully shaded by fine French tapestries and many decorative cloths. In its center, at the spot designated for the constable and his wife, was an especially fine tapestry of

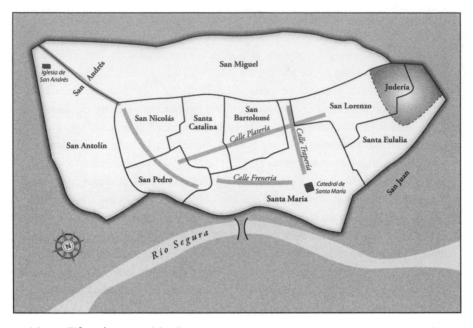

MAP 3. Fifteenth-century Murcia.

rich brocade.[71] Such preparations ensured that the *grandes* were comfortable and that they were part of the spectacle, as much on stage as the participants.

In Murcia, repeated efforts by the *concejo* to limit access to their *miradores* reveals how jealously they guarded this privilege. The main route for Corpus Christi processions in Murcia ran along the Calle de la Trapería to the cathedral (see Map 3). The feast usually fell in June, a notoriously hot month in the city. Members of the *concejo* were organizing shaded grandstands for themselves as early as 1419, but their efforts to separate themselves from the masses are recorded in detail beginning in the 1470s.[72] As recorded in their minutes, their reasons were prosaic enough: "Since, during the days of Corpus Christi, the *regidores* and officials of the *concejo* who accompany the Body of Our Lord Jesus Christ are so crowded among the people who gather there to see the *entremeses* in the procession that these officials cannot see the *entremeses* well enough, the said *concejo* orders *mayordomo* Juan Nuñes de Astudillo to have a wooden *catafalco* constructed so that the *concejo* officials can view the procession from it."[73] If the municipal council wanted a better view, however, so did others.

The *concejo* passed a series of resolutions in the early 1480s attempting to limit use of viewing platforms to themselves and approved guests, indicating that others were trying either to gain access to the official *cadalhalso* or to build additional ones. In 1480, they surrounded the platform with guards, a decision that would have heightened its visibility and unmistakably signaled its exclusive character.[74] Wealthier residents of Murcia, not deigning to trespass on the official platform, chose instead to construct their own, and the *concejo* moved quickly to regulate this practice as well. In 1481, they gave "the *jurado* (local representative to the council) Antonio Hurtado authority over the *cadalhalsos* which they have ordered to be built on the Trapería . . . and order that no one else may build a *cadalhalso* on the Trapería on the day of Corpus Christi without Hurtado's consent under penalty of a fine of five hundred *mrs.*, a third of which will go to the accuser and the other two thirds to the Hermandad."[75]

Three days later, they agreed to assess a fine of six hundred *mrs.* on anyone attempting to enter the official platform without permission and resolved that all nonofficial *cadalhalsos* should be at the same height with respect to the street.[76] Their ostensible reason for the latter was the risk that high platforms might block the views of those farther removed. Behind this practical rationale, however, was a fear that citizens with deep pockets might construct platforms that would dwarf that of the *concejo*. In 1482, the *concejo*'s arrangements for the platform included provisions for the *regidores* and *jurados* to be supplied with beverages throughout the day.[77] This was perhaps a wise precaution given the heat of a Murcian summer. It also further differentiated the members of the municipal government from their constituents. Hoisted above the masses on their platform, shaded by awnings, surrounded by guards, and now supplied with beverages as they reclined, they resembled nothing so much as the great magnates as they looked down on the sweating, standing, crowded, thirsty commoners. The *concejo*'s repeated need to legislate these markers of status, however, indicates that not everyone freely acquiesced to them.

The construction of temporary viewing platforms enclosed and ordered customarily egalitarian spaces on the Trapería. Works of ephemeral architecture did not function solely, however, as markers of spatial hierarchies. Spectacles that held an element of danger to the crowd, such as bullfights and the tournament games like the *juegos de cañas* that often followed them, required barricades to define the playing field and to keep spectators out of harm's way.[78] These barriers, constructed at significant expense, turned places where people lived, worked, and socialized into festive arenas where the quotidian could be forgotten and, through sport and theater, fantasy reigned. Barricades and *cadalhalsos* were, in fact, some of the most pedestrian ways in which such transformations were effected. As we will see in later chapters, nobles and *concejos* employed various means, from the cleaning and decorating of streets to citywide illumination to the construction of triumphal arches and fairy castles, to create provisional but overwhelming spatial associations among their subjects. Momentary structures bore the same attributes—deliberate rhetoric, emotional content, and limited access—as permanent edifices, but their temporary character made them all the more effective as bearers of meaning. Although retained in memory, their physical presence was fleeting and thus never became familiar or mundane, fading into the background of the cityscape. Ephemeral architecture thus reveals a central aspect of civic space: that it was simultaneously transient and durable. A new idea or a passing fancy could meld seamlessly with long-held associations and no building, space, or landmark was subject to a single interpretation.

*   *   *

The social and physical contexts of an urban spectacle were more than mere backdrops. They were an essential aspect of any performance. Miguel Lucas's extravagant commemoration of his son's birth provides a catalog of the many ways in which Castilian municipal authorities could exploit and subvert civic spaces as a means of influencing the people. There was nothing explicitly about the frontier in that particular set of performances and displays. But the constable's spectacles took place, as did those in Murcia and Córdoba, in places where the influences of the frontier were deeply felt. They made full use of their urban contexts in order to address tensions rising from the contradictory forces of *reconquista* ideology and religious acculturation. It was not an accident, for instance, that displays of piety and military skill played key roles in the celebration of baby Luis's birth and christening. These were everyday themes in cities constantly preparing for religious war. A full understanding, however, of how the realities of borderlands life conditioned not only the content but also the meaning of spectacles requires a closer look at the particulars of specific cases. The next three chapters detail the evolving role of urban spectacles during the last decades of the fifteenth century, a time when the well-established traditions of frontier life were challenged by a growing intolerance for religious minorities and a renewed push for holy war.

PART II

CHAPTER 3

Knights, Magi, and Muslims: Miguel Lucas de Iranzo and the People of Jaén

Miguel Lucas's career in Jaén, captured in lush detail by an anonymous biographer, was an encounter between Castilian court politics and frontier culture that was both atypical and emblematic. He was an outsider, the constable of Castile, who came to Jaén with the explicit intent of exacerbating hostilities with Granada in the hope of redeeming a sullied reputation. But he immediately embarked upon an extensive program of pageantry meant to deflect, rather than intensify, religious tensions in Jaén. His was, at the time, the most ambitious attempt yet to transfer the traditional entertainments of the nobility to an urban setting. It should be no surprise, then, that his spectacles were marked by an evolving relationship between the noble patron and the urban audience that fused traditional knightly and religious themes with the contradictory attitudes toward Islam that characterized Jaén and its environs. In these productions, the amiable enmity of the frontier found expression through spectacle.

The constable was, by all accounts, intensely pious. He viewed the conquest of Granada as a holy imperative while taking pains to faithfully attend Mass and often retiring to solitary prayer. He was also fully immersed in *caballeresca* culture, a staunch proponent of military exercises and an avid proponent of romances extolling the traditional knightly virtues: honor, courage, munificence, and loyalty. His strong inclination to act in the manner idealized by Cartagena, Valera, and Arévalo was balanced, however, by the imprint of his years at the royal court. These had shaped his public persona and approach to rule and instilled in him a love of fanciful theatrics as well as the admiration for Islamic culture that created such troubles for Enrique IV. Miguel Lucas was a pious man given to self-aggrandizement and a crusader who often emulated the dress, manners, and weapons of his enemies. Yet he also adhered to many of the knightly ideals he professed, remaining loyal to Enrique IV, for instance, throughout the faction fighting and civil wars of the 1460s and early 1470s.

The city in which he arrived in December 1460 was no less a study in contrasts. Overlooking Jaén and dominating its skyline was the imposing fortress of Santa Catalina, named for Catherine of Alexandria, whose medieval worship was strongly associated with crusading. In the fifteenth century, the fortress combined with an extensive system of walls and gates to give the appearance of a citadel to a city permitted since the fourteenth century to style itself the "guardian and defender of the kingdoms of Castile." As a frontier bastion and the major Castilian city most exposed to Granadan attack, Jaén was in a constant state of military preparations or active warfare throughout the 1460s; this was, of course, why Miguel Lucas had chosen it.[1] This military role resulted from the region's mountainous terrain and the nearby frontier. But those same environmental features also meant that Jaén, whose name likely derived from the Arabic Ŷayyān (جيان, place where caravans meet), was situated at the convergence of a number of trade routes connecting Castile and Granada.[2] The city was a hub of transfrontier trade in which much of the population maintained active and numerous contacts with Granada even as Morisco and Granadan traders were welcome throughout the year and especially at its annual fairs.[3] It was a provincial city whose relatively impoverished economy depended heavily on rural products and on trade with Granada, but which embraced elaborate spectacles that presented Jaén as a world dedicated to holy war and defined by abundance and profligacy. These contrasting inclinations conditioned life in fifteenth-century Jaén.

Within the context of Giennense society and the conflicts, both internal and external, of the 1460s, we should understand Miguel Lucas's pageants as attempts to articulate a vision of war against Islam in which the victors would not eradicate or expel the Muslims, but would instead force their conversion. This would permit Christians to fulfill their holy obligations while, in theory at least, preserving their commercial and personal relationships with Muslims. We do not have access to the thoughts or opinions of most of his subjects. We do know, however, that Miguel Lucas took great care to present well-crafted spectacles with a close eye to their popular reception. He succeeded, moreover, in winning provisional support for his ambitious civic projects and his struggles against Granada despite the heavy tax burden these implied, indicating that many found his perspective appealing. At the same time, the constable's vision of a society in which conversion to Christianity could erase all differences was out of step with broader social trends, in particular a growing desire for social homogeneity that would lead ultimately to the Inquisition and the expulsion of Castile's Muslims and Jews.

The social and physical contexts of Jaén conditioned the content and reception of Miguel Lucas's spectacles. This chapter centers on the interplay between sponsor and audience, both of whom held paradoxical attitudes toward other religions and cultures. I begin, therefore, with the constable's origins and career with the goal of determining, to the extent possible, the attitudes that lay behind his attempts to articulate ideas of holy war, religious identity, and Muslim culture through spectacle. Miguel Lucas's rise to prominence and to control of Jaén had been atypical, and his personal experiences influenced the messages he presented to the people of Jaén. There is no doubt, however, that he intended his spectacles to not only express his own perspective but also to be widely appealing. To this end, he employed a wide range of popular memes, which are considered later in the chapter. The record of Miguel Lucas's time in Jaén is a veritable catalog of such events. We can, therefore, only consider a small subset of them here, focusing on those presented in winter of 1462–1463, the months immediately following his first, and most successful, forays into Granada.

After the end of the campaigning season of 1462, Enrique IV signed a truce with Granada. Miguel Lucas, however, almost immediately began a plot to break this truce. This period of time thus corresponds to a critical point in his attempts to win the support of his new subjects. They had just experienced both an interruption in trade and the sight of the constable returning from battle laden with booty. The thought of renewed hostilities, now without even the hope of royal support, must have led to mixed feelings at best. The performances Miguel Lucas organized in order to redirect public opinion toward war therefore offer a window into elite understandings of the popular mind-set. While his perceptions were mediated by his high station and noble background, we should not discount the resources of a leader whose position depended on the support or, at least, the complicity of his subjects. Although the constable did not invent that combination of largesse and entertainment often known as "bread and circus," his idiosyncratic and often creative use of the approach merits close attention.

*　*　*

Miguel Lucas was a "new man," one of the many commoners and *conversos* raised to high positions in court by fifteenth-century Castilian monarchs, especially Enrique IV, who saw them as a means of countering the influence of the great magnates. His humble origins played an important role throughout his life, influencing his rise to prominence, his staunch support of the king, and his rule of Jaén. He was, according to several chroniclers, the son of Alonso Álvarez de Iranzo, a poor farmer, and was born in Belmonte, a town near Cuenca ruled by Juan Pacheco, the marquis of Villena. He joined Villena's household when still quite young, perhaps through his mother's status as a *hidalga*, and seems to have made an impression there. Villena soon proposed, in 1452, that he be taken into Juan II's court as page (*doncel*) to the infante Enrique. Villena's motives were clear—he wanted to surround the young prince with his people and thus extend his influence—and the penniless Miguel Lucas must have seemed a likely choice. Owing everything to Pacheco, he was expected to stay loyal to his patron.[4]

Miguel Lucas's role in the royal court was that of both a *criado*, or servant, and a member of the household. He received military training and participated fully in hunts, jousts, and the other elements of a young nobleman's education. Despite his humble role and penurious circumstances (his resources at this time consisted of only a *doncel*'s meager salary), his natural abilities, ambition, and willingness to please permitted him to outshine the *hidalgos* surrounding him, and he was soon a member of Enrique's circle of intimates.[5] He particularly distinguished himself during Enrique's many hunts and was made chief falconer (*halconero mayor*), a position that provided additional incomes.[6]

The real turning point in Miguel Lucas's fortunes, however, occurred in 1455, after what likely was his first experience of real combat. Enrique invaded Granada early in the year, in what was more a show of force than an attempt to conquer new territory, with a focus on causing economic damage and collecting booty while avoiding major confrontations.[7] On 12 June, a significant Muslim force attacked the Castilians near the city of Granada but was forced to withdraw after inflicting only light casualties.

In the aftermath of this battle, Miguel Lucas received an uncomfortable honor from the king. While fighting in one of the many skirmishes, "Garcilaso de la Vega, *comendador* of Montizón, killed a very valiant Moor in the presence of the king and knocked down another. He took the horse and shield [of the dead man] and presented the horse to the king, and the king gave it to Miguel Lucas."[8] Taking trophies after defeating an enemy in single combat was a custom of the frontier as was the presentation of a captured mount to the king, who would then receive the victorious knight with the appropriate honors. According to Alfonso de Palencia, Enrique IV regularly perverted this tradition by disdaining those who actually fought the Muslims in favor of his courtiers.[9] Enrique's repudiation of an established knight in favor of Miguel Lucas—still a mere *doncel*—was of a part with his support for other lowborn intimates. It also earned the youth the rancor of those who thought the king's act was arbitrary and that Miguel Lucas had been chosen more for his personal connections than the merit of his own victory.

This first public recognition was followed immediately by another with more tangible implications when, on that same day, Enrique ennobled and knighted Miguel Lucas in company with several others.[10] Miguel Lucas joined the expedition to Granada as an unknown courtier with no relevant familial connections; he had access to the king, it is true, but in the role of huntsman and *doncel*. He returned to Castile as a knight, aristocrat, and publicly acknowledged royal favorite. Nobles of old families might have resented his rise, but now they knew him as a person of import. Miguel Lucas had two circumstances to thank for his good fortune: Enrique's friendship and the frontier. Without the opportunity for distinction that the invasion had offered, the king might never have found a suitable excuse for honoring him. Enrique himself, in the patent of nobility, had declared that Miguel Lucas's military success led to his rise: "I am standing here in person in the field against the infidel Moors, enemies of the holy Catholic faith, and in sight of them . . . and ready to fight them in pitched battle . . . and you, Miguel Lucas, standing in my squadron, below my royal banner, have shown yourself courageous and eager to fight and do great deeds."[11] Miguel Lucas was transformed, in a real sense, through the ritual of investiture. His patent of nobility confirmed his new status and he never lost his respect for the written word, but it was the formal, public ceremony that truly and permanently turned the farmer's son into a noble warrior.

Given his later deeds, it makes sense to consider how this sudden change in circumstances may have affected his perceptions and priorities. He won his glory through frontier fighting, and it is not surprising that a few years later, he chose again to confront the Muslims, this time in the hope of salvaging his position. His later insistence on the outward forms of nobility—colors, emblems, and titles—and awareness of the power of public spectacle likewise suggest that his own dramatic investiture had made a deep impression. He had enjoyed the king's confidence in private for some time but only when this was openly recognized did he gain the fruits of this friendship. Some things, in other words, only mattered when everyone knew about them.

Enrique's support for Miguel Lucas knew few bounds in the mid- to late 1450s and this favor brought him into conflict with both established magnates and up-and-comers like himself. In March 1458, Enrique successively made him, in a single grand ceremony at the royal alcázar in Madrid, a baron, a count, and constable of Castile for life. Never before in any kingdom, marveled Diego de Valera, had anyone received such a set of promotions on the same day.[12] The office of constable of Castile, which had lain vacant since the death of Alvaro de Luna five years earlier, was essentially that of a commander in chief. By concentrating martial power in Miguel Lucas's hands as "president, leader, and governor of all the hosts, armies, legions, and military camps of Castile," Enrique may have hoped to give unity of purpose to his fading war on Granada in addition to rewarding his favorite.[13] Instead, he simply fueled ongoing rivalries as more established nobles sought to bolster their own positions.

Issues soon came to a head over another position vacant since Alvaro de Luna's death, that of Master of the Order of Santiago. The marquis of Villena, Miguel Lucas's old mentor, desired the title and expected no difficulties in obtaining it. Villena held immense power at this time, acting as de facto coruler with Enrique, and few opposed his ambitions.[14] He was to be disappointed this time, however. Palencia noted that, while the king was forced to publicly favor Villena, "In secret, he preferred the young Miguel Lucas, a man of low birth but not scorned for this, whom he had earlier distinguished with much affection. This exacerbated the rivalries common in those days, because [Villena] opposed the idea of raising someone from such humble origins to a post so high, and masked the worries that so agitated him so that the king would not suspect his secret plans. He could not, however, keep the envy often roused by such conflicts between powerful men hidden for long; and so the court was divided into two factions, with their respective candidates."[15] As happened often during Enrique's reign, struggles among his courtiers paralyzed the king. No one was appointed to the mastership of Santiago until 1463.[16] But the struggle over the position cost Miguel Lucas dearly. Only scant months after his investiture as constable, he withdrew completely from court politics and retired to Jaén, where he remained until his death. Why he did so is unclear; the chronicles disagree about the circumstances of his fall from grace.

According to the author of the *Hechos del condestable*, he was the victim of a plot conceived by Villena and his brother Pedro Girón, the master of Calatrava. The scheme centered on a man named Chávez, who claimed to be in the constable's service and was arrested carrying letters to the Granadan town of Moclín. These letters "contained many treasons and evils concerning the Constable." Chávez claimed innocence, saying he knew nothing about the letters other than that they came from "some nobles of the royal council that envied the Constable because his highness wanted to give him the Mastership of Santiago."[17] If this was, as the author of the *Hechos* assumed, a setup arranged by Villena, it was effective. After interrogating Miguel Lucas, Enrique placed him and several associates under house arrest. The king soon relented, however, and assured Miguel Lucas that he would be released and reinstalled in his various offices. After ten months, however, Miguel Lucas despaired, "seeing that his highness would carry out none of what he had pledged since . . . he would not displease those nobles who held so much power over him."[18] And so, in May 1459, Miguel Lucas absconded with his treasury and a few trusted squires, making his way to Aragón. From there, through mediators, he arranged a deal with the king. He would return to Castile but stay away from court, thus appeasing Villena's party. He would instead "choose and take for himself any city or town or place in all the realm. . . . With a great desire to be on the frontier, in order to make war on the Moors, he chose the city of Jaén."[19]

This account of Miguel Lucas's fall is not corroborated by any other chronicle or documentary source. In its depiction of a loyal knight undone by the envy of his rivals and the weakness of the king, it bears a suspicious likeness to the story of El Cid, who was similarly exiled by court intriguers. Indeed, Miguel Lucas's biographer explicitly modeled his history of the constable's exploits on the *Cantar de mio Cid*, recounting Miguel Lucas's struggles with his rivals, his daring feats against Granada, and his careful governance of Jaén in order to give his work the same theme as that of the epic poem: "God, what a good vassal! If only he had a good lord!" (¡Dios, que buen vassallo, si oviesse buen señor!).[20]

The *Crónica anónima*, in a more mundane explanation for the constable's withdrawal from court, suggested that he had left in a fit of pique after Enrique's failed attempts to court Francisco de Valdés, one of his *doncels*, and other young men in his circle.[21] While presenting the behavior of Miguel Lucas and the king in terms reminiscent of childish spats or lovers' quarrels, the chronicler also linked these events to the envy of the magnates. It is possible, in fact, that Villena brought these rivals to Enrique's attention, hoping that their novelty would turn the inconstant king from the constable.[22]

While Palencia also contended that Miguel Lucas absconded from court in response to Enrique's attentions to Valdés, he drew an altogether different conclusion. Of all Enrique's cronies, Miguel Lucas was the only one for whom Palencia had any regard. He saw Miguel Lucas's withdrawal from court as a redemptive act, the conscious choice of a young man who "renounced the primacy of [royal] favor" and the corrupting influence of the king and his degenerate lackeys. In his opinion, Enrique's unabashed pursuit of Valdés, to which he imputes a sexual motive, was the final straw: "Miguel Lucas, a young man who carefully observed religious precepts, saw all this with great disgust, and hating the causes of that [homosexual] inclination and embarrassed at the constant effort that it produced, fled the court and sought refuge in the kingdom of Valencia."[23]

Whatever the reason for Miguel Lucas's departure from court, he ultimately retained the king's goodwill, the title of constable, and an impressive set of incomes. And he appears to have welcomed the opportunity for a change of scenery, as indicated by his repeated requests for authority in Jaén rather than a full reinstatement of his former role. Perhaps he had, as Juan Torres Fontes suggests, simply tired of court politics.[24] In any event he had made arrangements for the construction of his palace in Jaén in time for it to be completed when he arrived there on 17 December 1460. Given the building's size and lavishness, it is possible that he had intended to spend significant time in Jaén even before Villena's machinations. Even if not, Miguel Lucas's plan to construct a suitable abode was a response of one excited by new prospects, not that of a demoralized outcast.

*   *   *

Jaén was a suitable destination for Miguel Lucas. He had personal ties in the region and the city; his brother commanded the nearby fortress of Montizón and he was betrothed to Teresa de Torres, a member of a prominent local *hidalgo* family and, as sole heir to the *señorió* (or lordship) of Villardompardo, a significant property owner in her own right.[25] His stated reason for going to Jaén, however, was to fight the Muslims. Jaén offered unparalleled prospects for autonomy and distinction in battle. It was a place where Miguel Lucas could embellish his reputation, win followers by deeds and generosity, and, if he desired, perhaps arrange a triumphant return to court. Perhaps most important, here he might emulate the heroes of old, especially the Cid, who had regained his honor in just such a manner.

Once settled in Jaén, he threw his energies into reorganizing the city's military forces and, when a truce signed by Enrique expired in 1462, immediately took the field. He would spend much of the next ten years on campaign but enjoyed only mixed success on his forays into Granada. He fought both independently and in alliance with other frontier nobles, particularly Cordoban magnate Alonso de Aguilar, but never as part of a major army, for Castile mounted no general expedition against the Muslims during this time. Miguel Lucas had better results in battle with other Christians, effectively defending the region from incursion by the Alfonsine or Isabelline factions and particularly embarrassing his old enemy Pedro Girón, the master of Calatrava, whose territories bordered his own.[26]

Miguel Lucas's success stemmed not from any tactical or strategic genius, but from organizational skill and an ability to inspire his troops, which he did through a carefully constructed public persona. Palencia reported on his efforts to field an army in Jaén with awe and not a little fear:

Certainly the Constable was known as a man of poor and limited ingenuity; but he employed an appearance of supreme authority, and his new kind of severity and eloquence ensured that he could never hold any of his citizens to the yoke of obedience without them obeying as if he were an illustrious king. He imposed strict penalties for the smallest failing; he spared no one from armed service. Even so, they obeyed him blindly; they did not protest poverty or neglect to buy horses and were always prepared to leave for sudden expeditions. They received no salary beyond the Constable's goodwill and never gave a thought to their expenses or hardships or to their own profit and pleasure, satisfied with earning the approval of their general. Such was his influence among those of Jaén that the citizens and commoners held such a high opinion of him that they forgot the lineage of the man they obeyed, whose inherited status was less than that of his subordinates, and would not deviate from his orders in the slightest way. A city that had never, even under the direst threats, produced five hundred horsemen now easily turned out a thousand, resolute and trained in all types of fighting.[27]

The author of the *Hechos* also extolled Miguel Lucas's ability to bring order to a chaotic situation. Before his arrival, Jaén "had become greatly weakened and destroyed by the widespread death, captivity, and robbery that the Moors had inflicted each day in times past. They charged right up to the [city] gates and killed the men, made off with prisoners and livestock, and burned or felled the fields, vines, and gardens."[28] Such attacks had gone on for decades. In concert with frequent outbreaks of plague, the most recent of which immediately preceded the constable's arrival, they had demoralized and nearly depopulated the city.[29] Little had remained, lamented the author of the *Hechos*, of a city once hailed as "Jaén, Jaén, the warrior." Miguel Lucas's arrival changed all this. From feeling abandoned by God, its residents soon came to consider they were "blessed by the coming, industry and aid of the Constable."[30]

Miguel Lucas also reformed Jaén's civic and judicial administration, embarked on an ambitious building program, and even improved educational opportunities by sending to Seville for masters of grammar, rhetoric, and logic. Through such works, according to the *Hechos*, he transformed the city. In a telling passage, the chronicler related how, upon Miguel Lucas's return from a successful raid, the people received him "with joy and happiness as great as that with which Rome received its emperors when they returned victorious from their conquests."[31] Here, free from vacillating kings and scheming courtiers, the constable could conduct affairs properly. If this work required a public image that presented him as Jaén's savior and a throwback to the heroes of old, so much the better.

Central to his image was an extensive program of spectacles. Building popular support in this way was not wholly new, but both the extent and content of his theatrics were idiosyncratic, reflecting his personal understandings of society, hierarchy, and holy war. To understand the intent behind his many productions, we need to consider the constable's own nontraditional route to a position of authority. His very reliance on spectacle, for instance, may well be tied to his personal experiences, particularly his investiture as a knight and promotion to constable. In each of those instances, a public ritual had transformed him. If ceremonies could enact such pivotal personal conversions, they might also remake an entire city.

Spectacles would also remind the citizens of Jaén of their ruler's status. Miguel Lucas was aware of the unease caused by his rapid advancement, aware of the whispers about his origins. He lacked useful familial ties; his authority was always open to challenge. This was the case even in Jaén. As

Palencia pointed out, the constable established his right to power through "his new kind of severity and eloquence." Palencia did not elaborate on what was innovative about Miguel Lucas's approach, but he could only have been referring to the theatrics through which the constable presented himself as both a man of the people and an exalted ruler.

All this was directed toward a purpose. Miguel Lucas had come to Jaén to rejuvenate the war against Granada, a task he saw as a religious obligation.[32] To do so, he needed followers willing to make the sacrifices required and therefore sought to inspire them with his own conspicuous religiosity. In 1464, for instance, he attended Mass on every day of Lent, in the process visiting all the churches of Jaén: "The first day of Lent, the lord constable went to the cathedral for terce, and there walked in the procession, heard the sermon, and received the ashes. Later, as Lent proceeded, his lordship heard Mass at all the churches of the city, in this manner: on the first Sunday of Lent at San Llorente, and the next day at Santiago, the next at San Juan" and so on through another fourteen examples. In addition to hearing Mass throughout Lent, moreover, he walked the stations of the cross at each church and with his full retinue.[33] Such a maneuver functioned on multiple levels. Not only did Miguel Lucas display his devotion while obligating his household to do the same; he also offered his personal attention to each parish, an itinerary that conveniently afforded him a chance to inspect the condition and management of the churches.

He linked this religious devotion to the military struggle with Islam and to his personal rule. At times, this was explicit, with the constable casting himself as a key player in the eschatological story of Christianity's ultimate triumph over Islam. At others, the connections were more subtle. Tournaments might be held on major religious holidays, such as Easter, or martial and religious themes would be combined without overt reference to Islam. Such was the case with the unorthodox *combates de huevos* presented on Easter Monday in 1461, 1463, and 1464, in which thousands of eggs were expended in battle between the constable's home and a wooden castle constructed nearby.[34] These "tournaments" preceded public banquets featuring eggs and cheese at which all comers were served and provided a welcome entertainment following the austerity of Lent while demonstrating the city's wealth and the constable's generosity. Moreover, they reminded the townspeople, at the start of the year's campaigning season, of the city's military role. Christ's sacrifice meant that they too must be willing to give their utmost to destroy his enemies.

Even as he rejected Enrique's policy of diplomacy with Granada as a form of appeasement, Miguel Lucas offered an ambivalent image of Islam in his spectacles. This was partly due to his efforts to present himself as the supreme authority in Jaén. The constable had few models on which to base a public persona and Enrique was his only example for how a ruler should portray himself as apart from and above the rest of the nobility. When determining his own image, Iranzo therefore presented himself in a manner akin to that of the king, who was notorious for his Moorish tastes. This was not by chance. His chronicler emphasized the care Miguel Lucas took with his personal appearance. To attend Mass one day in 1461, for instance, he was "dressed in a riding tunic of very fine yellow wool over a crimson doublet, and a blue cap whose hood was dyed with cochineal: dressed entirely as a Morisco, and very nicely too."[35]

His understanding of the trappings of power does not, however, explain the many other positive references to Moorish culture that suffused his spectacles. Rather, these expressed an understanding of the complexities of the frontier and respect for Granadan military, intellectual, and architectural prowess, predicting a future in which Muslims would convert to Christianity and all would live together in peace. This was not a vision of true tolerance; Miguel Lucas always emphasized Christian victory and dominance. Unlike Enrique, whose appreciation for Moorish habits led to accusations of secret apostasy, the sincerity of the constable's faith was never questioned. In his spectacles, Muslims were always both religious enemies and cultural brethren. Whether or not this reflected his personal feelings cannot be known. The dichotomy, however, reveals a sensitivity to local perspectives. Jaén's geographic and economic situation placed its people at the center of both the combative and acculturative tendencies of the frontier, and the constable needed to appeal to both to win their support.

*   *   *

His initial attempt to address this through drama came soon after his first campaigning season. With the expiration of Enrique's truce with Granada early in 1462, Miguel Lucas launched a series of generally successful attacks. These included not only profitable raids but also more substantial invasions that caused the Granadans to abandon a number of border posts.[36] In response, they appealed to Enrique. On 20 November, the king, despite Miguel Lucas's opposition, signed a new truce intended to last until the following June.[37] The constable, stymied, returned to Jaén, intending to pass the winter with celebrations, dances, and tournaments.

The first of these described by his chronicler was an elaborate joust held on 26 December in which two hundred knights took part. Half of these dressed themselves as Muslims, complete with false beards, and pretended to be a delegation accompanying a visit by the "king of Morocco." Joining them was the Prophet Muhammad who arrived "with great ceremony, riding on a lavishly adorned mule and bearing the Koran and books of his law in the shade of a rich tapestry borne on four poles by four *alfaquíes* [doctors of Muslim law]."[38] The procession entered the city to the sound of trumpets and kettledrums and two of the "Muslims" proceeded to the constable's palace. Dismounting, they entered to find him and his wife, well dressed and attended by a crowd of knights, squires, and noblewomen. The visitors kissed Miguel Lucas's hands before handing him a fictive chancery letter, a *carta bermeja*.

This missive, from the "king of Morocco," began by saluting the "valiant, strong, and noble knight, Don Miguel Lucas, Constable of Castile." The "king" then lamented that "I have heard of the great destruction and shedding of blood that you, honored knight, have inflicted on the Moors of the king of Granada, my uncle."[39] These defeats had driven Muhammad to despair. Therefore, he had come to deliver a challenge. If the Christians should prove victorious at a *juego de cañas*, then the "king" and his followers would convert to Christianity and become the constable's vassals. Miguel Lucas accepted the challenge and the game, which took place in the Plaza de Santa María and lasted for several hours, ended predictably, with Christian victory.

All the participants then paraded the length of the city to the Church of Santa María Magdalena. There, the putative king of Morocco and his knights were ceremoniously baptized while Muhammad, with Koran in hand, was dunked into a fountain for a more theatrical sort of baptism. Afterward, all the knights, including the newly Christianized Muslims, joined a large crowd of commoners and children at the constable's palace, where they feasted on wine and fruit.

Scholars have dismissed this performance as "frontier fantasy," a "wish-fulfillment piece," or "confirmatory magic."[40] Such characterizations emphasize the performance's whimsical nature while obscuring its political purposes. But the production, while playful and far-fetched, had serious goals. On a basic level, it promoted a high level of physical fitness and skill among the constable's knights. The *juego de cañas*, or "game of canes," was a rigorous form of military training that required knights to charge in formation while aiming nine- to twelve-foot lances at an opponent's shield and defending with their own shield. All this had to be done within the confines of the Plaza de Santa María and without, hopefully, trampling the spectators. Juan de la Corte's painting of *juegos de cañas* in Madrid (Figure 3), although it dates from much later, gives an impression of both the challenges faced by participants and the proximity of spectators and bystanders.

In using such entertainments to drill his knights, the constable ensured that he would have a fit, skilled, and cheerful fighting force. At the same time, he reminded all present that the object of all this martial energy was the defeat of Granada.[41] It also promoted what Angus MacKay has called a "frontier ideology," placing the constable's victories in the larger context of *reconquista*.[42] This tournament was not the first time Miguel Lucas had dramatized his contributions to the war on Granada. In 1461, for instance, he hosted a banquet that included a company of knights dressed in foreign clothes, pretending to be captives freed by the constable's personal intervention.[43] That, however, had been a private party in the palace. Now, with his first successful expeditions behind him, he openly professed a grandiose plan for the conquest of Granada.

Or did he? Despite apparent military successes in 1462, Miguel Lucas's policies disrupted long-standing commercial relations between Jaén and Granada and therefore threatened the financial well-being of many of his subjects, ranging from rural herders to his own relatives by marriage in the influential Torres family.[44] Unlike the *Hechos* and the constable himself, most residents of Jaén did not valorize the martial aspects of the frontier, instead preferring stability and conditions conducive to trade. Both Miguel Lucas's campaigns and his festivals were, moreover, quite costly. Some of this expense was offset by riches gained in battle. But most was covered by increased taxes on residents of the city and especially those living in the surrounding territories. These economic hardships, in concert with failed harvests and larger anti-aristocratic and anti-*converso* movements, would ultimately lead to popular unrest.[45]

There were no such disturbances in Jaén in 1462, but concern about internal strife was constant. One school of thought therefore sees a sinister side to Miguel Lucas's "frontier ideology," arguing that his festivals used popular motifs to direct lower-class discontent toward external enemies, both the Muslims of Granada and the constable's noble rivals in Castile.

Figure 3. Juan de la Corte, *Fiesta in the Plaza Mayor*, 1623. Courtesy of the Museo de Historia de Madrid. Although painted much later, this depiction of *juegos de cañas* gives some sense of how Miguel Lucas's tournaments may have appeared. Note the close quarters in which participants had to gallop, the elaborate attire, the barriers keeping spectators safe, and the onlookers watching from balconies.

The Christmas tournament, then, was but a cynical attempt to better bind the people to his authority, another example of how "those above continuously appropriate and transform popular unrest and culture for their own benefit."[46]

Miguel Lucas certainly sought to appeal to his subjects in the most effective manner possible; to do less would be pointless. That he consciously drew upon popular themes in articulating his vision is quite likely. But if he sought to disarm malcontents or portray himself as a champion of Christianity, why did he muddle the message by dressing as a Morisco? Why had he designed his palace in a Mudéjar style? Such affectations were not unknown at the time, but the mixed messages did not end with physical decorations.[47] The whole of the *carta bermeja* tournament was suffused with ambivalent references to Islam. Everyone rode *a la jineta*, or like Muslims, and the style of fighting, the *juego de cañas*, was of Islamic origin. Even the Church of the Magdalena had been built on the site of a mosque partly demolished during the Christian conquest of the city. The fountain that provided the water for the baptisms had once been used by Muslims for ritual ablutions.[48]

Perhaps most significant, all participants, both Christian and New Christian, joined together for a feast after their struggle. The sole object of contempt here was the Prophet Muhammad and his Koran. The only thing wrong with Muslims, Miguel Lucas seems to have been saying, was their religion. Take that away and there were no obstacles to peaceful interaction or to mutually beneficial cultural exchange. It would be wrong to present this as a vision of tolerance. After all, the central theme of the drama was Christian victory. But the defeated enemy was neither eradicated nor driven away, but converted and embraced.

To argue that Miguel Lucas sought to indoctrinate the people through pageantry therefore misses key aspects of his approach. He had come to Jaén with a particular and dissonant vision of Islam that drew on both his experiences at Enrique's court and his fervent support for holy war. Confronted with the amiable enmity that his new subjects evinced toward their Muslim neighbors, he sought to reassure them that he would not seek an unrestrained war against Granada that would destroy their livelihoods and expel their trading partners. In effect, the constable aimed to lower the stakes of holy war by suggesting that victory over Islam required the conversion but not the destruction of Muslims and would not entail the loss of Granadan culture. This was not a perspective he imposed on the populace; it was a proposed compromise.[49]

The emphasis on conversion and on the links between religious and secular concerns, moreover, was not limited to this one tournament. Christmas was one of the high points of the Christian festive calendar and Miguel Lucas marked the season with "the most significant festivals of all the year."[50] The *carta bermeja* tournament was only one event in a series that lasted from 24 December through 6 January and culminated with a dramatic enactment of the biblical story of the three Magi. It was not the first time the constable had presented the Magi play. In 1461, it had begun with a procession that moved the length of the city along an itinerary decorated with tapestries and lit by so many torches "that the brightness of the light made it almost seem like the middle of the day."[51] Spectators lined the route. Some, like Teresa de Torres and her ladies, enjoyed the scene from high towers. Others followed along on foot or horseback, watched from their windows, or sat on walls or roofs. Miguel Lucas himself was the centerpiece of the show, riding on a fine horse and "dressed in a gold-encrusted doublet and over it a short jacket adorned with his coat of arms made of fine yellow wool and very nicely outlined with black embroidery. On his head he bore a well-made royal crown with a mask and in his hand, placed carefully on the saddle as might a noble knight, was a bared sword." Preceding him were a pair of fifteen-year-old pages, each bearing a lance and wearing the same yellow jacket and brocade doublet, and in front of them a parade of twelve knights with lances and a thirteenth bearing a standard. All the knights wore, as did the constable, crowns and masks "in memory of the Magi kings, whose feast they celebrated."[52]

These fourteen Magi did not abandon their knightly personae in dressing for the occasion. Despite the crowns and masks, their mounts, swords, and personal devices meant that the transformation was incomplete. The actors were deliberately poised between the past and the present in an effort to incorporate the biblical Magi into their own chivalric world. The Magi became knights just as much as the knights became Magi. Once the procession reached the relative privacy of the palace, the play itself began. Here too, the boundaries between past and present were blurred as were those between stage and audience. Thus, the constable received the Virgin Mary in his own persona and escorted her and the Christ child to sit with the noble ladies of the court; and there the holy family remained when he returned in the guise of a Magus to offer gifts to the holy family.

The procession for the following year, that of the Christmas tournament, was largely the same, although a few new elements were introduced. Preceded by a troop of trumpeters and drummers, the dozen knights in the guise of Magi rode down the Calle Maestra, the city's main thoroughfare, followed by "a fool called the Master of Santiago."[53] Next were thirty torchbearers and then, as before, the constable appeared with crown and mask on his head and sword in hand. He was followed by a dozen musketeers firing their weapons into the air. When they reached the Plaza de Santa María, Miguel Lucas and his knights engaged in a lively game of *sortija* (in which the knights attempted to thrust a lance through an iron ring while charging at full speed) with rich prizes for the winners.

The Magi play, which occurred later that evening, had also been embellished. "The three Magi kings came on horseback, guided by a star hung on a rope that was strung along the street to the gate of the salon where the constable waited. Dismounting and entering, they found another guiding star and there offered their gifts to the child Jesus."[54] Just as it had done the year before, the play blurred past and present as the audience and players mingled, moving in and out of character.

The Christmas tournament presented Miguel Lucas's Granadan campaigns as directed at the eventual conversion rather than the destruction or expulsion of the Muslims of Granada. The emphasis he placed on the Magi story—whose central feature was the conversion of pagan kings—served the same end. Dramatic presentations of this biblical story were not unknown, but it was not a common choice for theatrics in Spain at this time; the shepherds' tale was vastly more popular. In bringing the Magi to the fore while dressing them in a fusion of exotic robes and chivalric accoutrements (which resulted in an appearance not unlike that of the "Muslims" in the *carta bermeja* tournament), Miguel Lucas linked his own martial efforts to the nativity story. The newborn Christ had converted pagan kings through the power of his divinity. The constable was, of course, unable to match such holy charisma, but the play made clear that his efforts to convert the infidels through the tools available to him were but attempts to imitate Christ himself. On a more practical note, the public processions preceding the play depicted the Magi as exalted and worldly rulers who bore the crowns and swords of their station. As the most prominent of their company, Miguel Lucas drew attention to his own powerful station. He emphasized the point, as he did on many other occasions, by making a timely exit from the public eye in order to complete the day's festivities among the civic elite.

The political import of the tournament and the Magi play is confirmed by the author of the *Hechos del condestable*. Although these events composed only a small part of a fortnight of revelry and theatrics, he devoted nearly his entire account of the Christmas season to them, summarizing "the other festivals" that occurred during the intervening days in only a short paragraph.[55] All of this was framed, moreover, by a discussion of the contemporary political situation that emphasized the constable's efforts to pursue the war against Granada despite royal vacillation. Immediately preceding the detailed descriptions of these two spectacles was the chronicler's account of Enrique's truce. Immediately following was an elaborate defense of Miguel Lucas's decision, made during the Christmas season, to violate it.

The terms of the truce required that Granada repatriate a number of Castilian captives. This transfer was to be overseen, as was customary, by *alfaqueques*, professional ransomers, from both sides. But, according to the *Hechos*, many prisoners were removed from the city of Granada to keep them out of the *alfaqueques'* sight. A number of these, perhaps thirty, were stashed in the castle of Montefrío where, taking advantage of lax guards, they staged a revolt and managed to barricade themselves inside the castle. Unable to escape Muslim territory without external support, they made contact with a Christian *alfaqueque*, asking him to find a frontier lord willing to send an expedition to their rescue. The *alfaqueque* chose Miguel Lucas, for he thought no one else would be willing to attempt such an audacious deed. Arriving in Jaén a few days before Christmas, he presented the situation to a receptive constable, who quickly drew up plans for an expedition of six hundred horsemen, two thousand infantry, and an artillery train.

As he organized and participated in the tournament and the Magi play, then, Miguel Lucas was planning to break a truce whose ink was not yet dry, and to do so in dramatic fashion. The size of the force he gathered was more appropriate for a significant campaign than for rescuing a few captives. It required a major outlay of funds as well as the active cooperation of Jaén's population. But, already unsettled by the disruption in trade caused by the previous summer's fighting and by their increased tax burden, they were likely to balk at any new demands, especially since this venture clearly lacked the king's blessing. The constable had used the Magi play to suggest the idea of conversion prior to his first raids the year before. Now he made the implications of the pagan kings' decision to follow Christ more explicit and with greater emphasis on his own role. This gambit was successful, insofar as no indication of unrest or lack of cooperation is recorded.

The actual invasion did not work out so well. The expedition set out late in January but accomplished little. Bad weather and lack of supplies plagued the army and, after a few skirmishes and the destruction of some minor fortifications, it returned to Jaén. The captives at Montefrío were forced to surrender and eventually converted to Islam. There was, moreover, no major response from Granada, meaning Miguel Lucas had even failed to conclusively break the truce.[56]

He was unable to follow up on this expedition due to a struggle with the bishop of Jaén, Alfonso Vázquez de Acuña, for control of the city. In order to ease Miguel Lucas's transition to Jaén, Enrique had ordered Acuña to withdraw to Begíjar, near Baeza. From there, however, the displaced bishop marshaled support for an attempt to retake Jaén. While ultimately unsuccessful, this ploy occupied the constable's attention for much of 1463, leaving little time for military adventures. In early spring that year, he thus found himself in the ironic position of hosting a Granadan delegation to Jaén to negotiate hostage exchanges and resolve local transfrontier disputes.

On the Sunday of carnival, the *alcaide* of Cambil arrived in Jaén with representatives of the king of Granada. Miguel Lucas immediately organized a *juego de cañas* in their honor. This was meant in part to impress the visitors with the size and preparedness of Jaén's garrison, and they responded as expected. The *Hechos* recorded that "the Moors were not a little frightened and amazed, seeing the ferocity of the game and the confidence and number of the knights of the city."[57] While intended to overawe the emissaries, the proceedings also bore a distinctly informal character. After the *juego*, for instance, the guests and their hosts moved in procession to the palace with the appropriate level of pomp. They rode "with many torches, and all the streets full of lances topped by burning flambeaux so that there was not a single shadow in all the city, and six pairs of kettledrummers, and many trumpets, flutes, and tambourines."[58] For such events, the Constable usually marched or rode in a majestic pose, bearing his sword and displaying his heraldic devices. On this occasion, however, he rode a pony (although a very fine one, to be sure) with his wife perched behind him on the animal's haunches. His brother and sister-in-law rode in a similar manner, as did Teresa's uncle Juan de Torres and his wife María Cuello. The scene as described in the *Hechos* is a familial, comfortable one, a mood that persisted during the carnival revelries throughout Jaén that followed. Mimes and actors performed in the plazas, townspeople danced and sang, and trumpets and drums pierced the air. The visitors wandered through these street parties until midnight, and then retired for a meal at the palace.

The next day brought further festivities. The nobles and their Granadan guests occupied an elaborately decorated stage in front of a vast bonfire on the Plaza de Santa María, while the constable's knights played at *sortija* and crowds thronged in the adjoining streets. The "master of Santiago" made an appearance as the game's judge, directing a group of pages to beat the winner of the contest, Miguel Lucas's mace-bearer Pero Gómes de Ocaña, with "clubs" made of wool stuffed with cotton. After a luxurious dinner (at which food was provided "in such great abundance that the people began throwing it at each other"), "a band of one hundred fifty men entered with baskets on their heads and clean round skullcaps, each with three or four large, dry gourds."[59] They proceeded to engage in a vigorous burlesque melee that involved hitting each other on the head with the gourds to the sound of trumpets, a struggle "that seemed to be the fiercest fight in the world. Such seemed to all to be the case, especially the Moors, who exclaimed among themselves."[60]

The author of the *Hechos* clearly assumed that the constable intended to use the spectacles and games already planned for carnival as a means of impressing the Muslim diplomats. But his willingness to bring the visitors into his home as honored guests and to treat them to events defined more by playfulness than grandeur betrays an ease at odds with the idea of Muslims as religious enemies. The absurd oversupply of food, for instance, demonstrated the city's wealth: Jaén provided so much food that, not only could all eat to excess, they could play with it, a point driven home by the grand gourd battle that followed. But the very silliness of this behavior would have undermined this message. If the constable wanted the Muslim knights to return home with an image of a wealthy and fierce enemy, would not a staid but opulent meal and a repeat of the first day's intense *juego de cañas* have served him better? Instead, he treated his guests to "a kind of mockery of the knights' own mock battles."[61]

By permitting the emissaries to join in the town's carnival fun, Miguel Lucas treated them as truly honored guests rather than barely tolerated representatives of an illegitimate infidel ruler. He did so publicly, sharing his *cadalhalso* with them and letting the people of Jaén see the vision he had presented in the Christmas tournament made into reality. If Christians and Muslims could eat and play together even while fighting continued, then the future might be bright indeed. Such, too, may have been the message he hoped the delegation would bring back to Granada: that the constable was a fierce, dangerous foe but also a generous and noble leader who did not reflexively hate Muslims.

*   *   *

Miguel Lucas's penchant for burlesque tournaments and ambivalent references to Islam did not end here. In February 1464, he put on one of his most elaborate shows to commemorate King Enrique's visit to Jaén. As the king's party approached the city, they met five hundred mounted knights dressed like Muslims who entertained them with mock skirmishes. Continuing along their way, the royal party met thirty other knights dressed as Muslim women and playing tambourines. Finally, they encountered a huge crowd of children riding wicker hobbyhorses in white Muslim robes or wielding wicker crossbows. Joined by this young multitude, the king entered Jaén in a triumphal ceremony.[62] Such mass events were not solely reserved for special visitors but also marked particular moments in the ecclesiastic calendar. The feast days of San Juan (24 June) and Santiago (25 July), for instance, usually saw mock battles with some participants in Muslim attire while Epiphany celebrations continued to feature the Magi play and tournaments. Significant moments in the constable's personal life, such as the birth of his daughter in 1465, could also inspire mock battles. On that occasion, the usual configuration of costumes, torches, and music included *añafiles* (Moorish trumpets).[63]

Despite their regular place in Jaén's festive life, these games should be seen in the context of the winter of 1462–1463, when the pattern they would thereafter follow was set. Miguel Lucas was then flush with his first successes against Granada and considering an open rejection of the king's truce. But the local population looked forward to the security and commercial opportunities a continued truce would provide. The combination of Miguel Lucas's personal background and his perceptions of popular fears created a novel result. His experiences in Enrique's court had given the constable a familiarity with Moorish culture that allowed him to use a variety of Islamicate motifs and to embrace the Granadan visitors as fellows, while the need to assuage popular concerns forced him to temper his zeal for holy war with considerations for what would come after the (for him) inevitable Christian victory.

In proposing that conversion would put an end to meaningful differences between Muslims and Christians (or more properly, given his professed expectations, between converted Moors and "Old Christians"), he drew on an understanding of conversion that assumed baptism effectively removed the taint of Islam. Once a Christian, the convert would suffer no social or legal disabilities. Such was the case already, in theory at least, with the communities of Mudéjares in or near Jaén and such was the situation of the more significant population of converted Jews in the city. But Miguel Lucas's vision ran against the temper of the times. Christians remained eager to engage in trade with Muslims, but their willingness to live on equal terms with recent converts or members of other faiths, long a hallmark of the frontier, was fading.

The Jewish community of Jaén seems to have nearly disappeared after destructive pogroms in 1391, but the city boasted a significant and economically prominent *converso* population that lagged only those of Seville and Córdoba.[64] The constable put his ideas about conversion into practice in his relations with these "New Christians," backing individual *conversos* in their efforts to join the ruling councils or to hold municipal office. This support provided ammunition to his numerous enemies, who accused him of unduly favoring the *conversos*. These rivals, who included the Marquis of Villena and his supporters as well as the bishop of Jaén and other local notables distressed by Miguel Lucas's military and economic policies, sought to undermine the constable's popularity by identifying him with the *conversos*, whose success had inspired widespread popular envy.

Such machinations first came to a head in 1468, when the constable uncovered a plot to assassinate him and spark a riot. The account of the conspiracy given in the *Hechos* demonstrates how anti-*converso* sentiments could be mobilized to serve political ends during the civil war that erupted after the Farce of Ávila:

> As the Constable so diligently persevered in his loyalty and service to the lord king, the Marquis of Villena, who was now Master of Santiago, wished to destroy him and have the city of Jaén in his hand, believing that, if this could be accomplished, the king would be lost in every way and have nothing in Castile that could sustain him. And so Villena made a deal with a knight named Fernán Mexía, a native of Jaén, and also the *comendador* Juan de Pareja, whom the king had fostered and rewarded, for it was through his highness that the man held the town and castle of Pegalajar, which is in the domain of Jaén, as well as other natives and citizens of Jaén. They agreed and conspired to kill the lord Constable through

treachery *and to rob the conversos, so that the populace of that city would wish to join them.*[65]

The attack was to take place as the constable left the vespers service on the feast of San Lázaro (the day before Palm Sunday). But he attended church that day with a large entourage and, "by a miracle of God," Mexía faltered at the key moment and was taken into custody, whence he revealed the details of the scheme.[66] Although the assassination attempt came to naught, several conspirators escaped and the episode illustrates Miguel Lucas's increasingly insecure position as well as the vulnerability of the *conversos*. The conspirators' confidence that the populace would rise against him if offered the opportunity to pillage their *converso* neighbors implied a dangerous level of tension that could explode under the right circumstances.

This came to pass in 1473, when an anti-*converso* riot in Córdoba inspired a wave of similar attacks across Andalucía. By 20 March, the violence had reached Andújar, a town near Jaén, ruled by Miguel Lucas's confidant Pedro de Escavias.[67] The constable wrote to Escavias the next day, exhorting him to act decisively in protecting the *conversos*. This letter, as Michel García has pointed out, reveals that Miguel Lucas saw the violence as a challenge to his own authority. Escavias was one of his deputies; refusal to obey him amounted to a rebellion against the constable.[68] The uprising next broke out in Jaén, where, according to Palencia, anti-Semitic sentiment had hitherto been repressed due to the constable's resolute defense of the *converso* community: "The example of the booty gained in Córdoba greatly encouraged the people of Jaén, who were eager to throw themselves into a similar attack, and they were contained only by the energy of Constable Miguel Lucas."[69]

However, Palencia continued, Miguel Lucas's star had lost much of its luster. He had recently taken the field against a Granadan incursion led personally by Sultan Abū al-Hasan ʿAlī (Muley Hacén to Castilians). Encountering the Muslim army in the pass of La Guardia and possessing an army that could easily have overwhelmed the enemy, he was "seized by fear" and withdrew his forces.[70] The political ramifications of this failure were profound, for "the people of Jaén converted this shame into disdain for their leader and soon enough began to plot disorder with more boldness than was their habit, for they were losing their earlier docility. On 22 March they took advantage of a conspiracy against the unsuspecting Constable in order to eagerly join together in robbing the *conversos* of their goods."[71] Led by several of the constable's local enemies, a mob of residents fought a running battle with his troops through the streets that eventually reached the cathedral. There Miguel Lucas was hearing Mass and, "when he knelt [to pray], one of the conspirators who was nearby dealt him a wounding blow to the temple with a crossbow, and then many of those present tore at him with swords and spears so much that his body barely looked human. Meanwhile, the crowd gave themselves to looting the homes of the *conversos* and killing them."[72]

It may well be that there was a conspiracy against him, that his earlier defeat at La Guardia had weakened the constable's reputation in the city, permitting his enemies to build support for their plans to remove him. All sources agree, however, that his death was linked to popular anger against the *conversos*. His passing signaled carte blanche to rob and kill the New Christians of Jaén. Even those seen to support the converts were targeted; Miguel Lucas's family and many members of his circle were forced to take refuge in the Castilla de Santa Catalina overlooking the city.[73]

*   *   *

Christians in Jaén, like those elsewhere on the frontier, had long struggled to define clear social boundaries between different religious groups. In response to this dilemma, they often resorted to contradictory extremes, ranging from unrestrained violence toward enemies to the rejection of fixed religious identities. Miguel Lucas's program of pageants proposed a middle ground in which Muslims (and Jews) who converted to Christianity would live in peace under Christian rule. He adopted this message as a means of making religious warfare more appealing to the people of Jaén, assuring them that his campaigns would interrupt trade only temporarily. His spectacles and heavy-handed methods of governance succeeded in securing at least the tacit support of Jaén's populace despite the cost of his military endeavors, his civic building programs, and the spectacles themselves. But his role in noble factional struggles won him a number of enemies who took advantage of waning tolerance for the sort of *convivencia* he espoused. Enrique IV's maurophilia led many of the high nobility to reject Islamic culture in all its aspects, while a generalized reaction against Castile's *conversos* undermined the security of not only the *conversos* themselves but also those nobles who supported them too prominently. This popular disaffection, manipulated by his aristocratic enemies, led to the constable's death at the hands of the populace on whom he had lavished such attention.

Miguel Lucas's willingness to turn so often to the pomp and splendor of elaborate spectacles was a product of his own past. Never entirely comfortable in his exalted position and ever aware of the gossip regarding his humble birth and his dependence on the king's largesse, he presented himself not only as noble in appearance but as a paragon of the noble virtues of generosity, piety, and courage. But the content of his theatrics owed much to his perceptions of the people of Jaén. Although his experiences in Enrique's court meant he was familiar with Mudéjar and Morisco dress and manners, there is little evidence he shared the king's deep feeling for Islamic culture. He appreciated the finer things in life, and many of these in fifteenth-century Castile were products of Muslim hands and Mudéjar artistry. But at heart he was a holy warrior who fully embraced the idea of a Christian-dominated Iberia. The spectacles, therefore, were less an expression of his own feelings than an attempt to win broad support, to convince his subjects that his purposes were not at odds with livelihoods built on frontier accommodations.

Although they were amenable to trade and contact with the Muslims of Granada, the people of Jaén ultimately rejected Miguel Lucas's vision of a society in which conversion to Christianity could erase all differences. The *converso* community in Jaén recovered somewhat after 1473 but remained vulnerable. The Tribunal of the Inquisition was established in Jaén in 1483 (only those in Seville and Córdoba came earlier) and was first housed, ironically, in the constable's palace, amid his Mudéjar decorations. Jaén's autos-da-fé were conducted on the Plaza de Santa María, where Miguel Lucas first proposed that one day Muslims and Christians might live in peace, competing on the practice ground instead of the battlefield.[74] These events, like those of the constable, were meant to shift public sentiment toward religious minorities in a particular direction.

CHAPTER 4

A "Chance Act": Córdoba in 1473

The anti-*converso* violence that raged through Jaén, and indeed all of Andalucía, in 1473 was sparked in Córdoba by what Alfonso de Palencia called a "chance act" (*un hecho casual*). In early March of that year, Córdoba's Cofradía de la Caridad (Brotherhood of Charity) conducted a procession down the Calle de la Feria bearing an effigy of the Virgin Mary. As they passed through the Cruz del Rastro, a small but busy market square near the river, a young girl spilled some fluid, likely water, from a window overlooking the square (see Map 2). The home in which she stood belonged to a *converso*. The liquid spattered the statue, causing Alonso Rodríguez, a blacksmith who was part of the procession, to cry frantically that the girl had deliberately thrown urine on the Virgin as an insult to Christians. "I sympathize with you," he shouted, "honorable citizens, for the evident derision that these detestable heretics have dared to present to the holy religion, with no fear of punishment for their crimes. Let us now avenge it on these reprobate enemies of the faith and of charity."[1]

The gathered crowd at once set about firing the offending house as well as others owned by *conversos* in the surrounding streets. Almost immediately, Pedro de Torreblanca, a knight well known in the city and especially popular among the "Old Christians" who made up the mob, sought to dispel the tension. Playing on his reputation, he pleaded with the crowd to leave off the fighting, which could do nothing but disservice to God and king.[2] As Torreblanca spoke, however, Rodríguez struck him and the disturbance developed into a running battle between the rioters and townsfolk coming to Torreblanca's aid. The blacksmith and his supporters fled to the church of San Francisco, located a few streets away on the grounds of the Monastery of

San Pedro el Real. At this point, the chief magistrate (*alcalde mayor*) of the city, Don Alonso de Aguilar, came onto the scene.

Both Palencia and Diego de Valera described Aguilar as incensed by the disturbance and the injury to Torreblanca. He managed to convince Rodríguez to leave the sanctuary of the church with an offer of mercy and then, perhaps after the blacksmith offered some intemperate words, stabbed him with a lance. Friends and relatives bore the wounded Rodríguez home, where he soon died, while the *converso* community prepared for the worst. Palencia, who evinced no love for the New Christians, described their precautions from a perspective likely shared by many Old Christians, that is to say, as evidence of their guilt: "The *conversos*, fearful by nature and through knowledge of their wicked deeds, organized defenses in their most populous neighborhoods; they armed themselves and hid away their treasures, most of which had been accumulated by their immoral wiles."[3]

Drawn by rumors, a large crowd gathered near Rodríguez's home, where a macabre reinterpretation of the Passion was enacted as "some of the more hotheaded among them, having the gullibility of the common folk, began to shout that he had risen from the dead and that he implored those present to avenge his unjust death and also the outrages committed against the sacred religion by evil men."[4] Inspired by this fresh infusion of religious enthusiasm, the crowd renewed and expanded the assault on *converso* homes. Aguilar returned to the scene, confident that his personal authority, combined with a squad of mounted knights, would suffice to disperse the crowd and end the troubles. He was confounded both by the rioters' fervor and by the efforts of *veinticuatro* Pedro de Aguayo, described by Palencia as "a fractious man and a friend to the *converso* tanners," who had aided the *conversos* in their efforts to organize a defense and now rallied them to resist the attackers.[5] Embroiled in a pitched battle in the streets, neither side heeded Aguilar's interventions and instead turned on him and his retainers. Under a hail of rocks and arrows, Aguilar fled to his headquarters in the Alcázar, in the western end of the city and far from the fighting.

With the city government now taking a passive role, the situation settled into an uneasy standoff that lasted several days. The anti-*converso* ranks were augmented by sympathizers who gathered from throughout the city and even the surrounding countryside with the hope of "earning their pay" (*a cobrar sus jornales*) by looting the *conversos*.[6] Aguilar, meanwhile, advised his friends among the New Christians that they might take refuge in the city's old castle, the Alcázar Viejo, and many of the wealthier were able to do so. Others defended themselves as best they could in the streets, barricading intersections near the old walls that ran through the heart of the city and afforded some protection. Unable to regain control of the city, Aguilar and other civic leaders acquiesced to the anti-*converso* faction's demands and disowned the *converso* community, leaving the rioters free to vent their wrath on their New Christian neighbors.

And this they did, as Palencia related in graphic detail:

> No one among the Old Christians now favored the *conversos*;
> indeed, they hurried to burn their homes, to steal their treasures,
> and to plunder in general. They violated maidens and cruelly
> stripped the matrons or made them suffer horrible deaths. Finding
> a certain beautiful young woman, already stripped of all her clothes
> save a fine shirt, decorated like a newlywed's with intricate lace, one
> of them tore it from top to bottom with his sword, opening her
> chest and stomach and killing her instantly. It is said that there was
> even one man who violated the corpses of the young women; and
> many older residents were killed as well. No form of cruelty was
> omitted on that disastrous day of 16 March 1473, the sixteenth since
> the troubles began.[7]

After the violence, which left the heavily *converso* neighborhoods near the Calle de la Feria and the Plaza de las Tendillas de Calatrava in ruins, many of Córdoba's New Christians fled to Seville. Meeting with further violence in Seville, many continued on to Gibraltar and emigrated to Italy or Flanders.[8]

Historians have traditionally explained this outbreak of violence and the disturbances across Andalucía that it provoked as part of a larger trend of increasing anti-Semitism that culminated in the Inquisition and the Edict of Expulsion. This stemmed both from theological understandings of Jews that cast them as the enemies of Christ and from social tensions that marginalized and isolated religious minorities in general. The breakdown in the circumstances of the Jews, from this perspective, was part of a general crisis in medieval Castile that began with the incomplete colonization of Andalucía in the thirteenth century and was exacerbated in the fourteenth by plague and civil war. These dislocations led to the scapegoating of Jews and to widespread violence in 1391 that devastated Jewish communities throughout Castile, forcing many survivors to convert. Despite a somewhat more congenial atmosphere in the early fifteenth century, the rapid rise of *conversos* who left

behind the legal restrictions placed on Jews aroused popular envy, and, when
harvest failures and renewed civil war again stressed Castilian society, these
converts found that their new status was poor protection against old prejudices. As an explanation, this argument has much to commend it and goes
far in explaining why Córdoba's people turned upon their neighbors with
such ferocity.

It does not give us insight, however, into the *moment* when these long-
term tensions exploded or explain how and why Palencia's "chance act" was
the catalyst for an outpouring of rage against *conversos* in a city where their
position had been secure for three-quarters of a century. To dismiss this as
happenstance or historical contingency overlooks the importance of the
Cofradía de la Caridad's ill-fated procession and the reactions of onlookers.
The mere existence of ideas about Jews and *conversos*, moreover, is insufficient
to explain these events. People mobilized these discourses for particular reasons in a particular place at a particular moment in time. We must therefore
look to the specific motives of Rodríguez and his fellows as well as those of
local *conversos* and the Old Christians who sought to defend them. But we
should extend this line of reasoning to consider how the articulation of traditional discourses gave them power, discounting neither the significance of an
apparent insult to the Virgin's dignity nor the appeal of Rodríguez's strident
call to arms.

In the face of such visceral stimuli, protagonists and onlookers could
respond in multiple ways. The spilled water may have been provocation enough
for those ready to exploit the slightest opportunity to assault the *conversos*.
The success of Alonso Rodríguez's harangue, however, suggests that less-hostile
onlookers were also open to his message. Part of the answer lies in ritual elements of the procession and initial disturbances that took advantage of their
timing. The Cofradía de la Caridad's march took place on 1 March, or just
before the start of Lent in a year when Easter fell on 18 April.[9] The licenses of
carnival and the religious passions of Lent might explain why the initial attacks
and rumors of the blacksmith's resurrection so effectively moved the crowd to
action. But even these associations do not suffice to explain the extraordinary
power of a moment that induced even some *conversos* to turn against their
peers. One of these was the poet Antón de Montoro who, in a regretful and
sarcastic poem addressed to Aguilar, lamented that "I, how unfortunate I was, /
was the first to put on / the livery of the blacksmith."[10]

Montoro, an outspoken critic of the tendency to view *conversos* "more as
Jews than Christians," would hardly have agreed that the New Christians

must be punished for Christ's death.[11] Yet the waves of resentment that swept the city caught him up, at least for a time.

Unscripted though much of it was, the opening events of the assault (including the procession, the spilled water, Rodríguez's speech, Torreblanca's rejoinder, Aguilar's attack, and the rumors of Rodríguez's resurrection) functioned as a public performance complete with a plot, characters, and moral message. Its success depended on the reactions of spectators. To understand these, we must closely examine the context, both social and physical, in which it occurred. Those contexts were defined by Córdoba's proximity to the frontier with Granada. As this chapter shows, the ambivalent religious attitudes of the frontier were not limited to Christian-Muslim relations. The Old Christians of Córdoba viewed converts with both resentment and affability. They held, in other words, an amiable enmity strikingly similar to that displayed toward Muslims by the Christians of Jaén. This in itself is perhaps unsurprising, but the particular conditions in Córdoba exacerbated this situation. For the frontier did not only condition residents' perspectives on members of other religious groups, it also played a significant role in shaping all the social structures of the city.

Córdoba of the 1470s was marked by both cohesion and division. On the one hand, a powerful self-mythology of unity and shared pride in Cordoban heritage was enhanced by a frontier ideology that offered citizens a collective purpose and role within the larger drama of *reconquista*. On the other, Cordoban society was controlled by a military elite that held jealously to the reins of urban power even while embroiled in disputes over access to privilege and in factional struggles that led at times to bloodshed. The populace was drawn into these noble conflicts and was itself divided into small corporate bodies defined by occupation, locality, and religion. Individuals could belong to several different such clusters, and the drama of March 1473 played before an audience in which each person had alliances with multiple groups while harboring resentments against several others. An attack against the *conversos* could thus serve to attack the nobles who protected them, the municipal government into which they had purportedly paid their way, the trade guilds to which they belonged, or the parishes in which they lived. Such aggression by proxy had real benefits for it allowed effective expression of resentment against inconvenient targets. It also demonstrates that we cannot reduce Córdoba's divisions to simple binary oppositions, such as noble versus popular or New versus Old Christians.

The physical setting of the procession and the fighting was as significant as its social context. It would not, in fact, be overmuch to suggest that the city itself was a player in these dramas. The spatial organization of the city exacerbated competition, both friendly and not, among groups by geographically segregating and thus limiting contact between them. This contained latent discord by preventing the lower classes from coalescing as a unified whole but also prevented the full assimilation of Córdoba's *conversos*. Moreover, the streets, buildings, and plazas of Córdoba held various associations for the residents who lived in and visited them. These connotations—in concert with the actions of the protagonists, their use of both positive and negative discourses about Jews and *conversos*, and the larger contexts of the city and the frontier—enabled viewers to order events into a coherent narrative in which they played a role.

*   *   *

Contemporary images of Córdoba, like those of many late medieval and early modern cities, presented a bounded and unitary space in which internal divisions were subordinated. These drawings of Córdoba drew on a mythology of cities as communal entities, whose citizens lived together in fellowship, free from feudal hierarchies.[12] There were a number of factors that would have encouraged Cordobans to think of themselves in these terms. The municipal government was, in theory at least, representative. The *concejo* had two chambers. The first consisted of the *regidores*, crown-appointed councilors who held their office for life and who were known generally as *veinticuatros* (because there were supposed to be twenty-four of them). The second was made up of *jurados*, parish representatives who could be elected by the *vecinos* (male property owners of the parish) or, as was usually the case, appointed by the crown. At times a *corregidor*, another royal appointee, held precedence over the council as de facto governor of the city. While there was regularly a *corregidor* in place near the end of the century, long periods during the reigns of Juan II and Enrique IV saw the position vacant.[13] Despite the reality of royal authority in the city, however, the semblance of popular involvement on the council seems to have fostered some sense of belonging. Moreover, there were a great many other municipal offices whose holders were named without royal or even *concejo* influence, but were elected by the *caballeros de cuantía*. These included the *alcaldes* (judges) and *fieles* ("reliable men") who supervised the markets and workshops, as well as the constables who provided public order.[14]

The frontier provided another impulse for civic solidarity, uniting a large part of the population through a shared religious identity and nearly all of it through the perception of potential physical danger. Córdoba was not as exposed to attack as were other frontier cities, and there were few panics such as that which gripped Jaén in the late 1470s. It did act, however, as a rear base and, during the war with Granada in the 1480s, was headquarters for the Catholic Monarchs and their extensive retinue. Throughout the century, then, the city and its territories were never able to relax their guard fully. Córdoba's constant military preparations, moreover, had a notable impact on its demographic and social makeup, ironically providing sources of division and confusion.

Cordoban society in the fifteenth century was dominated by its military classes, which included the *hidalgos*, or hereditary nobles, as well as the *caballeros de cuantía*, commoners of means obliged to provide horse and weapons for themselves, receiving in return exemptions from some taxes. Together, the privileged groups were a sizable minority within the city. *Hidalgo* families, along with the clergy and military orders, the other tax-exempt groups in Córdoba, made up about 5 percent of an overall population of perhaps twenty-five thousand. The *caballeros* and their families composed another 5 percent.[15]

While the *caballeros* acted, in theory, as no more or less than a mounted militia, their privileges denoted some level of status and their social position over time became confused with that of the *hidalgos*. These groups were not closely aligned, however. *Hidalgos* saw themselves as willing servants of the king, paying for their weapons and mounts and often providing contingents of followers to serve as well. The *caballeros de cuantía*, in contrast, usually served when compelled (through legal requirements or public shaming) or bribed (through tax exemptions). And, although the *caballeros* remained relevant in this region at a time when they had mostly disappeared in northern Castile, they were clearly subordinate to the *hidalgos*, who dominated the *concejo* and held most key municipal offices.

But *hidalgos* did not form a homogeneous class, instead ranging from penniless knights to magnates who owned vast estates, wielded regional influence, and were active in court politics. In the late fifteenth century, the most prominent of these in Córdoba were the houses of Cabra and Aguilar, both branches of the illustrious Fernández de Córdoba lineage. Their struggles for preeminence lasted throughout the period. The fortunes of these families (of which the chief figures were, respectively, Don Diego Fernández de Córdoba, third count of Cabra, and Don Alonso de Aguilar, *alcalde mayor* of Córdoba) were based in large estates to the south of the city. Both controlled extensive *bandos* (groups of relatives, vassals, and supporters) through which they could influence the municipal government. A favored method was to pay retaining fees to officeholders in return for their votes and support. When Aguilar and Cabra were at odds, therefore, conflict invariably spilled over into the city itself. This struggle for local supremacy divided the citizenry in deep and lasting ways and encouraged wide-ranging seignorial interference in civic politics. Even after direct royal rule was imposed during the reign of the Catholic monarchs, the magnates and their opposed *bandos* continued to act as significant forces in the city.[16]

In contrast, the position of the minor *hidalgos*, those without titles and often without lands, was insecure. They held a virtual monopoly on the office of *veinticuatro* and enjoyed a social stature often at odds with their economic status. Many were quite poor, in fact, having few viable means of earning money while retaining their rank. To "live nobly" required landholdings sufficient to support an appropriate lifestyle. Failing this, warfare offered the best prospects, while competing in tournaments was an option for the young. Many *hidalgos*, however, could not afford to arm themselves and were forced into common trades, the "rank or vile offices" forbidden to nobles since Juan II's reign.[17]

The *caballeros de cuantía*, a class that included perforce nearly all wealthy commoners in Córdoba, meanwhile found themselves excluded from higher municipal offices. Viewing *hidalgos* as pretentious or idle and resentful of their tax exemptions, they repeatedly attempted to have the credentials of all *hidalgos* inspected, in the hopes of bringing some down to their own social standing. They also began to present themselves as defenders of the traditional liberties to frontier cities. In this role, they clamored for a more even-handed distribution of the tax burden while demanding access to the *concejo*. Whether these actions point to the "radicalism" of the *caballería*, as some have suggested, is open to debate.[18] It is clear, however, that there was no harmonious privileged class in Córdoba; the dichotomy between economic and social status kept the *hidalgos* and *caballeros* in constant tension.

Much less is known about those Cordobans who lacked wealth sufficient to require mounted military service. The laconic administrative records offer little insight into the experience of living in fifteenth-century Córdoba. The data that is available suggests a prosperous city but one whose population was often at odds with privileged groups.[19] Despite latent unrest inspired by social inequalities, however, there were no popular protests in the second half of the fifteenth century other than in 1473. This was in marked contrast to the repeated uprisings that had occurred over the course of the prior century.[20]

While this relative tranquility may be attributed in part to aristocratic efforts to control tension and in part to the myth of civic solidarity, we might also consider an urban layout that divided the populace into small, physically segregated corporate bodies. Occupational zoning meant that those engaged in a particular trade worked and lived together, with particular streets often named for their specialties. In Córdoba, for instance, we have already seen the Calle de la Feria's cloth merchants as well as the Tannery in the Ajerquía. There were also, among many others, streets named for silversmiths (the Calle de los Plateros), blacksmiths (de la Herrería), butchers (de los Carniceros), boatmen (de los Barqueros), and so on. There were practical reasons for such groupings. They facilitated quality control, training of apprentices, and guild business. Access to particular resources also influenced civic layout. Tanning, for instance, required vast quantities of water as well as a means to dispose of waste and so more than 90 percent of Córdoba's tanners lived in the parishes adjacent to the Guadalquivir.[21] Such spatial organization, common in medieval cities, effectively prevented broad class struggles by limiting contact between those of different trades. Unrest, when it occurred, required a catalyst.

In Córdoba, as in most cities, the spatial distribution of these enclaves reflected local hierarchies. The wealthiest and most influential lived in the city center. Here too was the pinnacle of civic architecture, with the townhouses and compounds of the affluent rubbing shoulders with the cathedral, the bishop's palace, the Alcázar, the exchange, and the guildhalls. Córdoba's marginalized groups, including the unemployed, day laborers, prostitutes, and the non- or newly Christian, were relegated to the outskirts of town or carefully demarcated regions within it. Together, these arrangements resulted in a city of cliques, with neighborhoods and parishes defined by residents who worked in the same trades, had equal social and economic standing, and knew each other well. All this confirmed social differences and inequalities while minimizing contact and open confrontation.

Even parishes in close proximity could exhibit striking differences, as a comparison of San Nicolás de la Ajerquía and San Pedro reveals. Three trades—textiles, leather production, and metalwork—employed nearly 70 percent of San Nicolás's workforce, while a further 10 percent worked in the hospitality industry centered on the Plaza del Potro and Calle Mancebía.

Some of the same trades were well represented in San Pedro, directly to the north. But the area had an altogether different character. The clergy who staffed the parish's many religious houses composed a significant portion of the population, and holders of public offices made up the largest single group of recorded residents. Military officers, *veinticuatros*, judges, *fieles*, tax collectors, and inspectors were attracted to this neighborhood both by its proximity to the city center and by its lively commerce. Its weekly markets and seasonal fairs employed many others in the parish, not only the merchants who owned the stalls but also scribes and notaries to record transactions and carters to move goods. The parish was therefore diverse in terms of the occupations represented, but in practice its various aspects remained separate. Its mercantile centers and affluent residents were concentrated in its west end, near the Calle de la Feria and the Plaza de la Corredera, while the majority of artisans and producers lived farther east.[22]

Home to its centers of ecclesiastic, royal, and municipal authority, Santa María was Córdoba's largest and most populous parish. Like other waterfront parishes, it housed many leather and textile workers who needed access to the river. Away from the Guadalquivir, however, were the streets where Córdoba's most prestigious artisans worked in ceramics or precious metals, where the *veinticuatros* lived and met, where wealthy merchants had their townhouses, and where the region's true elite, the bishop and *grandes*, stayed when in the city.[23] In this one parish, only a short walk from the tanneries, were nearly half of Córdoba's clergy, a majority of its merchants, and two-thirds of its goldsmiths, enamelers, and jewelers. Here too were far more domestic servants, butchers, and construction workers than any other district. Santa María was the city's center in another sense; its residents literally owned the rest of Córdoba. Both its institutional and individual inhabitants were major landlords both within and without the city. Precise figures are difficult to come by, but the bishop, the cathedral chapter and other religious houses, the *concejo*, and a number of the *hidalgo* families combined to own as much as 80 percent of Córdoba's dwellings.[24]

Local homogeneity was reinforced by the division of the populace into a series of corporate groups. In Castile, these were generally defined by internal hierarchies, public displays of solidarity, and privileges that might range from preferential access to civic spaces (such as markets) to monopolies on certain products to the right to solicit charitable donations. Such clusters were often close-knit, commanding a loyalty that at times compared to the devotion given the nuclear family and lineage.[25] The most prominent and powerful such organization in Córdoba was the urban government, composed of social (although not economic) equals, with the *hidalgos* controlling nearly all of the key offices. It was also, in some regards, the least integrated of Córdoba's constituent groups. Yet the elites, while often internally divided, presented a unified front when facing challenges to their political and economic privileges, striving successfully to retain what amounted to a military hegemony that controlled civic political, economic, and social life.

That they were able to do so reflects the inability of Córdoba's other groups to wield effective political power. The most significant civic corporations among commoners were guilds and confraternities. Little is known about their internal workings in Córdoba as few records have survived, leaving only external sources that offer scant insight into their activities, memberships, or agendas. Broadly speaking, however, there were *gremios* (trade organizations or guilds) and *cofradías* (lay religious brotherhoods and charitable organizations). While the references to such groups in *concejo* records use the terms indiscriminately and their functions and memberships likely overlapped, it makes sense here to describe each separately with the caveat that contemporaries did not see sharp distinctions between them.

The major trade guilds were those of the cloth workers, with separate organizations representing the weavers, dyers, fullers, and shearers. The records do not mention other significant guilds, and it is possible that artisans practicing other trades either joined one of the existing cloth guilds or did not organize.[26] The manufacture of cloth, however, was one of Córdoba's most lucrative industries and was tightly regulated by municipal and crown authorities. This required the cooperation of the guilds in order to insure effective quality and price controls, and it is in this regard that those guilds appear in the records. It is therefore probable that smaller or less formal organizations that dealt with less prominent products existed, but they left few if any imprints on the surviving sources.

Confraternities offered their members services similar to those of the trade guilds. These included practical assistance in times of penury, sickness, and death as well as social and business support networks. Like guilds, confraternities generally required that members show evidence of good character, be willing to work harmoniously with other members and adhere to a code of conduct, and be able to pay dues. Both guilds and confraternities also marched in civic processions, held banquets, and conducted charitable works.

Despite their comparable structures and benefits, however, there was a meaningful difference in emphasis. Guilds existed for trade purposes and, despite their many other activities, retained a focus on the economic well-being of their constituents. Confraternities developed to permit the lay expression of religious devotion. Groups might organize penitential processions to celebrate saints' days or particular aspects of the Passion in displays ranging from luxurious banners and statues to flagellants who proclaimed their solidarity with Christ and atoned for their sins through ritual scourging.[27] They might also focus on charitable deeds, using their monies to supply dowries to poor or orphaned girls, feed and bury indigents and convicts, endow hospitals, and generally ensure that the marginalized populations of the city had at least minimal comforts and so would be less likely to cause disruptions. There were at least a dozen such organizations in fifteenth-century Córdoba, of which the best known and most influential was the Cofradía de la Caridad.[28]

Groups defined by their religious, as opposed to their social or economic, character were segregated to a degree from the life of the city. These included the Christian clergy as well as all Muslims and Jews. The institutional church was a powerful presence in terms of both its wealth and its raw numbers. While it is impossible to determine with precision how many priests, nuns, and monks lived in fifteenth-century Córdoba, the number was substantial, at least 5 percent of the population. The 1502 grain investigation offers precise numbers for one community, the staff of the cathedral. Not counting members of the bishop's staff, this document enumerates no less than seventy-two canons, officials, and chaplains, a number in keeping with contemporary norms. There were, moreover, fourteen parish churches in Córdoba and at least seventeen monastic houses. All of these entities were property owners, with the result that the organized church's economic role in the city resembled that of the wealthier *hidalgos* and *caballeros* who collected rents and redistributed the proceeds in the markets or as charity. The central vehicles of such charity were the many hospitals—at least eighteen—whose work was closely aligned with that of the confraternities.[29]

In contrast, the city's Mudéjares were physically and economically segregated from the Christian majority. Shortly after Córdoba's thirteenth-century conquest, the Muslim population was deported, though a small number of artisans soon returned. The continued survival of this community confirms their economic contributions to the civic community, to which they brought highly prized skills not readily available from other sources, including masonry, gardening, and veterinary medicine. The Mudéjares traditionally lived near the Plaza de las Tendillas de Calatrava, on the border between San Nicolás de la Villa and San Miguel parishes north of the cathedral. In the 1470s and 1480s, however, successive attempts were made to increase their tax obligations, to more effectively segregate them from the Christian majority and, ultimately, to force their conversion. Some of these measures, such as a requirement that Muslims wear distinguishing marks on their clothing, had been law since the early part of the century but only now were vigorously enforced. Other laws, such as that of the segregation, or *apartamiento*, of Muslims into *morerías*, were revivals or extensions of earlier approaches.

The first attempt to restrict the Mudéjares from the Christian population occurred in 1479, when *corregidor* Francisco de Valdés moved them to the Alcázar Viejo in San Bartolomé parish, a location whose tight quarters were physically separate from the rest of the city and without access to fresh water. The order not only required the Muslims to reside there but forbade them from leaving for any reason without permission. Isolated not only from society but from their means of earning a living or of worshipping (their mosque was closed at the same time), the Muslims of Córdoba appealed to Isabel and Fernando for relief in 1480. Their petition, addressed to the monarchs in their traditional role as protectors of the Muslim community, had mixed results. Although the Catholic monarchs agreed that conditions in the Alcázar Viejo were unacceptable, they declared that the Muslims must remain segregated in a new *morería* in San Nicolás de la Villa. Here they remained, faced with ever-increasing tax burdens, until formally expelled in 1502.[30]

These moves against Córdoba's Muslims were not, however, of local origin. Despite the *concejo*'s willingness to tax them, policies intended to isolate the Mudéjares usually stemmed from royal prerogatives. Local elites, on the contrary, tolerated and sometimes even admired the culture of the city's former rulers. Jerónimo's fervent praise for the Mezquita, whose minaret and arcades proclaimed it to be a work of Islamicate architecture, is but one example. Perhaps no other city of fifteenth-century Castile retained such a distinct Moorish flavor in its architecture and layout. Why was this so? Córdoba's former glory as capital of al-Andalus and consequent monumental architecture might be one explanation, but there were few conscious efforts at preservation. Córdoba was instead notable for a relative lack of deliberate attempts to efface the past. Its rulers treated the Muslim minority in the same way: with benevolent neglect, failing to harass them overtly but also failing to defend them against crown edicts. Moorish influence in Córdoba is illustrated best by its ultimate fate. Only after the fall of Granada and the expulsion of the Muslims was its

Great Mosque, long since converted to a Christian cathedral, defaced. In 1523, and despite the protests of many in the city, Carlos V approved a plan to construct a chapel within the existing structure, destroying the central part of the original mosque. Yet even this proved to be a suggestive statement of Córdoba's Moorish heritage, with the new grafted onto the old but unable to erase it completely.

The Jewish population in late fifteenth-century Córdoba was also quite small, having never recovered from attacks that nearly destroyed it in 1391. The riots, which began in Seville but soon spread throughout much of Iberia, began with anti-Semitic religious rhetoric. Most perpetrators, however, were motivated more by the prospect of robbery than by the goal of creating a homogeneous Christian society uninfluenced by Jewish "heresy." Ultimately, thousands of Jews were killed or displaced and the Jewish quarters of many cities, including Córdoba, lay in ruins. The long-term effects were devastating. Castilian Jews had long endured policies that limited their social and economic activities, but this stark display of their vulnerability led many to convert to Christianity. In doing so, they would, in theory at least, remove all barriers to full acceptance into Christian society.[31]

In Córdoba, this meant a physical as well as religious and social relocation. While some Jews remained in the old *judería* and formed a small community that survived until the early 1480s, the converts moved to other parts of the city, especially Lozana's neighborhood of San Nicolás de la Ajerquía and the streets around the Plaza de las Tendillas.[32] For much of the fifteenth-century, it seems that they faced relatively little overt hostility, although the lack of detailed records for the period means that this cannot be stated with confidence. Freed from legal barriers, some *conversos* achieved prominent positions in church, court, and civic hierarchies, and more than a few married into notable Old Christian families.[33]

Opposition to *converso* success began, in some Castilian cities, as early as the 1440s. The example of Toledo, where this shift was most dramatic, foreshadowed trends that would become more widespread in the following decades. There, Old Christian agitators claimed that the *conversos* had purchased positions in the municipal government and succeeded in banning them from holding office. In this and other campaigns, intended to expand legal proscriptions on Jews to include *conversos*, Old Christians argued that conversion could not make a Jew into a full member of society. In effect, they attempted to transform a religious distinction into a racial one that would ultimately be articulated as the idea of *limpieza de sangre*, or "pure blood."[34]

Complementing this was the often-repeated assertion that the *conversos* were not really Christian at all but had converted under duress or for temporal gain and continued to practice Judaism in secret. This was no doubt true of some converts, and it is equally certain that some became sincere Christians. Many former Jews and their descendants, however, lay open to charges of heresy or Judaizing simply because they knew little about the faith to which they had converted.

For the most part, however, Old Christian suspicion of former Jews had little to do with their actual religious behavior. Antón de Montoro, for instance, offered a visceral description of the difficulty of ever gaining acceptance as a true Christian:

> O sad, bitter Ropero
> who does not feel your sorrow!
> Seventy years since your birth,
> and, in all of them, you always said
> "[the Virgin] remained immaculate,"
> and never swore by the Creator!
> I recited the Creed, I worship
> pots of pork fat and
> eat rashers of half-cooked bacon,
> listen to Mass and pray,
> cross myself every which way
> and never could I slay
> this stain of *converso*.
> On bent knees
> and with great devotion
> in all those holy days
> with great devotion I pray
> and recite
> the stations of the Passion,
> adoring the God-and-Man
> as my highest Lord,
> so that my guilt be removed,
> but never could I lose the label
> of the old faggot Jew.[35]

Montoro's closing words—"puto y judio"—neatly encapsulate the position of the *conversos*. They do not suggest he was accused of homosexuality but instead linked two outcast groups. As Rafael Carrasco notes, "behind the sodomite, bearer of pestilence, is the outline of the converso. They are joined in the worst popular insult that could be hurled: 'faggot Jew!'" The term "faggot," moreover, cannot fully express the connotations of *puto*, a masculinized form of *puta* that cast the Jew or *converso* as both prostitute and passive partner in the homosexual act.[36]

Anti-*converso* attacks took place in Toledo in 1449, in Toledo and Seville in 1465 and again in 1467, and throughout Andalucía in 1473 and 1474. Such violence was often associated with social and economic pressures, notably harvest failures and related hikes in food prices.[37] Even so, the increasing frequency with which the Old Christians blamed them in times of trouble reveals a significant erosion in the *conversos'* security.

For a time, many municipal councils and nobles in Andalucía protected the New Christians who held often-vital positions within the community.[38] These protections, however, could not overcome the deep suspicion with which some Old Christians viewed the *conversos*. After several abortive attempts during Enrique IV's reign, the Inquisition was established in Seville in 1480. The appointment of inquisitors in Córdoba in 1482 soon followed. The Inquisition's jurisdiction over *conversos* replaced mob violence with the rule of law, a transformation facilitated, ironically, by converts' legal status as Christians. Although baptism was seemingly unable to remove the taint of Judaism, it did permit the trial of suspected backsliders as Christian heretics.[39]

The transfer of persecution to the public sector did not go entirely unchallenged, but few criticized it openly. Hernando del Pulgar, for instance, was scandalized that the church, having failed to educate these putative Christians, now proposed to punish them. Writing to Cardinal Pedro González de Mendoza of Seville, he argued that "I am certain, my lord, that there are ten thousand young girls between ten and twenty years of age in Andalucía, who from the time they were born have never left their homes or heard of or learned of any doctrines save that which they have observed of their parents indoors. To burn all these people would be a very cruel thing."[40] But the Inquisition's defenders responded by impugning Pulgar's loyalty and ultimately forced him to admit that the intentions behind the tribunals were good.

In Córdoba, the Inquisition initially secured the support of local civic and ecclesiastic leaders and successfully prosecuted a number of suspected heretics. While the practice of distributing goods confiscated from these victims to local notables no doubt facilitated their acquiescence, their interest waned with the escalation of trials that followed the appointment of cathedral canon Diego Rodríguez Lucero as inquisitor in 1495. Lucero, convinced that Judaism continued to be widely practiced, cast his net widely, implicating important local figures and conducting multiple mass autos-de-fé. This roused the joint opposition of the *concejo* and the cathedral chapter, who managed, in 1508, to have Lucero removed from office. At the same time, however, his activities divided the city, with popular feeling in support of the arrest of so many *conversos*.[41]

* * *

The 1473 attacks transformed the condition of Córdoba's *converso* community. Old Christian prejudice predated this moment, but was mostly implicit. In the wake of the violence, Aguilar immediately declared that henceforth no *converso* could hold public office, indicating that this had been a point of contention.[42] But there had been few prior efforts to exclude them from civic life. The 1466 will of Ferrán Ruiz de Aguayo, precentor of the cathedral, founded a chantry there with the proviso that New Christian clergy be prohibited from serving at its altar. Aguayo, however, softened the blow by noting that he made this restriction "notwithstanding that in this generation of *conversos* there are many virtuous and good persons, and of good conscience and life."[43] The 1470s found this real, but relatively painless, form of discrimination replaced by violent and systematic repression. Córdoba's *conversos* were first attacked by the mob, then rejected by the nobility, and finally criminalized by the legal system.

Was this sudden transformation the result of a cascade of nascent expressions of discontent that, once begun, could not be reversed? Did each person who condemned the *conversos*, beginning with Alonso Rodríguez, encourage the next to do the same? Perhaps, but even if this is so, we need to consider how the groundwork was laid for this mobilization of anti-*converso* sentiment. In doing so, we can clarify how the frontier, the general Castilian situation, and the particular circumstances in Córdoba enabled the anti-*converso* faction to translate personal animosities into effective mass action that united people from disparate social and economic backgrounds. They did so both by enlisting religious passions and by transforming the meanings of quotidian surroundings. And so the bustling Calle de la Feria became a holy procession route, the Cruz del Rastro with its fish market, booths, and tanneries the site for a deadly insult to the Virgin, and the Church of San Francisco and a blacksmith's abode the setting for a new Passion story.

Before exploring the "how," we must determine the "why," specifically the identities and motives of those most intimately involved in the violence. At the heart of the initial disturbances was the Cofradía de la Caridad, whose ferocious reaction to a supposed insult to the Virgin sparked the whole affair. This group, founded in the first half of the fifteenth century, was based at the Monastery of San Pedro el Real, to which Alonso Rodríguez fled.[44] The Caridad's charitable works included maintaining inmates in the city prison, providing burials for paupers and travelers, and arranging dowries and marriages for poor but respectable girls. In 1493 the brotherhood, whose members were mostly commoners, received permission from the bishop of Córdoba to construct the still extant Hospital de la Santa Caridad and a bell tower in the Plaza del Potro, where masses might be said and the brothers have suitable headquarters.[45]

In contrast to this image of a typical, if highly successful, confraternity, chroniclers presented the Caridad as an organization unusual in its dedication to Old Christian dominance and close engagement with national and local politics. By about 1470, Alonso de Aguilar and his supporters had emerged as de facto rulers of Córdoba, forcing his adversaries Diego Fernández de Córdoba, count of Cabra, and Pedro de Córdoba y Solier, bishop of Córdoba, to leave the city. The struggle for local predominance, however, continued by proxy, with nearly everyone in the city drawn in through familial, military, or economic links. Even geography played a role, as particular streets or districts tended to support the same faction. In addition to his other clients, Aguilar enjoyed the support of Córdoba's *conversos*. Palencia used stereotypical language to describe "a certain reciprocity of services between them and Don Alonso de Aguilar," in which the *conversos* would enlist, arm, and pay three hundred horsemen, and Aguilar would turn a blind eye to their Judaizing and purchase of offices.[46] In response to this supposed alliance between Aguilar and the *conversos*, Cabra and his supporters presented themselves as champions of the Old Christians.

Both Palencia and Valera claimed that external influences played a crucial role in these developments. At the time, Castile was divided between those who supported the right to succession of Enrique's daughter Juana of Castile and those who preferred his sister Isabel la Católica. The dispute had led to civil war in the previous decade, but the early 1470s was a time of uneasy peace and shifting alliances. The Cordoban magnates kept their options open and both enjoyed, at one time or another, the favor of each monarch. In 1473, when the anti-*converso* violence erupted, Aguilar was loosely linked to Enrique's party while Cabra was in the Isabelline faction. Their approach was typical of the frontier nobility, who used this period of weak central authority to extend their traditional autonomy. In Murcia, for instance, Pedro Fajardo refused to recognize any king after 1468 and ruled unencumbered for a decade. In Seville, the Duke of Medina Sidonia forced Isabel to promise him the mastership of Santiago before committing to her cause. Only in Jaén did either candidate have a real base of support, as Miguel Lucas remained faithful to Enrique.[47]

Quarrels in one part of the region, moreover, could easily spill over into others. Valera saw the Cordoban troubles as stemming partly from disputes in western Andalucía and partly from deliberate attempts to sow discord and weaken Isabel's position: "From the differences and past struggles between the duke of Medina Sidonia and the marquis of Cadíz came great evils, not only to the city of Seville, but also in Córdoba and in Sanlúcar and much of Andalucía. And, since the monarchs Fernando and Isabel were much loved in those cities, some that did not desire their service tried to cause trouble between the Old and New Christians, especially in the city of Córdoba, where there was great enmity and envy between them."[48] Palencia put a name to those troublemakers, claiming that Juan Pacheco, Marquis of Villena and now master of Santiago, "who knew no equal in the art of plotting sedition and tumults," decided that unrest in Córdoba would further his own ends. Noting that Old and New Christians were already at odds, he sent some knights sworn to his nephew Rodrigo Téllez Girón, master of Calatrava, to "throw fresh fuel on the fire."[49]

The Cofradía de la Caridad would prove central to Villena's plans, though Palencia is not clear whether this was by chance or design. Directly after describing Villena's intent, he noted that, "For their part, the Old Christians, apparently moved by religious zeal, founded a devotional confraternity dedicated to Charity and such was the people's fervor that in only a few days its members were numerous; they conducted weekly processions to the churches and liberally distributed their wealth as alms to the needy."[50] Valera was more direct, arguing that New Christian arrogance and anti-*converso* feeling "caused a conspiracy to be formed in the city under the color of devotion, into which the greater part of the population entered, which they called the Brotherhood of the city. They conducted processions on certain days, thus demonstrating their great devotion."[51] Alonso Rodríguez was a prominent figure in this organization. As Palencia observed, "Notable among those possessed by this religious fervor was a certain blacksmith who was very hospitable to the poor and to travelers. His charity had earned him the affection of the masses, and he had acquired, through his passion against the *conversos*, a remarkable degree of authority among the brothers; whoever he praised they considered the more worthy; whoever he condemned they found despicable."[52]

If Palencia and Valera were accurate in their descriptions of the Caridad's purposes—and there is no reason to suppose that they were not, as Palencia, in particular, was clear about his lack of sympathy for the victims—then the procession was a deliberate provocation. Both authors described the Cofradía de la Caridad's numerous processions as related to the organization's anti-*converso* stance. Given their route through the heavily *converso* neighborhood adjoining the Calle de la Feria, we can surmise that its regular marches, including the one that led to the troubles, were planned with an eye for taking full advantage of any disruptions that might come about either by chance or because of the New Christians' perceived hostility to the Old. Palencia was correct in describing the young girl's spilling of water as a "chance act," but the Caridad was already prepared to use it as a pretext to attack both the *conversos* and Aguilar's party.

By manipulating popular resentment over Aguilar's supposedly preferential treatment of the *conversos*, Rodríguez and his supporters placed the *alcalde mayor* in a difficult position. He could either side with the *conversos* against the majority of the city's population or abandon them to their fate and thus lose a key base of support. For Cabra and the Old Christian party, it was a win-win situation; Aguilar's prestige would be reduced in either case. Aguilar's personal inclination was to stand with the New Christians, as revealed by his attack on Rodríguez and offer to shelter at least some of the *converso* population. Faced with the mobilized and well-organized Old Christians (whose ability to bring in reinforcements from the countryside and to maintain a cohesive force for several weeks is further evidence of both prior preparations and expert support), he was forced to accede to their wishes in order to save his own position. If the initial disturbances following the Caridad's interrupted procession were political theater instead of a spontaneous outpouring of hostility, it makes sense to understand it as the improvisational performance that contemporaries suggested it was.

Rodríguez's original call to arms aroused the townspeople by asking them to avenge what he called a deliberate affront to the Christian faith. An insult to Mary was an especially effective tool with which to rally the faithful, playing on both the devotion with which she was commonly held as well as fears that the *conversos* secretly despised Christianity. The sense that it was a ritualized insult only intensified their anger. In the tense atmosphere surrounding *conversos* in late medieval Castile, their every action was scrutinized for evidence of Judaizing or heresy. Their modes of dress, of eating, and of worship acquired a ritual significance that proved their religious conformity or dissent. As Angus MacKay has noted, "the predicament of the *conversos* and *moriscos* meant that a chance remark or an inappropriate action, even if uttered or performed by a child, might have the most serious consequences."[53] It was inconceivable to Old Christians that a *conversa* could spill water on the Virgin by chance; such an act must bear a deeper significance that implicated the whole of the *converso* community, for the child must have been put up to the task or had learned disrespect for Christianity from her elders. Rodríguez's words fit the expectations of his audience, directing them to act in a manner many already thought appropriate. They were sufficient to spark violence and sustain it in the face of Torreblanca's opposition. They may not, however, have induced the demonstrators to carry on after Aguilar's intervention.

The insult had, arguably, been avenged once the houses surrounding the Cruz del Rastro were plundered and burned. Aguilar's daunting force of veteran soldiers were in the streets, and their leader, the man who instigated the fighting and had also, according to Palencia, inspired much of the anti-*converso* sentiment, was injured and dying, no longer able to rally them. By presenting Alonso Rodríguez's death as a modern recurrence of the Passion, however, his supporters were able not only to continue the insurrection but to widen its scope and redouble its fervor. In doing so, they took full advantage of the timing of events. The Easter season was a time of intense religious fervor in which biblical experiences came to life for Christians. These were as much emotional as cognitive responses. Ritual self-flagellations on Holy Thursday, for instance, were not simple simulations of a long-ago event but representations of a living past that continued to reverberate through physical pain and emotional release in the present.[54] Easter was also a dangerous time for Iberian Jews. The idea that all Jews, past and present, were complicit in Christ's death was widespread; the annual emphasis on the continued reality of the Passion reminded Christians that the Jews' "crime" was not a thing of the past. If Christ's suffering and death were symbolically renewed in the hearts of the faithful, then he was also murdered again and again by his enemies.

Easter was a season "in which the sacred was physically experienced, relations of power were criticized, the past became the present, and urban space was transformed."[55] The rumor of Rodríguez's rebirth was not a premeditated attempt to exploit this mood—no one could have known that he would be mortally wounded—but it was an extemporaneous response to events that placed them in a coherent order and assigned allegorical roles to the main figures. For if Alonso Rodríguez represented the slain Christ, then those responsible for his death were Christ's killers. Aguilar's attack on the blacksmith with a lance placed him firmly in the role of the Romans, both the soldier who used his lance to stab Christ's side and Pilate, unwilling to take a stand against Jewish attempts to see Christ killed. But the Romans were not the villains in contemporary readings of the Passion and the Roman soldier was even honored as Saint Longinus. In the Gospel of Matthew, moreover, Pilate washed his hands of the execution while the Jewish people willingly accepted responsibility for the crime: "All the people answered, 'his blood is on us and on our children.'"[56] Just as their forefathers were responsible for Christ's death, so the *conversos* caused Rodríguez's and their associative guilt was confirmed by the rumors that described his deathbed cry for revenge. To an audience incensed by present-day events as well as experientially engaged in the religious mood of the season, a call for retribution would have seemed appropriate; it was what Jesus might have wanted, perhaps what he *should* have wanted.

All this, moreover, took place on a frontier where millenarian visions were commonplace and not solely the province of Old Christians or those who saw victory over Islam in Iberia as the first step of the Apocalypse. Palencia ends his account of the violence by noting that "a wonder that had occurred a little earlier had inspired among the *conversos* the belief that the coming of their false Messiah was near. They were the Andalucíans most given to such imaginations and, as it came to their attention that an enormous whale had died while chasing a ship on the coast of Portugal near Setúbal, it appeared to them that this whale was the one named Leviathan, heralded by the prophets, and therefore their Messiah could not be far distant."[57]

We can, perhaps, leave aside the reference to a "false Messiah" and Palencia's underlying assumption that the *conversos* were relapsed Jews. It is equally likely that the *conversos*, whose religious knowledge, in many cases, consisted of a jumble of Jewish traditions and incompletely understood Christian doctrines, had developed among themselves a reading of this whale sighting that loosely conformed to Christian theology. In relating the story of Leviathan to present hopes for a Messiah, the *conversos* of Córdoba could just as easily have been speaking about the second coming of Christ as about the Jewish Messiah. Millenarian expectations in general accorded with those of the general population, for whom the current famine and civil war signified the impending apocalypse. In this, we can perhaps gain some insight into the experiences of Antón de Montoro and others tempted to raise arms against their fellow *conversos*. It was not only that they faced a pressure to conform to Old Christian social and religious conventions that intensified the typical human impulse to follow a crowd.[58] They also shared the experiential understanding of the Easter season that transformed Córdoba into a New Jerusalem and helped drive the mob to a sustained and destructive passion.[59]

That Palencia (and presumably many among the Old Christians of Córdoba) failed to consider the possible Christian origins for *converso* apocalypticism and instead dismissed it as yet another sign of unrepentant Judaism indicates their general distrust of New Christians. It was also a function of the *conversos'* physical and social separateness. To some degree, their separation was consciously fostered by many *converso* authors, who took pride in the idea that they composed their own "nation." They defined this in terms more racial than religious, presenting themselves proudly as descendants of the ancient Israelites and members of Christ's own *linaje*. Diego de Valera thus referred to the *conversos* in the words of Deuteronomy—"Is there any nation so noble?"—while Alfonso de Cartagena described the Virgin Mary as "my blood-relative." Such pretensions led to a predictable backlash and Andrés Bernáldez, for one, grumbled that the *conversos* "entertained the arrogant claim that there was no better people in the world than they."[60] Villena claimed that "the *conversos* spoke openly against the Christian religion, while they secretly devised despicable crimes, as a nation apart (*como nación aparte*), which nowhere cooperated with Old Christians. Instead, as a people with completely antagonistic aims, they openly and with the greatest boldness supported whatever was contrary to them [the Old Christians], as demonstrated by the seeds of bitter fruit spread throughout the cities of the kingdom."[61]

Fears inspired by the *conversos'* self-definition as a nation differed little from those directed at Jews throughout Iberia and Europe. But they were intensified by their status as Christians, which removed the social limitations placed on Jews, and confirmed by their physical separateness. The dissolution of the *judería* and the large number of converts at the beginning of the century created a wave of internal migrants too large to be successfully dispersed and assimilated throughout the city. Córdoba's de facto occupational zoning helped maintain the spatial integrity of the population over time.

In fact, the *conversos* would have resisted attempts to break up their social networks. A spate of new construction early in the century provided accommodations in previously underpopulated areas of the city, while the converts endowed their own churches and formed their own confraternities. Their proximity encouraged communal solidarity. *Conversos* married, worked, worshipped, and socialized among themselves. This segregation provided a social and economic safety net, but also left them vulnerable to attacks by the Old Christians. The perception that they formed "a nation apart" meant that they were an alien people, one necessarily at war with the larger Castilian nation and whose willingness to betray Castile for their own ends was taken for granted.[62] Lacking personal connections among the *conversos*, Old Christians were willing to believe the worst about people they hardly knew, and all rumors, no matter how fantastic, were given some credence.

That the *conversos'* pride in their status as a separate and exalted nation played a role in the 1473 assault is suggested by the emphasis on sexual violence in the sources. Sexual tension was a constant feature of interconfessional relations. Marriage and sexual contact between members of different faiths often raised high emotions, and all the various religious communities invested a great deal of energy in defining and maintaining sexual boundaries.[63] The *conversos* did not, in theory, compose a distinct religious group, and there is ample evidence of intermarriage with Old Christian families among the economically privileged, but there was a general tendency to marry their own that stemmed from the social forces that isolated them from the rest of the civic population. Antón de Montoro, in verses dedicated to his wife, commented on how this limited one's potential partners while revealing the hidden advantages of the situation, presenting it as an ironic source of good fortune that permitted him to wed a younger woman who lacked alternatives:

> Since God wished you
> and me to be unlucky
> and of little value,
> much better that we pervert

one house only, and not two.
It would be a waste of time
and an offense to reason
for you to enjoy a good husband,
and so I, old, dirty, and crippled,
can caress a lovely woman.[64]

The actions of the mob in 1473, however, were not meant to protect
their daughters from contagion. Palencia in particular emphasized the sexual
violence exercised against *conversas*, which ranged from rape to public stripping to violation of corpses. There are several ways to read his graphic
descriptions, not least of which is a prurient interest on the part of Palencia,
who certainly never shied away from such details. But even if he emphasized
relatively isolated incidents, Palencia did not invent these crimes. We could
explain them as the work of individuals who took advantage of a chaotic
situation or were carried away by the passions of the moment. Rhetoric
against the converts prior to the violence, moreover, may have demonized
them to a degree that induced some to assume that any license could be taken
against them. The tone of all the accounts, however, suggests something more
systematic: either a planned campaign of rape or a sense that this was a
particularly appropriate way to attack *conversos*. The efficacy of rape as a
means of destroying social and familial ties would not have been lost on the
Old Christians of Córdoba, who were well aware of the shame and loss of
honor that this sexual contact, forced though it was, meant for victims and
their families.

Conversos' pride in their ancestry offers another reading of these attacks,
one implied by Valera, who summarized the violence by noting that "there
was no kind [*linaje*] of cruelty that was not practiced that day by the looters."[65] The term *linaje* is not entirely inappropriate here, but it is a curious
choice, as the term most often referred to family or ancestry. In a sentence
with almost precisely the same sentiment, for instance, Palencia wrote that
the perpetrators failed to omit "any form [*género alguno*] of cruelty." Valera's
wording is particularly striking when one considers the rape of the *conversa*
women as an assault on their own *linajes*, an attempt to dilute the "Jewish
blood" that was a font of communal pride but was also viewed fearfully by
Old Christians as a source of pollution. It would be too much to suggest that
the rapes of 1473 were a form of ethnic cleansing; that it was, in other words,
a conscious and systematic effort to breed a community out of existence. It

is, however, no stretch to view this as an attempt to undermine the integrity of the *converso* community.

What other advantages did the Old Christians seek in the *conversos*' misfortune? Just as in 1391, many contemporaries saw it all simply as a "robbery." Palencia used the term, and Valera noted that "many came to plunder." The minutes of the cathedral chapter, which met a fortnight after the events to discuss what should be done with rental properties that had been let to *conversos*, spoke of the "robbery of the *conversos* which was committed in this city." Likewise, *veinticuatro* Luis de Córdoba's will acknowledged that he was involved "when the robbery of the *conversos* happened in this city," and the testaments of other notables who felt deathbed remorse described events in the same way.[66] These wills describe significant plunder—5,000 *mrs.* in one case, 1,500 in another, and a silver cup in a third—at a time when an scribe earned about 300 *mrs.* a year, a lawyer 2,000, and senior municipal officials no more than 3,000.[67] Such wealth would have tempted many even in good times. In the early 1470s, when the price of cereals had skyrocketed, it would have been especially relevant, inspiring both the envious and the desperate. Rioters also claimed that *converso* wealth justified their actions—how, other than by dishonest means, could they have accumulated so much in such hard times? Even Alonso de Aguilar and his brother Gonzalo Fernández de Córdoba, the *conversos*' erstwhile defenders, joined enthusiastically in the search for buried or hidden valuables and in the systematic robbery of fugitives. They did so both for the monetary gain and to show Old Christian solidarity and thus effect "a reconciliation with the frenzied masses."[68]

The void created by the flight of the *conversos* and their subsequent absence from civic life benefited Old Christians of all social classes. For artisans and merchants, the riots removed a number of successful competitors. An examination of cathedral properties rented to *conversos* and abandoned in 1473 indicates the trades affected. The twenty-seven documented examples include a pair of blacksmiths (which implies, perhaps, that Alonso Rodríguez's motives were not wholly religious), several cloth merchants, leather workers, and a carpenter, as well as a surgeon and an innkeeper.[69] Aguilar's decree in the aftermath of the violence, that *conversos* were henceforth ineligible for public office, similarly profited the minor nobility and *caballeros de cuantía*, who saw the pool of applicants for such positions dwindle.

The Cofradía de la Caridad as an institution was also a beneficiary. Palencia described it as founded solely to act against the *conversos*, but, in fact, it predated the events of the 1470s by several decades. It did, however, experience an influx of new members in the late 1460s and early 1470s, and may have acquired its anticonvert character at that time. As it was based in the heavily *converso* San Nicolás de la Ajerquía parish, the Caridad's leadership may have felt itself in competition with the New Christians in defining the character of the neighborhood. In conducting their processions through the streets of the Ajerquía, the Caridad not only sought to provoke confrontation but also to embed the idea that it was an Old Christian neighborhood. The Calle de la Feria was the epicenter of the *converso* business community. These merchants and other wealthy New Christians lived in Cruz del Rastro. The brothers of the Caridad hoped not only to displace the *conversos* but also to replace them. The strategy was successful: the decades after 1473 saw the Caridad embark on a building program that transformed the parish into an Old Christian bastion.

* * *

Using a perceived insult to the Virgin as pretext for an assault was an effective means of gaining widespread Old Christian support. As such, it clarifies the nature of their distrust for *conversos*. Many scholars have noted that the Inquisition was more concerned with outward behaviors than inner belief.[10] This emphasis extended beyond formal religious ceremonies to include the ways in which recent converts ate, drank, and interacted with others, thus emphasizing social conformity as well as doctrinal orthodoxy. It was, of course, a practical approach; it is far easier to judge a person's deeds than his or her heart. As ritual actions were central to Islam and Judaism as well as Christianity, moreover, proper conduct was seen as a reasonable proxy for adherence to Christian beliefs, while retention of behaviors associated with a convert's former religion implied recidivism. Old Christians, firmly convinced that *conversos* secretly continued to hold Jewish beliefs, were ever watchful for meaningful "slips": a convert who avoided pork, an improperly made sign of the cross, the casual use of a Hebrew name. Nothing could be attributed to chance, all gestures bore symbolic overtones, whether intended or not. And so a young girl's spilling of water on the statue of Mary could be nothing other than a deliberate and ritualized attack on the Virgin, an insult that, in the context of the general religious insecurity of the frontier and more specific concerns about the *conversos'* ties to Aguilar and their supposed recent "arrogance," held the portent of incipient *converso* action against the faithful. This was met first with a formal call to arms and then, poetically enough, with a ritualized solution, a reworking of the most sacred of Christian rites, the remembrance of the Passion.

In Córdoba, despite a number of related factors that may have inclined the Old Christians to act against the *conversos*, including the agrarian depression, ongoing anti-Semitic polemic, and political upheaval, the Old Christians did not lightly turn on their *converso* neighbors. These problems certainly laid the groundwork for violence, but they proved insufficient on their own. Only a public performance that illustrated the *conversos'* treachery could induce the Old Christians to action. The success of this performance was based on its perceptive exploitation of local social and physical contexts.

On one level, the choreographers of the procession and the subsequent assaults took full advantage of features unique to the frontier, including a local tradition of defending the faith, physical and social anxiety, the absence of effective monarchical power, and the *bando* politics that facilitated alliances between influential nobles and a grassroots religious movement. While the frontier provided a receptive audience, the social and physical topography of Córdoba isolated the *conversos* from the networks that defined Old Christian public life, leaving them particularly vulnerable to coordinated action. Finally, the procession and initial disturbances played out at specific times and in specific locations within Córdoba that held multiple associations for residents and intensified their emotional responses to these events. Once released, these emotions led to a horrific wave of violence as the Old Christians lost all inhibitions regarding their *converso* neighbors. Their brutality should not, however, be seen as evidence of a deep hatred of *conversos* that must inevitably have resulted in bloodshed and expulsion. On the contrary, in revealing long-pent tensions that had not been released in nearly a century, it confirms that such an outburst was difficult to spark. The 1473 attack was possible only with a particular confluence of circumstances and the presence of individuals willing to make use of them.

Many of these circumstances, of course, were present throughout the realm. The influence of Córdoba's position on the frontier on the unfolding of the violence is illustrated by what happened (or, rather, what did not happen) in other cities. After his success in Córdoba led to violence against *conversos* throughout Andalucía, Villena (whom Palencia had fingered as the mastermind behind the violence) attempted to do the same in Segovia, which had recently declared for Isabel. In seeking to turn the populace against the New Christians, he used several of the arguments that had proved so effective elsewhere: he alleged that the *conversos* had bought their way into municipal power, that this was detrimental to the public good, that they were an alien people bent on undermining the Old Christians. Villena, moreover, made the most of the precedent set by disturbances in Andalucía, word of which had reached more northerly cities, including Segovia. It did not work. "In no way could he persuade the Old Christians in Segovia" to turn against the *conversos*. They responded that converts in Andalucía were wholly different from those in their region, who were known for their piety and had produced some of the most significant churchmen of the time. Villena next went to Toledo, where he met much the same response.[71] The Andalucían population, it seems, was more open to such arguments at this time.

Fifteenth-century Córdoba was dominated by the frontier, which created what John Edwards has called a "society organized for war and taxation" that was completely controlled by the military elite. In this context, he continued, "it was hard for a merchant or an industrialist to live, and virtually impossible for a faithful Jew or Muslim."[72] Despite, or perhaps because of, a century of social and economic success, Córdoba's *conversos* found themselves increasingly defined as enemies of the faith. Attempts to defend themselves through political alliances or, in the last resort, with arms were seen as further proof of their perfidy. Even attempts to accept their diminished status were unsuccessful. Antón de Montoro, in a pitiable passage of his poem to Aguilar, described the lengths to which the *conversos* might go in order to be accepted into Christian society:

> We're willing to give [you] tribute,
> be captives and serve.
> We'll be beggars, cuckolds, and faggots . . .
> so that we can live.[73]

Montoro and other Cordoban *conversos* had depended on the goodwill and occasional active support of those Old Christians who bore them no grudge. This protection melted away in the face of adversity. Without it, the social organization of Córdoba left few other avenues of defense.

A religious outlook defined by frontier conditions lent strength to popular resentment of the *conversos*' social and economic success. For notwithstanding the social, economic, and political dimensions of the 1473 attacks, it was ultimately an attack on a religious minority by a religious majority in which theological understandings of Jews came to the fore, specifically their continued responsibility for the death of Christ. That is why, despite ongoing conflicts with Granada, it was the *converso* and Jewish residents of Córdoba, and not the Muslims, who bore the brunt of Old Christian anger. Renewed intolerance for Muslims under Christian rule at this time radiated from the core areas of Castile, particularly from those irritated by Enrique IV's policies, and only gradually wore away at established modes of coexistence at the frontier. But the rejection of Castile's *conversos*, although begun in Toledo in the 1440s, was rooted in attitudes at the periphery, where the need to protect Christianity from real or imagined attacks was deeply felt. Frontier dwellers, although divided about how to put the idea into practice, agreed on the need to end the Muslim political presence in Iberia. But within their own society, it was the *conversos* who posed the greater threat to the faith. Arguments that acknowledge only secular motives for anti-*converso* violence fail to explain its ritual character and its explicit religious content and thus obscure the beliefs and actions of Córdoba's Old and New Christians.[74]

CHAPTER 5

Murcia and the Body
of Christ Triumphant

During Enrique IV's reign, internal conflicts and a lack of political will had made a sustained war of conquest against Granada impossible. The king's brief campaign in the 1450s was more an attempt to display the trappings of holy war than a serious effort to displace the Muslim presence in Iberia. Later in his reign, even this was beyond Enrique's capabilities as he sought truces in order to focus on wayward nobles, leaving the war, such as it was, in the hands of frontier lords whose resources or inclinations rarely permitted anything more ambitious than traditional border raiding. This state of affairs persisted through the 1470s. Alfonso de Palencia later wrote that Fernando and Isabel held an unshakable resolve to conquer Granada even before they took the throne in 1474. Even if this is true, however, they were unable to act on this immediately as they had to stabilize the realm and their rule even while embroiled in a war with Portugal. The frontier situation in the early years of their reign, therefore, resembled that of Enrique's time. There was a general hardening of noble sentiment against Granada caused in part by a reaction to Enrique's policies, and a few energetic aristocrats, such as Miguel Lucas in Jaén and Rodrigo Ponce de León in Cádiz, attempted to organize campaigns explicitly aimed at conquest. For the most part, however, life on the frontier remained as it had been: defined by vacillation and a contradictory set of attitudes about religious differences.

By 1480, however, the Catholic monarchs had successfully concluded the Portuguese war and stabilized the most serious of Castile's internal disputes.

In particular, they limited the power and autonomy of the nobility, rationalized the royal administration through the Cortes of Toledo, and brought
anti-*converso* feeling under their control by establishing the Inquisition.[1]
Although these acts were not completely or immediately successful, the rulers
next turned their attention and the resources of the realm against Granada,
entrusting Diego de Merlo, *asistente* (chief magistrate) of Seville, with the
task of inciting a war. Merlo's first expedition, against Ronda, failed to
achieve any significant gains. In response, however, a Granadan force under
the personal command of Abū al-Hasan 'Ali (or Muley Hacén) captured the
citadel of Zahara on 27 December 1481, using it as a base for further raids.
This galvanized the Catholic monarchs and the nobility. While Fernando
traveled to Córdoba to take control over the war, a coalition of frontier
magnates, including Ponce de León and Alonso de Aguilar, captured the
critical fortress of Alhama, located between the cities of Granada and Málaga,
and repulsed a Muslim attempt to retake it. This began what would be a
costly and laborious, but also a sustained and ultimately successful, Castilian
campaign.[2]

   This newly aggressive pose toward Granada inspired fresh approaches to
representing ideal relations between members of different religious groups.
Attempts to sway public opinion toward war by predicting future harmony
between Old and New Christians, such as in Miguel Lucas's spectacles, were
no longer relevant for a populace that had lost interest in welcoming converts.
Nor did the enemies of the *conversos* find further attempts to rouse public
indignation necessary or expedient. The Inquisition had effectively suborned
crowd violence as the accepted means of preventing religious recidivism and
of ensuring that New Christians would now find it difficult to establish bases
of power, if indeed they ever had done so. But residents of the frontier did
not break cleanly with their past culture of amiable enmity nor was there was
a broad consensus regarding the proper place of converts or religious minorities in Christian society.

   The war with Granada was prosecuted under the auspices of well-
respected monarchs and with the full backing of the nobility. Yet public
support was still required to conduct an expensive, long-lasting campaign
that threatened, even if successful, to destroy traditional modes of frontier
life. This support could be garnered only by convincing Castilians, especially
Old Christians, that the war would result in a better and more Christian
society, that what was to be gained would far outweigh what must be lost.
To that end, municipal *concejos* celebrated victories with exuberant festivals

that explicitly linked the progress of the war to popular religious practices and proclaimed a vision of a Castile that was triumphant and unabashedly Christian. In this imagined society, Jews, Muslims, and recent converts would have, at best, a tenuous position.

This vision comes through clearly in the galas conducted in Murcia to commemorate the conquest of Málaga in 1487 and Granada in 1492. The highlights of these events were a series of plays mounted on moving carts known as the *juegos de Corpus*, the "game," customarily reserved for the festival of Corpus Christi. Corpus was Murcia's most popular celebration, featuring grand and expensive processions in addition to the *juegos*. The Murcian *concejo*, which organized these events, was careful, throughout the fifteenth century, in its approach to the city's diverse population. In one sense, Christians used Corpus to affirm their faith in a public and ostentatious manner that reminded Muslims and Jews that Murcia was a Christian city. But religious minorities were not excluded from the processions and games. All members of the civic community could, and often did, participate actively in the celebration, and the fame of the event was such that it often attracted an influx of visitors from the heavily Muslim countryside.

The use of Corpus mysteries to commemorate key victories against Granada was partly a matter of pragmatism. The *concejo* needed to arrange an appropriately extravagant gala on short notice and already had significant experience in organizing Corpus. The decorations, mysteries, and performers already existed; rather than create an entirely new event, they used what was at hand. Even if this was the primary motivation, however, the *concejo* was aware of the potential significance of the choice. For in symbolically linking the veneration of Christ's body to military victories, they declared, in a visceral manner no formal proclamation could replicate, that these were religious conquests. More meaningful than any temporal success, they were triumphs over the enemies of Christ. The association between Corpus Christi and conquest, moreover, ensured that the annual holiday would henceforth serve as a reminder of these occasions and of the dubious position of the Jews and the now-defeated Muslims.

Murcia occupied a unique position within Castile. Situated on the eastern end of the frontier with Granada, with Aragón to the north and the Mediterranean to the east, it was segregated from the rest of the realm. This, and the city's role in Mediterranean trade and the business of provisioning frontier garrisons, sheltered its significant Muslim and Jewish populations, for a time, from external anti-Muslim and anti-Semitic sentiments. But the war with Granada was fought as an integrated campaign under royal over-sight.[3] This curtailed noble autonomy while bringing Murcian troops into contact with contingents from other parts of the realm, opening the region to external anti-Semitic and anti-Muslim discourses. The very success of the war, however, eroded the Jews' and Muslims' economic importance and opened land to settlers from the north, who began to displace Mudéjar peasants. The triumphalist message of the galas heralded a significant shift in Murcia's relations with the rest of Castile. Its integration into the wider realm meant that the amiable enmity of borderlands culture was no longer viable.

*   *   *

In some respects, fifteenth-century Murcia was a typical Castilian frontier city, subject to social and political tensions akin to those found elsewhere. Its administrative structure, like that of Andalucían towns, was centered on a *concejo* composed of *veinticuatros* and often led, in the fifteenth century, by a crown-appointed *corregidor*.[4] At the same time, true power in Murcia through much of this period was held by the Fajardo family, through the office of frontier *adelantado* (military governor). Struggles between the Fajardos and the rival Manuel and Calvillo families, however, resulted, as in Córdoba, in destabilizing *bando* politics.[5] By the late 1470s, faction fighting had become so problematic that King Fernando ordered all *bandos* disbanded.[6] Also like Córdoba, Murcia was a rear base for military operations rather than a frontier citadel. Even so, its people lived in a near-constant state of physical insecurity. Despite numerous truces, skirmishing continued throughout the period, leaving little faith that agreements to cease fighting would endure or be honored. In March 1475, for instance, the Catholic Monarchs ordered Pedro Fajardo to ready his forces for war. When, just ten days later, they informed him that a truce had been signed, they ordered that he keep his forces in the event of renewed hostilities.

That same month, the crown rejected a petition by Murcian Jews and Muslims seeking to end their required military contributions, noting that the city was "so near to the Moors, the enemies of our holy Catholic faith," that the request could not be granted.[7] It was not only the Jewish and Muslim residents of the city, however, who tried to lift the burdens of military obligation. *Caballeros de cuantía* and *peones* (commoners required to serve as foot soldiers) often tried to circumvent their responsibilities or, failing that, simply ignored them. And, as elsewhere, transfrontier accommodations were the rule rather than the exception. In times of truce, robust trade produced significant tax revenues, while smuggling and illicit commerce thrived during both peace and war.[8] Such activities supplemented an economy based, like those of Andalucían cities, primarily on agriculture, ranching, and cloth production.[9]

Despite these parallels, Murcia was not the mirror image of an Andalucían frontier city. The region's maritime trade fostered a more diverse economy and cosmopolitan society but also left it vulnerable to piracy and seaborne raiders.[10] More significant, the unusual circumstances of Murcia's incorporation into Castile meant that its demographics differed markedly from any other part of the realm. Although it had been conquered by Castile in the 1260s, the initial Christian settlers came mainly from Catalonia and Provence. After three decades under Castilian rule, moreover, Murcia briefly became part of the Crown of Aragón until the treaties of Torellas and Elche returned it to Castile in the early fourteenth century. The result was a Christian settlement even less complete than elsewhere on the frontier and an urban population linked culturally and economically more to the Crown of Aragón, especially Valencia, than to Castile.

Moreover, the Mudéjar and Jewish communities in Murcia and its surrounding territories dwarfed those of most Andalucían cities. The process of settlement left intact a sizable Muslim peasantry, which played a vital role in the agrarian economy, while the Arrixaca *morería* in the city housed artisans whose contributions were similarly important. The Islamic community in Murcia itself varied in size over the course of the fifteenth century. By midcentury, poverty, intermarriage, plague, and political instability had pushed it to a nadir of fifteen households. It recovered somewhat in the 1470s and 1480s, only to decline again with an outbreak of plague in 1489. The *concejo's* subsequent request that the monarchs relocate some Muslims from newly conquered territories to Murcia, made in January 1490, underscores the contemporary perception that a Mudéjar community was necessary for the city's continued growth and prosperity.[11]

Although tolerated for this contribution, Murcian Muslims were often caught in the middle of frontier hostilities, widely mistrusted by both Christians who questioned their ties to Granada and Granadans who did not understand their continued willingness to live under Christian rule. In 1477, for instance, a major Granadan force entered Murcian territory and forcibly carried away a large number of Mudéjares, leaving some rural areas, such as the Val de Ricote, effectively depopulated. Although the crown actively sought, on account of their economic value, the repatriation of these captives, those who did return found themselves attacked by local Christians. Royal protection of Murcian Mudéjares also had limits. During the Granadan war, suspicions that they provided aid to enemy raiders led to regulations prohibiting them from carrying arms or having Muslims from Granada in their homes.[12]

The Jewish population was also both economically essential and socially vulnerable. Although the surviving evidence is not conclusive, it appears that the 1391 pogrom against Iberian Jews did not extend to Murcia or, at the least, spared most of the city's Jewish inhabitants. Thus, while Andalucían cities saw mass conversions to Christianity in the wake of these attacks and a new population of *conversos*, Murcia's Jewish community remained vibrant well into the reign of the Catholic Monarchs. While precise figures are lacking, scholars have estimated the Jewish population of Murcia as ranging from 750 to 2,000, a significant enclave in a city housing, at most, 10,000 to 12,000 residents.[13] Nor were the Jews an invisible minority. A number of Murcian Jews held prominent positions in the municipal and regional administrations as late as the 1470s.

In 1476, for instance, the crown appointed Gabriel Israel, a Jewish *vecino* of Murcia and an interpreter and scholar of Arabic letters, its herald on business transacted in Murcia with local and Granadan Muslims. That Israel enjoyed royal favor was made clear through a letter intervening in a lawsuit involving him in Lorca, in which Queen Isabel pointedly hinted that the magistrates should rule in Israel's favor.[14] Don David (or Daví) Aben Alfahar enjoyed at least as much influence. As a wealthy landlord and tax collector, he had numerous dealings with the municipal *concejo* as well as royal representatives.[15] Murcia was also an attractive locale for Jewish merchants of less exalted status, offering opportunities beyond those to which Jews were traditionally limited, such as medicine and moneylending. The constant frontier skirmishing and especially the extensive campaigns of the 1480s created a market for provisioners in which the Jews of Murcia and Lorca played a prominent role. Many worked in trades as well, especially the wool and metalworking industries.[16]

Even so, Jews in Murcia were not free from the discrimination faced by their coreligionists elsewhere in Iberia. Extensive legislation imposed taxes on them, denied them access to some professions, and erected social barriers that defined their status as inferior or foreign. The situation worsened in the late fifteenth century. Although Jews had, in theory, been physically separated from their Christian neighbors since the city's conquest, enforcement of this requirement was short-lived, fading after the end of the thirteenth century. In 1481, however, the crown, contending that continued proximity between Christians, Muslims, and Jews would result in great damage and inconvenience for all, enforced separate living areas for Jews and Muslims according to laws passed in the 1480 Cortes of Toledo.[17]

The segregation of Murcia's Jews was but one step in a series of attempts to reinstate or more strenuously enforce restrictions on the community. As early as 1473, for instance, the *concejo* noted that physical proximity was both an "unpleasant situation" and a "bad example" and ordered that all Jews living outside the boundaries of the old *judería* move back within them. Earlier that year, just a few days after the Córdoba riots had raged out of control, the *concejo* passed a series of other limits on Jews, including the provision that no Jew should serve as legal counsel for a Christian, or vice versa. Even so, these legal and social disabilities must be seen in the contexts of a general policy of protection on the part of both the municipal *concejo* and local church authorities.[18] Together with the region's relative isolation, their policies prevented the overt physical violence seen elsewhere in the kingdom.

Murcia's Muslims and Jews had reason to hope that the wave of new restrictions would be fleeting and that their traditional protections would continue. Indeed, the city had a history of periodic legal attacks on its Jews that soon passed, most recently after Saint Vincent Ferrer's preaching tour of Castile in 1411–1412. Ferrer's visit to Murcia and its environs, made at the invitation of Pablo de Santa María, bishop of Cartagena (himself a *converso*), lasted from 19 January to 25 February 1411 and included at least thirty public sermons. These talks focused on the Apocalypse, and Ferrer encouraged the people to prepare their souls for its imminent coming through immediate and wide-ranging reforms.

In response, municipal *concejos* throughout the region passed measures meant to improve public morals. The new laws were, like Ferrer's sermons, hardly unique. They included prohibitions against swearing, blasphemy, gambling, and witchcraft as well as attempts to limit faction fighting and bring popular festivities under tighter control. The clergy was to limit their contact with women and to teach parishioners some basic prayers. In addition to this push for social discipline, however, Ferrer emphasized the need to convert Jews and Muslims to Christianity, arguing that their presence lay at the root of many social problems. This, too, led to legislative programs, and the Murcian *concejo*, on 24 March 1411, passed, but ultimately did not enforce, ordinances directed at the isolation and eventual conversion of the city's religious minorities.

Many of the restrictions emphasized physical separation. Jews and Muslims could no longer own property outside the *judería* or *morería*; any real estate they currently possessed must be sold within one month. Christians were not to cohabitate with Jews or Muslims, attend their weddings, or enter the ghettos for any purpose. Christians who maintained businesses in the *judería* or *morería* would be relocated to new facilities elsewhere in the city. Other regulations undermined the economic and social status of minorities. Not only were Jews and Christians forbidden to sell wine or meat to each other, but Jews were no longer permitted to own pharmacies or to practice surgery or medicine among Christians. Still other laws, such as one directing Christians to no longer light fires or bring food to Jews on the Sabbath, stressed doctrinal differences between the faiths. They had the additional, and not unwelcome, effect of making Jews' lives more difficult.[19]

Taken as a whole, these legal disabilities should have posed a significant threat to the long-term viability of the Jewish and Muslim communities in Murcia. If stringently enforced, they would be effective means of encouraging conversion. This was, in fact, the case in many towns and cities elsewhere in Castile that passed similar programs in response to Ferrer's preaching and saw a wave of conversions similar to that which followed the 1391 pogroms. In Murcia, however, efforts to implement the new ordinances were half-hearted, short-lived, or both. This permitted the Jewish and Muslim communities to thrive for several more decades.

In the early 1480s, the Catholic Monarchs' policy of imposing effective royal control throughout the kingdom and especially on its frontier regions had already proven successful. When, therefore, royal representatives renewed efforts to impose physical and social separation, the protective influences that had hitherto sheltered Murcia's Jews and Muslims lacked their former strength. The war itself had an effect as well. The anticipated end of the frontier meant that the need to provision armies and garrisons, still critical in the 1480s, would soon be lessened and the cessation of Granada's ability to raid Murcian territory opened the land to settlers from the north who began to displace Mudéjar peasants.

By the end of the decade, with Málaga conquered and Granada besieged, Murcian Jews and Muslims were viewed more as remnants of the past and symbols of the defeated than economic assets deserving of protection. They no longer posed a perceived threat to a triumphant and invigorated Christian population. But they were still aberrations who espoused heretical ideas and were therefore a spiritual contagion that might infect the Christian body social. And so without directly attacking them, Murcian leaders sought to emphasize that Jews and Muslims were not true members of the community but outsiders who could, at best, play only a marginal role in society. Public performances offered Christians the opportunity to celebrate their own religion while displaying its power to those outsiders. It was therefore an effective complement to legal restrictions and physical segregation. The feast of Corpus Christi, the most elaborate and popular event in fifteenth-century Murcia, proved an ideal forum for expressing this vision of an exclusively Christian society.

*   *   *

Corpus Christi was a relatively new feast, added to the liturgical calendar only in 1264.[20] In Castile, it was celebrated in some locales by the late fourteenth century and in most larger towns by the fifteenth. In Murcia, a commemorative procession was conducted regularly at least by 1406, and perhaps earlier.[21] At this point, celebration was likely a simple affair focused on the liturgical elements of the feast. Over the course of the fifteenth century, however, it became progressively more complex and ostentatious, involving secular and clerical processions, the plays known as the "games" of Corpus, a resplendent banquet for municipal elites, and even, on occasion, bullfights. Its essential purpose was to confirm Christian faith and unity. It highlighted the status of the official church and instructed the faithful. But it also proclaimed the wealth of a city that could present such a flamboyant display and confirmed the social order through spatial hierarchies, not only of participants but also of spectators.[22]

Christians in fifteenth-century Murcia viewed their particular celebration of Corpus Christi as an essential statement of their corporate identity and acted vigorously to ensure that it be conducted in an appropriate manner. It required the active participation of all social strata, coordination between the municipal *concejo* and the cathedral chapter, or *cabildo*, and, above all, money. The economics of Corpus were an issue throughout the century, with the *concejo* assuming responsibility for most of the expenses. These included wages for musicians accompanying the civic banner, viewing platforms, or

cadalhalsos, installed along the Calle de la Trapería for the use of local notables, banquets, the cleaning and decorating of streets along the route, as well
as sundry other costs. In addition, the *concejo* regularly provided financial
assistance to the *cabildo*, which was responsible for the procession itself. This
subvention was initially quite small; from the 1420s to the early 1460s, it
ranged from 100 to 200 *mrs*.[23]

From that point, however, the costs expanded dramatically as the *concejo*
increasingly saw Corpus as tied to municipal honor. Between 1462 and 1469,
the amount sent to the *cabildo* rose from 360 to 1,000 *mrs.*. By the end of the
century, the *concejo*'s direct contribution to *cabildo* expenses, in addition to
the costs of its own areas of responsibility, was 4,500 maravedis.[24] The rise in
costs was due, in large part, to the desire to present a greater number of ever
more elaborate mysteries. This impulse coincided, however, with a series of
economic crises occasioned by crop failures and currency devaluations and
meant that the *concejo* struggled greatly to raise the necessary funds.

It approached this problem with a variety of strategies. In 1469, for
instance, the *veinticuatros* delegated half of their contribution to Murcia's
Jewish community.[25] This was a stopgap measure, however, and two years
later the *concejo* imposed a special Corpus tax on meat for a period of eight
days.[26] The logistical measures required to obtain this money in advance gives
a sense of the total cost of Corpus. In June, the relevant tax collector, the
Jewish *arrendador de los carnicerías* Ysaque Abenturiel, advanced 14,000 *mrs.*
on the condition that the *concejo* not cancel the tax until he had recouped
his investment. Given that annual municipal budgets generally ranged from
130,000 to 200,000 *mrs.*, this was no small sum.[27] Special taxes henceforth
became a regular means of raising the required funds. In 1480, the meat tax
was imposed only for the day of Corpus. To supplement it, the council
ordered contributions from a number of groups in the city, including those
working on church construction, various tax collectors, Jews, and Muslims.[28]
A sizable proportion of all these monies was spent on the mysteries of Corpus.
Accordingly, the *concejo* occasionally tried to limit their number or richness
by threatening to withhold contributions to the *cabildo*, which was in charge
of the mysteries. Popular outrage, however, put an end to these attempts,
forcing the council, on several occasions, to postpone municipal improve-
ments in order to fund the Corpus procession.

At times, particularly during the war with Granada in the 1480s, economic difficulties meant that the festival had to be canceled. Such was the
case in 1483, and the *concejo*'s response to the situation reveals the popular

enjoyment of the event as well as its ties to civic pride and the war effort. They declared that "no person, man or women, should go to [the nearby town of] Orihuela this feast of Corpus Christi because [by staying in Murcia] they thus fulfill their duty to our lords the King and Queen."[29] The *concejo* underscored how seriously they took this issue by setting the fine for violators at a staggering 2,000 *mrs*.

The issue recurred in 1484 when Murcia was made responsible for housing and provisioning a sizable Castilian army poised for an attack on Granada. Because Corpus was to fall relatively late that year, on 17 June, the *regidores* put off a final decision on whether or not to hold the procession as long as they could. Finally, on 29 May, *vecinos* Sancho Manuel and Ruy García de Harronis appeared before the *concejo* to formally ask that the full show be conducted, both because it would provide a much needed morale boost and because people would just go to Orihuela to see the mysteries if they could not do so at home. Pushed to a decision, the *concejo* cited a lack of funds in telling them it would be impossible to provide money for the mysteries.[30] Three days later, on 1 June, the same men appeared again, this time to propose that they organize the mysteries themselves and at no cost to the city. All they needed was permission to borrow the *carros*, the wagons on which the mysteries were mounted and which were stored in a city-owned warehouse. They were again rejected but apparently attempted to remove the *carros* without permission, for on 3 June, *alcalde* Lope Alonso de Lorca ordered Alonso Hurtado, who was responsible for both warehouse and *carros*, not to lend them to anyone and to take measures to ensure that they not be stolen.[31]

Lope Alonso de Lorca was subjected to a great deal of public criticism for this decision, leading him to present a letter to the *concejo* defending his actions on 5 June. He described at length the dubious state of municipal finances and the difficulties of providing assistance to the military forces in the area. He cited his attempts to work out a more amenable bargain with their commander, Juan de Benavides. Benavides, however, had responded not only by emphasizing his authority as a royal deputy but also by noting the sad state of his troops, who had little to eat and would take what they needed by force if it was not freely offered. He, Lope Alonso, had had little choice in the matter but to spend the money required to provide the army with the requested provisions and therefore protect the property of Murcia's citizens.

Given that it would, he argued, be impossible to also fund the traditional elaborate Corpus procession, he had worked out an agreement with Bishop

Lope de Rivas to replace it with an austere and solemn rogation procession
in which the citizens of Murcia could join together to ask God's forgiveness
and pray that the Christian armies would prove victorious in their struggles.
The mysteries, therefore, were no longer appropriate, even if funded by private citizens, "because they are meant to relax and delight the people rather
than bring them to devotion." His efforts came to naught, however, for he
was not the only one under pressure from the public. The entry in the *actas
capitulares* containing the text of his letter concluded with the terse notation
that, "once the said document had been presented, the members of the *concejo* said that, despite what had previously been ordered, they now directed
that the games be held that year."[32] Where they obtained the money to
finance them is not mentioned; their earlier strategies suggest that it was
through a combination of special taxes and the cancellation or delay of other
municipal business.

The debate over the 1484 Corpus festivities reveals both how highly the
event was regarded and the various meanings it bore in Murcia. The plays
were its most popular aspect, so important that many were willing to travel
to Orihuela to see them. The *concejo* saw them as an expression of the community and a focus of civic pride worth the risk of bankrupting the city or
shortchanging the army. The mysteries, moreover, represented the city, and
so no one but the *concejo* (which, in a legal sense, *was* the city) should have
control over them, nor should they be presented unless this could be done
properly. Indeed, the council generally preferred cancellation to a substan-
dard presentation.

Yet Lope Alonso's letter reveals another strain of thought regarding the
significance of Corpus, a feeling that the mysteries had, in their popularity
and growing pomp, obscured the holiday's religious aspects. In proposing a
"solemn procession," he and the bishop sought to return the commemoration of Corpus to its simpler and more pious antecedents, a shift that had
the welcome corollary of costing far less. This was linked, of course, to the
war with Granada. In praying for Christian victory while demonstrating their
own faith and austerity, the people of Murcia could use Corpus as a means
of advancing the Christian cause. The failure of their proposal in the face of
popular pressure indicated that this was a minority view. For many, the Corpus plays trumped all other considerations and were what the holiday was all
about.

Lope Alonso's was a minority viewpoint, but one that was beginning to
gain ground. Concerns that the plays drew too much attention from the

Host, ostensibly the point of the holiday, led church authorities to formally divide these components in 1482, culminating a process of gradual separation that had been going on since the 1460s. Under the new rules, the day commenced in the cathedral with a solemn celebration of the office of Corpus Christi, followed by a formal procession bearing the Host in triumph through the city, ultimately returning to the cathedral. The focus of this procession was the vessel, or *ostensorio*, containing the Host. This container, carried on a covered litter and draped with a rich tapestry (purchased in 1461 at the cost of 4,000 *mrs.*), was borne by six *regidores* and headed a closely regulated parade of nearly all the city's recognized corporate entities. First came the city's clergy, all of whom were obliged to attend dressed in their finest vestments, who carried with them the relics and treasures of Murcia's churches. They were followed by the civic corporation, composed of the *regidores* and senior officials, bearing the official banners of the city and the realm.[33] The *regidores'* prominent role in the procession as Host and standard bearers seems to have been more of an onerous duty than a privilege, however, a testament to the physical strains of an ever longer and often delayed procession. The *concejo* had difficulty finding volunteers to carry the litter and repeatedly passed legislation chastising and punishing *regidores* who laid the civic and royal banners on the ground or abandoned them entirely. The remainder of the procession consisted of contingents from the city's guilds, each with its own banner and arranged (often contentiously) according to seniority. Interspersed throughout the procession were musicians and, on occasion, actors dressed as angels or saints.[34]

Traditionally, this procession was preceded by the Corpus Christi plays. In theory at least, stops for performances meant that the plays and the religious procession could be timed to join and move along the Calle de la Trapería together. In addition to the predictable delays and difficulties in coordinating the two groups, however, spectators lining the Trapería often flocked to the plays, leaving the formal procession to march nearly unattended along the final stretch to the cathedral. After the new regulations passed in 1482, the plays embarked on their tour of Murcia only after the Host had been formally ensconced in the cathedral.

The plays were always religious in nature. Some brought to life biblical passages, from both the Old and New Testaments, while others depicted saints' lives. But all touched, in one way or another, on the mystery of transubstantiation. Their purpose was to edify the crowd, to bring the soul to better knowledge and devotion. But even church authorities acknowledged that the plays were popular chiefly because they were enjoyable. Indeed, the idea was to catechize in the most appealing and effective manner possible and so the *cabildo* was a tireless proponent of efforts to make them more elaborate, lifelike, and entertaining. To a degree, this strategy backfired as the emphasis came to be more and more on the plays' appearance rather than on their pedagogical potential.

The plays were performed from atop carts, or *carros*, constructed for the purpose, that varied in size according to the needs of a particular performance but generally had two axles and were dragged by a group of men hauling long ropes.[35] The carts stopped several times over the course of the procession route, with performances each time. The locations and number of performances varied from year to year. In 1470, for instance, with provincial *adelantado* Pedro Fajardo in attendance, the *concejo* planned a total of eight performances and "ordered that the presentation of the mysteries of Corpus Christi be conducted in this manner: the first performance in front of the Host, the second near the gentlemen [accompanying the] *adelantado* and Doña Leonor [Manrique, Fajardo's wife], the third near Alfonso de Vallebrera's property, the fourth near Cabezón's estate, the fifth at the houses owned by Rodrigo de Soto, another at San Lorenzo, another in front of the Plaza de Almenara, another at the houses of Diego Tomas, and another at the houses of *regidor* Alfonso Carles."[36]

Later *concejo* records provide titles for some Corpus plays, but none are mentioned until 1447, when cathedral chaplain Juan Valero appeared before the *concejo* to report that the props for *Paradise* had been stolen.[37] *Paradise*, which told the story of Adam and Eve's expulsion from Eden, was one of the core plays of Corpus, presented on all the occasions for which we have records. In 1471, for instance, it was performed alongside *Los santos padres* (the harrowing of Hell), *Sant Geronimo* (Saint Jerome and the lion), *El belem* (the Nativity), *El Juyzio* (Judgment Day), *El Aguila* (perhaps related to Saint John the Evangelist), *Sant Miguell*, *Sant Jorje*, and *Sant Françiso*. *The Holy Fathers*, *Paradise*, and *Saint George* were also presented in 1480, as were *La desenclavación* (the removal of Christ from the cross), *La Salutación* (the Annunciation), and *La destruycion del mundo*. The records from 1481 do not include the full slate of plays presented that year but do mention a new title: *La misterio del Drago* (likely the Saint George play). In 1492, we hear of *Ynfierno* and *Calvario* plays but as separate from *Los Santos Padres* and *El desenclavamiento*. Other titles mentioned in the records include the biblical stories of Abraham and Mary Magdalene, and plays dedicated to Saints Anthony, Joseph, and Martin.[38]

There are no surviving scripts for any Corpus Christi plays conducted in Murcia during this period. There is, in fact, almost a total lack of extant medieval Corpus texts for the whole of Iberia, a circumstance some have explained by noting that these were working documents, owned by traveling companies and cut up to be distributed among the players, each of whom needed to know his own lines.[39] But we have some details concerning how these mysteries were staged. The "Holy Fathers," for instance, were usually eleven in number and wore embroidered skirts and breeches, with gauntlets on their hands, beards and wigs made of canvas strips, and diadems of lace-covered paper. The cart for *El juicio*, meanwhile, included a ceiling of clouds constructed over a wooden framework, atop which was an angel bearing a bouquet of flowers and meant to represent Our Lady of Salvation (Nuestra Señora de la Salvación), who intercedes on behalf of sinners.[40]

The evidence also allows us to gain some sense of the content and style of these presentations. Over the course of the fifteenth century, Castilian Corpus Christi plays developed from painted images mounted on carts to *tableaux vivants* narrated by a speaker who sat to the rear of the cart and was often joined by a musician to something akin to a "play" in the modern sense of the word.[41] The timing of these transformations, however, is uncertain and likely varied from place to place. By the 1490s at the very latest, scripted performances were conducted in Toledo, as attested by script outlines and the sole surviving fragment of a Corpus script, a *décima* from the *Auto de los santos padres*, which has Jesus addressing the Holy Fathers and rescuing them from Hell.[42]

Extant scripts from similar performances written for other religious occasions can suggest the potential length, structure, and sources for Corpus plays. The *Auto de la Pasión*, for instance, was composed between 1486 and 1499 in Toledo. Its several hundred lines were divided between ten characters and included several laments and meditations on the Passion. Though it was meant to be performed on Good Friday, its lyrical tone, limited cast, and lack of physical action made it, as Josep Lluís Sirera suggests, well suited for staging atop a mobile cart, and we can therefore surmise that similar structures were used in Corpus Christi performances. Late fifteenth-century religious plays performed in monastic settings, such as the *Auto de la huida a Egipto* and the *Auto de San Martín*, offer further clues to potential Corpus styles, including varied meters that kept the dialogue lively, emotional appeals, and songs.[43]

There is a greater survival rate of Corpus plays outside of Castile, particularly in France but also in England. The French examples, however, offer little insight into the composition or content of Iberian plays for they were unified works rather than loosely connected series of skits. They were, moreover, literary works composed by prominent authors and meant to be read as well as staged. Surviving texts for English Corpus Christi cycles, including the York, N-Town, and Coventry cycles, however, share structural and compositional traits with what we know of those in Iberia. They may, therefore, clarify the intended and received messages of Murcian Corpus plays.[44] Given the differences in physical, cultural, and linguistic milieus, such a comparison is necessarily limited. But the central themes of the Corpus celebration—the mystery of the body of Christ and the social unity implied by a shared devotion to this miracle—were common to both locales.

The picture of Corpus Christi plays that emerges from the English texts is one centered on the physical body and on violence, themes linked to medieval understandings of the Eucharist and also present in Castilian commemorations of Holy Week and other Christological feasts. The "spectacle of suffering," as scholars working on England and Castile have independently described it, was intended to evoke emotional responses and even experiential understandings of Christ's suffering, from the perspective of both the victim and the torturer. The vicarious experience of pain echoed spiritual practices through which the actual mortification of the body demonstrated one's true devotion, denied the flesh and all it represented, and brought one into closer communion with Christ. Bodily violence could thus represent a quest for higher spiritual virtues free of the base connotations more familiar to modern observers. But it did not necessarily do so. In both England and Castile, the emotional energies mobilized through representations of violence found resonances in social realities and thus bore the risk of spilling beyond the boundaries of the performance.[45]

Although violence was prevalent throughout the English Corpus scripts, it was generally relegated to certain groups. The most common victims were Jews, usually attacked in the course of transgressions against Christians or Christian symbols; women, particularly female martyrs; and Christ. The perpetrators of violence were more diverse, but Jews played a role here also as enthusiastic torturers of Christ. Violent acts were represented as graphically as possible in order to heighten the emotional experience: actors playing Christ, for instance, wore skintight, flesh colored suits on which horrific injuries were painted; scourges were made from birch branches dipped in red dye that would leave "bloody" stripes.[46] This vividness played a role in the plays' popularity. But it was not simply that medieval people enjoyed depictions of violence for their own sake, that torture and blood "attracted rather than repelled men and women of the Middle Ages," and that Corpus Christi plays were "violent theatre for a violent era."[47]

Instead, theatrical representation of violence served multiple social purposes. On one level, as Claire Sponsler has argued, the plays warned those who might transgress against the social order, using children, women, and Jews as subjects in order to emphasize the masculine, dominant power of authority. But there were ambiguities here, particularly as the plays rhetorically linked Jesus to those groups. He, too, was a powerless victim and presented as passive, naked, and weak: silent in the face of his torturers' taunts and disembodied even as his body was the focus of attention. The plays therefore challenged the social order even while confirming its authority. People could tolerate, even enjoy, spectacles in which Jews and women were tortured or violated. Such treatment of Christ's body, however, emphasized that anyone might be subject to authorized physical attack. Spectators, moreover, were reminded that, as passive witnesses, they were complicit in the represented and implied abuses. By exposing the ways in which social structures controlled and objectified the body, Corpus Christi pageants offered the possibility of resisting those structures and reversing the authoritarian logic of those who sponsored the Corpus plays.[48]

Christ's body also represented the Christian body social, an association that was particularly powerful on Corpus Christi. By displaying this body, the Corpus Christi itself, in a broken and abused state, the English plays suggested that Christian society was under attack and pointed to the culprit: the Jews who took such joy in buffeting the helpless Christ. The plays linked biblical tales of the Passion with the experience of Christian worship and the unity of Christian society, and depicted Jews as a threat to all of these. Seeing Jews stabbing and beating the wounded Christ reflected familiar narratives, including the belief that Jews bore continued guilt for the death of Christ and that they regularly participated in ritual murder and Host desecration.[49] All this played into doubts about the doctrine of transubstantiation.[50] In reflecting the imagined image of a bleeding Host stabbed by Jews, the bleeding figure of Christ confirmed the Eucharistic miracle.

*   *   *

Without scripts, we cannot know if the Corpus plays performed in Murcia depicted violence or Jews in a manner similar to those in England. Their themes, as shown by the titles, certainly provided ample scope for the graphic depiction of brutality and torture. The display of Christ's broken body would have been appropriate in *El Calvario* and *El desenclavamiento*, while *El juicio*, *Ynfierno*, and *La destrucción del mundo* would hardly have been complete without mention of the fate awaiting Jews, Muslims, and heretics. Saints' tales were likewise full of possibility in this regard. Violence and suffering, moreover, were common themes in Castilian drama and in the experience of popular religion.[51]

There were, however, no Jews or Muslims in England. All Jews had been expelled from the kingdom in 1290, and there never had been any significant Muslim population. English playwrights, actors, and audiences could project particular ideas onto these religious others from a distance, without the need to confront them directly. In Castile, and especially in Murcia, Jews and Muslims were present at and even participated in Corpus Christi theatrics. This limited the freedom with which Jews and Muslims could be presented— fanciful statements were less likely to ring true—but it also ensured that even subtle statements about them would be socially relevant and emotionally powerful.

Religious minorities were central to the meaning of Corpus Christi in Murcia in multiple ways. In one sense, it acted as a way for Christians to publicly and ostentatiously proclaim their faith to their Muslim and Jewish neighbors. But Corpus could also serve to bring members of different faiths together. As one scholar has noted about the festival in Murcia, "even though [Corpus] was in essence a Christian ceremony, its scope and resonance extended to people of different faiths, and this day, perhaps the only of its kind in the year, was considered exceptional and the Muslims and Jews who were invited to contribute felt attracted by the magnificence of the celebra- tion. . . . No one was excluded from the festival; on the contrary, the joy of some infected the rest, and in a certain way all competed to adorn their homes and streets and to wear their finest clothes. This meant that the Thurs- day of the celebration produced, even if only for the single day, an authentic and fraternal *convivencia*."[52] This is perhaps an overly idealistic reading of Corpus in Murcia, but it is true that Murcians were unusually open to the presence and even participation of religious minorities in Corpus festivities for much of the century. Elsewhere in Iberia, strict laws either forbade the Jewish and Muslim involvement, even as spectators, or forced them to join in this Christian act of worship. In Saragossa, for instance, Jews and Muslims were forbidden to view the procession, even from their own windows. In 1445, attempting to tighten control over the event, the *concejo* there banned "all manner of [unauthorized] *entremeses*, masks, Jews, and games nor should anyone launch fireworks, under penalty of imprisonment."[53] Authorities in the then-small town of Madrid adopted the opposite strategy when, in 1481, they ordered that the Jewish and Muslim communities present musical and dance performances or face a fine of 3,000 *mrs.*[54]

We cannot know the zeal with which Murcia's Jews and Muslims decorated their homes, but their voluntary involvement was a regular feature of Corpus. Musicians, for instance, were a key part of all aspects of the celebration: they accompanied the procession, provided the score for the plays, and entertained guests at the closing banquet. Organizers particularly prized Muslim players, who were renowned throughout the region for their skills. In 1425, the *concejo* "commanded majordomo Juan Ferrandez de Campo to send to all the *morerías* so that all available musicians come eagerly to the festival in order to honor it in the accustomed manner."[55]

It was common practice in Murcian society to hire Muslim musicians for important events; they played trumpets, kettledrums, and tambourines, as well as stringed instruments, at banquets in private salons, at the festival of San Juan, to celebrate civic appointments, for the king's anniversary, and so on.[56] Corpus Christi organizers therefore secured the services of as many Muslim players as possible in order to maintain the festival's reputation. In 1430, the majordomo brought eleven minstrels (*juglares*) from the Ricote Valley; in 1466, the search was cast even farther, as far as La Albatera in Valencia. Those hired included women as well as men; in 1440, a number of Muslim women were contracted for Corpus and later references to "juglares y juglaresas" likely indicate Muslim women as well, given restrictions on the activities of Christian women.[57] For these services, they were well paid; the 1425 order noted cost was not a primary concern.

Non-Christians did not view Corpus only as an opportunity for paid work. In May 1480, for instance, a Muslim delegation argued before the council that "the Moors have, since this city was won from them and they came to the *morerías*, been accustomed to wear robes of Morisco silk . . . and to never come out in other attire." They therefore requested that "the committee permit them to wear their robes and silk head coverings on the day of Corpus Christi without fear of consequences."[58] After three days of deliberation, the *concejo* lifted restrictions on attire for all in the city, regardless of

religion, proclaiming that "for the day of Corpus Christi and for the honor
of the festival, any and all persons, whether Christian, Jewish, or Muslim,
may wear all clothes restricted and reserved under the law of the *hermandad*
without any penalty."[59] With its careful phrasing, this decision skirted religious issues and instead indicated a general easing of restrictions for a festival
day. Yet the request indicates that Muslims participated willingly in Corpus,
and the seriousness with which the request was taken confirms the *concejo*'s
desire to ensure that participation while perhaps revealing some pleasure at
the thought of colorful Muslim robes lending a touch of the exotic to the
festivities.

This did not, however, mean that Jews and Muslims were considered to
be truly equal participants. In 1468, the *concejo* decreed that "that Jews and
Muslims who are in the street when the Host is carried past or when its
procession comes through the city are obliged to move away from that street
or to hide themselves or to kneel." Any Christian observing a Jew or Muslim
failing to do so was obliged to arrest the offender and bring him or her before
a local magistrate. The agreement of two witnesses was enough to confirm
guilt, and the penalty was a stiff fine of 200 *mrs*. In addition, the guilty
party's clothes were given to the accuser.[60] In addition to providing an easy
pretext for any small group of Christians to dispossess a Jew or Muslim of
his or her clothing, this edict demonstrated to Murcia's religious minorities
that they were tolerated guests only, not full participants.

We should not read too much into it, however. Jews and Muslims *were*
guests at a Christian religious ceremony. For Christians, the Eucharist was a
holy object worthy of vigilance, especially in regard to non-Christians, who
could not be expected to feel the proper sense of adoration toward it. Compelling the outward signs of respect was aggressive but not necessarily intoler-
ant. Jews and Muslims, who also had rules about nonbelievers and sacred
objects, texts, and spaces, could interpret the Corpus restrictions as similar to
their own. All this was of a part, moreover, with other attempts by authorities
to control spectator behavior. In 1482, the *cabildo* chastised anyone—
Christian, Muslim, or Jew—who engaged in shameless acts (*deshonestidades*)
during Corpus.[61] Special taxes imposed on Jews and Muslims perhaps fell
into this same category. In times of financial need, the *concejo* noted that
they took part in and enjoyed the show, yet paid no parish taxes. The levies
were a means of correcting this situation. If Corpus Christi demonstrated
civic solidarity, from this perspective, Jews and Muslims should demonstrate
respect for the Host as a symbol of that unity and contribute appropriately.

The clearest indication that Corpus Christi in Murcia, prior to the 1480s, was not a flashpoint for interfaith tensions occurred in 1472. Just after the procession ended, a Jewish man by the name of Yehuda drew a sword and attacked, for reasons unknown, a priest in front of the church of San Bartolomé. The priest, Pedro Gómez (or Fernández, according to another witness who appeared before the *concejo*), avoided his assailant's charge and ducked into the church, while bystanders subdued and detained Yehuda. The *concejo* immediately met to take statements and determine the appropriate punishment, but they were preempted by *adelantado* Farjardo's deputies, who claimed that Yehuda was in the service of Doña Leonor and that their lord, known for his protection of the Jewish community, thus had jurisdiction over the case. The *concejo*, resenting the perceived usurpation of their authority, then wrote to Fajardo with an outline of events and a firmly worded note stating their jurisdiction over all Jews and Muslims residing within the city's *juderías* and *morerías*.[62]

Concejo records do not mention the case again: Fajardo's response and Yehuda's fate are not recorded. Given the timing and sensational nature of the assault, this silence is notable. A Jew had, in broad daylight, attempted to murder a priest on the steps of a church during the festival honoring the body of Christ, a body whose sufferings at the hands of Jews were likely relived in the Corpus plays. Yet there was no popular outrage, no unrest, no attacks on Jewish homes. Less than a year later, a far less dramatic offense in Córdoba would lead to pogroms throughout Andalucía. The conclusion is clear: in Murcia in 1472, tensions between Jews and Christians were so minimal that even a dramatic assault did not lead to further trouble.

*   *   *

This situation shifted dramatically in the 1480s, a change intensified by its expression in civic festivities. Even as policies were promulgated that weakened the position of Murcia's Muslim and Jewish communities, their role in Corpus diminished. It was during this period, also, that the *concejo* began to use the *juegos de Corpus* to commemorate various significant events in the war with Granada, creating an explicit connection between Christian victory over the enemies of the faith and the mystery of Christ's body. Records of *concejo* preparations for these special events reveal that they no longer saw Muslims and Jews as valid, if marginal, members of society. They were now financial resources to be exploited as fully as possible or ornaments whose participation was compelled.

The first links between Corpus and military victory were forged in 1485 to honor the Castilian conquest of Ronda, a key stronghold in western Granada. The *concejo* wanted to publicly acknowledge the victory in order to raise civic morale, but their ongoing financial struggles made this difficult. They were barely able to fund Corpus and other events already on the annual calendar; adding an additional spectacle would be impossible. They compromised by extending the festivities of Corpus while cutting what costs they could. They ordered the majordomo, for instance, to purchase no beverages for the postprocession banquet and used the money instead to purchase a bull that "would be run on the Trapería on the Sunday after Corpus for the celebration of the capture of the city of Ronda and the other conquests that the King our lord has made in the kingdom of Granada."[63] This was not a complete innovation; indeed, there were recent precedents both for publicly commemorating military victories and for linking them to established religious holidays. The 17 March 1452 battle of Los Alporchones, for instance, became associated with Saint Patrick, who was consecrated as a patron of that city. Thereafter, saint and battle were jointly honored with an annual procession.[64]

The capture of Málaga in August 1487, however, inspired a more dramatic celebration. Málaga was the second city and major port of the kingdom of Granada; its surrender after a lengthy siege seemed to presage the final end to Muslim independence in Iberia.[65] The *concejo* therefore abandoned fiscal restraint in organizing a series of events that culminated in a grand three-day gala. The preparations, which took nearly a month to complete, are unusually well documented, likely because this was a special occasion for which customary arrangements could not be assumed. On 4 September, just two weeks after Málaga's capitulation, the *regidores* appointed a small group of delegates to organize a presentation of the Corpus Christi plays on Sunday, 9 September, and ordered "that [these men] have the authority to command all that should be done in order to present the plays."[66] Only after the gala was over did the *concejo* address the costs for this spectacle, which were immense, by instituting a tax on meat.[67]

The special rendition of the Corpus plays, however, paled in comparison to the ambitious plans they made for an extended party from Friday, 28 September, to Sunday, 30 September, coinciding with the feast of Saint Michael the Archangel, a figure long associated with the triumph of good over evil.[68] The celebration was to begin on Friday with the ringing of all the city's church bells and a fireworks display. On Saturday morning, there would be a solemn procession to honor Saint Michael featuring the civic, royal, and guild banners. The council went on to order that "on Saturday afternoon the Jews and Muslims would dance." The day would end with bonfires, church bells, and an additional fireworks display "just as is done for Carnival." The gala culminated on Sunday morning with another perform-ance of the Corpus plays.[69] Here, too, the expenses were enormous, but the *concejo* did not haggle, instead directing their subordinates to pay all the monies needed.[70]

Just a few months later, the *concejo* put on a similar show to celebrate a visit by Fernando and Isabel, who had come to oversee the conduct of the war. The royals were greeted with bullfights, a full array of Corpus plays, and Jewish dances. These last were organized by *jurado* Alonso Hurtado, who was directed to ensure "that they be enjoyable."[71] Hurtado, it should be noted, had no particular connections with the Jewish community. He was a munici-pal servant experienced in organizing Corpus and perhaps other civic specta-cles. In 1484, he had overseen the depot housing the Corpus *carros* and, together with his brother Diego, also helped plan and present the galas for Málaga and Granada. Jewish participation in this event was not a form of inclusion; rather, Jews, along with the bulls, were one of a number of entertainments.

The most elaborate and carefully planned special presentation of the Corpus plays took place in January 1492, shortly after the fall of Granada. Granada's surrender, after an eight-month siege, was, for Castilian observers, an event of momentous proportions. It marked the end of a seven-hundred-year struggle, the conclusion to the Muslim political presence in Iberia, and a victory of Christians over Muslims that seemed to foreshadow the conquest of Jerusalem and to fulfill apocalyptic prophesies. In a more prosaic, but no less significant, sense, it concluded a decade-long war that had consumed immense resources and countless lives while disrupting agriculture and sti-fling trade.

Upon hearing the news, Murcia's *concejo* immediately began preparing a gala that would last nearly a week, from 10 to 15 January, and include multiple processions as well as Corpus plays and bullfights. In order to make the arrangements as quickly as possible, they delegated authority to several of their own number as well as experienced *jurados* such as Alonso and Diego Hurtado. To emphasize that these celebrations marked a religious triumph by Christians over the enemies of Christ, and not simply a military victory that could be embraced by all residents of the city regardless of confession, the *concejo* ordered that, "for those three days, all officials, workers, and women not involved in putting on [the festivities] should behave as they do on Sunday or face a penalty of two *mrs.* toward the expenses of the revelries."[72]

The first event, on Tuesday, 10 January, was a procession to Santa María de la Arrixaca, an effigy of the Virgin housed in the church of San Andrés in the Arrixaca, or Muslim quarter of the city (Figure 4). The statue was closely associated with the thirteenth-century conquest of the city and the subsequent failure of the Muslims to retake it. According to Alfonso X's *Cantigas de Santa María*, the Muslims had resented the church in the midst of their community and repeatedly attempted to destroy it, only to be foiled by Mary's miraculous protection (Figure 5).

The *cantiga* linked Mary's powers to the failure of the Mudéjar rebellion of the 1260s as well as an attempt by the army of Abū Yūsuf Yaʻqūb ibn ʻAbd al-Haqq, the Marinid ruler of Morocco, to capture Murcia through the treachery of those in the *morería*. In response, Mary drove the Muslims out of the Arrixaca, leaving only a few behind. Although the text does not directly reference the effigy, it is clear from the accompanying illumination that it is the source of the miracles described. The Virgin of the Arrixaca, moreover, was not only a symbol of defense against Muslim aggression; she was an allegory of irreversible Christian triumph in Iberia and beyond. The *cantiga* concludes that Mary's church is forever free: "Muhammad can never have power there because she conquered it, and, furthermore, she will conquer Spain and Morocco and Ceuta and Asilah."[73]

In the context of the fall of Granada and contemporary plans to push forward into North Africa, the procession to Santa María de la Arrixaca celebrated the long-delayed fulfillment of Alfonso X's plans for such conquests. It also was intended to remind the Muslims of Murcia that their defeat was permanent. Neither the Virgin nor the Christian rulers of the city would permit any insurrection or reversal. This was emphasized by the procession route, which went from the cathedral to San Andrés through the *morería*. The royal and civic banners headed the procession itself; at the rear, in the position occupied by prisoners of war in a military triumph, were Jews and Muslims ordered to dance and make merry while dressed in their finest attire.

The remaining two processions also passed conspicuously through Muslim and Jewish neighborhoods while honoring sites linked to reconquest

Figure 4. *La Virgen de la Arrixaca*. Courtesy of the Iglesia de San Andrés, Murcia.

FIGURE 5. Muslims attempt to attack the Virgin of the Arrixaca. Alfonso X el Sabio, *Cantigas de Santa María: Edición facsímil del Códice T.I.1 de la Biblioteca de San Lorenzo de El Escorial*, fol. 226v. In this detail from the illustration for *cantiga* 169, an effigy of the Virgin Mary protects a church in Murcia from Muslim rebels. The celebrations marking the fall of Granada began with a procession to this statue.

ideology. On Wednesday, a similar (*de la misma manera*) procession terminated at the church of Santiago, also in the Arrixaca. Thursday, the destination was the Trinitarian house, dedicated to the redemption of captives. It lay on the far side of the *judería* from the cathedral, requiring the procession to cut directly through the Jewish quarter.[74]

The *concejo* issued a proclamation on Saturday stating that "all trumpeters and minstrels and players, both Muslims and Christians of whatever quality and station" were not permitted to leave the city until the festivities had ended. Never before had the *concejo* hired so many musicians that they feared a lack of supply. They had, it is true, previously imported Muslim players from surrounding areas, but that was on account of their reputed skill. Now the emphasis was on quantity rather than quality. The grand finale came on Sunday, 15 January, with six Corpus plays—*El paraíso, Infierno con los santos padres, La desenclavación, San Jorge, San Martín,* and *Abrahán*—and carnivalesque revelries, headlined by a bullfight featuring eight animals.[75]

No doubt the fines collected from those violating various decrees helped offset the costs of such mammoth galas. But the scope of those expenses clearly exceeded that of any prior celebrations. The *concejo* made no attempt to impose a short-lived tax on meat or any other product. Instead they deflected the costs onto those they deemed not fully part of Murcian society. The Genoese merchant community, for instance, was required to contribute 15,000 *mrs.* But pecuniary demands focused particularly on Jews and Muslims. One aspect of this was a property tax on all Muslims in Murcia's jurisdiction. On Monday, 9 January, the *concejo* directed Juan de la Cueva to inform the various Muslim communities of this new levy and organize immediate property appraisals to ensure that each paid a share suitable to his or her wealth. Any who failed to pay faced further fines and taxes.[76] These appraisals took place the next day, perhaps while the triumphant procession wended through the Arrixaca.

The tax levied on Murcia's Jews was communal. During their planning meetings, the *concejo* instructed *regidor* Pedro de Zambrana (who was also in charge of the Sunday Corpus plays) and the knight Alfonso de Palazol to "speak with the Jews and command them to pay, within three days, the 50,000 *mrs* that they owed as their share of the war, of which they had been informed but said they did not owe."[77] "Their share of the war" referred to contributions to the Santa Hermandad (Holy Brotherhood), a national militia force used by the Catholic Monarchs as a supplemental means of raising money and troops for the Granadan war. Hermandad taxes were calculated on the basis of population and paid by municipal *concejos*, who were then responsible for collecting individual payments.[78]

The Jews and Muslims of Murcia had recently appealed the Hermandad tax, arguing that they should have the same tax-exempt status "as widows or orphans or other miserable persons."[79] Their original claim does not survive, so we do not know the basis upon which they made this argument; it may, however, have rested on their general poverty or inability to engage in particular trades. In this particular case, the *concejo* had directed their claim to court administrators, who affirmed the tax and ordered that Jews and Muslims pay the same rates as their Christian neighbors. In previous instances, however, the monarchs had ruled in favor of Murcian Muslims, fearing that heavy tax burdens would induce them to emigrate to Granada and thus deprive Castile of their economic contributions. In 1487, for instance, when confirming the Muslim community's existing privileges, the crown noted that "because of the wars and other evils that have beset the land of Murcia, the majority of the Muslims are dead and the rest have fled, leaving the land very depopulated and diminished." The *concejo* should therefore impose no unusual or burdensome taxes, since if "the Muslims who live outside of my territory [i.e., in Granada] would like to come and all be happy and prosperous, they can do us a great service."[80]

While this restriction did not prevent the *concejo* from levying special taxes on Muslims, it did discourage attempts to impose rates so high that the Muslims would appeal to the monarchs. Under Fernando and Isabel, the Jewish community had few such protections and so the *concejo* moved aggressively to collect the 50,000 *mrs.* they claimed to be owed, returning to the issue several times in their deliberations on 9 January, arguing that the monies were both "for their share of the Granadan war . . . and for the revelries and entertainments that are made in this city for the surrender of Granada." They went on to add that failure to pay within three days would lead to an additional fine of 20,000 *mrs.*[81] Soon thereafter, after Zambrana reported that Samuel Abulafía, the *jurado* of the Jewish community, had protested against the demands, the *concejo* raised the penalty for noncompliance to 50,000 *mrs.*[82] No further comments on this special tax are recorded in the *actas capitulares* and it remains unclear whether payment was made or penalties imposed.

In any event, the Jews were in no position to appeal this tax, nor did the *concejo* have many further opportunities to exploit them. In a document dated 31 March 1492, Fernando and Isabel accused Castilian Jews of attempting "to subvert and to steal faithful Christians from our holy Catholic faith." They argued that recent converts from Judaism to Christianity were particularly susceptible to apostasy due to contact with Jews. Prior efforts to deal with this problem, specifically physical segregation and the Inquisition, had proved to be insufficient barriers; the Jews continued to win adherents to "their own wicked belief and conviction." As all this was "to the great injury, detriment, and opprobrium of our holy Catholic faith," the monarchs resolved that the only remaining course of action was to require that all Jews in their lands leave, convert, or face draconian penalties. This decree, generally known as the Alhambra Edict or Edict of Expulsion, was to take effect on 31 July. As it was not publicized throughout the kingdom until late April, however, the Jewish population effectively had only three months to depart.[83] In Murcia, the *concejo* duly copied and publicized the initial edict as well as various decrees issued by the monarchs regarding the logistics of this mass emigration, including regulations for the sale of Jewish property and arrangements for their protection until they should depart.[84] Through the victory galas, the council had treated the Jews as outsiders in Castilian society; the Edict of Expulsion made this status official.

*   *   *

The expressed rationale for the Edict of Expulsion, namely the danger of *converso* recidivism as a result of contact with their Jewish neighbors, was not particularly relevant to Murcia. While its Jewish community was larger and more vibrant than many in Castile, there were also fewer *conversos* who might revert to their old religion. Further, the Muslim population of Murcia and its surrounding territories was Castile's most significant and an essential part of the rural economy. The city had been no idyllic haven for Jews and Muslims. They had never been fully accepted and had to deal with periodic efforts to isolate them, such as Vincent Ferrer's 1411 campaign. Even so, Murcia's maritime economy and relative isolation had permitted a mixed society to a degree unmatched elsewhere in Castile.

The situation changed in the 1480s. The region was the object, along with all other frontier zones, of efforts to firmly establish royal control over territories that had been virtually autonomous during the preceding decades. The war with Granada intensified this process. The city served as a base for operations in eastern Granada, bringing the *concejo* under the eye of royal deputies and, on occasion, the monarchs themselves. Contact with incoming soldiers exposed the Murcian population to the growing anti-Semitism of Andalucía and other parts of Castile even while fears of fifth columnists led Murcian authorities to curtail the freedom of local Muslims. There was, moreover, a sense that this war with Granada would bring a final end to the frontier and therefore to the peculiar accommodations of frontier life.

The victory galas were a means of recognizing changed conditions, and special presentations of the Corpus Christi plays were an apt tool for the purpose. There are no recorded instances of their performance on any day but Corpus nor of any extensions of the Corpus festival before the capture of

Ronda in 1485. After this date, however, they became an almost regular feature of Murcian life, emphasizing that the victories commemorated were
world changing and beyond the scope of normal events, thus requiring
extraordinary celebrations to give them meaning. The new role of Muslims
and Jews in these performances similarly echoed the shift in attitudes. By
forcing them to dance in apparent joy at the tail end of each procession,
Murcian Christians assured themselves that these groups no longer posed a
threat to the body social; they were marginalized but also tamed.

The victory galas were more than social barometers. They not only
reflected changing attitudes about Murcian society and religious minorities;
they helped to create those attitudes. By choosing the Corpus plays to represent Christian victory on the frontier, the Murcian *concejo* deliberately
invented associations between popular religious practice and royal policy.
They did so in a manner well calculated to resonate with the people. Corpus
plays were immensely popular not only because they were enjoyable but also
because the visual representation of Christ's sufferings spoke to fundamental
aspects of their beliefs. By linking Christ's torments to the triumphs of the
Catholic Monarchs, the *concejo* also affirmed royal policy toward putative
enemies of the faith within Christian society. The body of Christ represented
the unity of Christian society. So too did the Corpus procession, but in
hierarchical terms. The relegation of Muslims and Jews to a subordinate and
humiliating position within it affirmed that Murcia's was a dominantly
Christian society. Just as Holy Week permitted the faithful to vicariously
experience the torments of Christ, the Corpus processions, as planned by the
concejo and included in the victory galas, offered a means of symbolically
expelling undesirables.

That such an association was intended is indicated in the *concejo*'s planning meetings in early January of 1492. The discussion returned repeatedly
to the role of Muslims and Jews: their place in the processions, their attire,
their financial contributions. Whatever else the celebrations of victory over
Granada might accomplish, the *concejo* meant them to convey a particular
message regarding these religious minorities. The *actas capitulares* are silent
regarding the overall reception of these events, a silence that points toward
general acquiescence. Yet it is unlikely that the import of the galas escaped
participants or spectators. The role of non-Christians in the new order was
made clear by the sight of Jews and Muslims, attired in their finest clothes
by order of the Christian *concejo*, made to dance in celebration of a victory
in which they would not share.

Charlotte Stern has characterized the Murcian Corpus Christi festival as a "puzzling mix of ecumenism and bigotry."[85] If we put it into the context of the amiable enmity that marked frontier relations between Christians, Muslims, and Jews, the city's celebration of Corpus is no longer puzzling, but a function of the social confusions engendered by the frontier. Furthermore, the fact that the Murcian presentation of this holiday began to tend strongly toward bigotry rather than inclusion in the 1480s reflected the increasing influence of broader Castilian trends. The galas commemorating victories in Ronda, Málaga, and Granada demonstrated the *concejo's* understandings of these new external pressures as well as its desire to articulate them to the general population. Yet the Murcian processions and plays did not express fear or hatred of religious minorities. There were no incitements to violence, no overt rejections, nor even an attempt to ban Jews and Muslims from attending. Instead the revelries expressed the irrelevancy of non-Christians in Murcian society. They were barely tolerated guests required to convey their insincere joy at the triumph of Christian arms. Tellingly, the *concejo* passed an order forbidding anyone to wear mourning clothes at the gala marking the fall of Granada.[86] With the end of the frontier would come an end to frontier coexistence.

Conclusion

Why this sudden restlessness, this confusion?
(How serious people's faces have become.)
Why are the streets and squares emptying so rapidly,
everyone going home so lost in thought?

Because night has fallen and the barbarians have not come.
And some who have just returned from the border say
there are no barbarians any longer.

And now, what's going to happen to us without barbarians?
They were, those people, a kind of solution.
— C. P. Cavafy, "Waiting for the Barbarians"

It is perhaps a bit passé to end a book on Spanish history in 1492, but it is appropriate here. As discussed in the previous chapter, the fall of Granada at the beginning of that year had profound implications for the amiable enmity that had characterized the frontier zones of Castile. In addition to removing or, at the least, greatly lessening the physical anxiety that had intensified contradictory reactions to religious minorities, the conquest gave legitimacy to those factions within Castilian society who aimed to remake it into an exclusively Christian one. This push toward social and religious uniformity resulted in the expulsion of Jews and the increasing marginalization of Muslims living under Christian rule. Those Jews and Muslims who converted in order to avoid social and legal disabilities, moreover, faced a powerful and aggressive Inquisition. Spain, as defined by its temporal and religious rulers, was to be not only a Christian kingdom but one that zealously defended orthodoxy and orthopraxy. But this is not to say that the hybrid culture of the frontier suddenly disappeared. Far from it. In fact, as Barbara Fuchs has shown, interest in and engagement with Moorishness intensified during the sixteenth century as people at all levels of Spanish society continued to struggle to reconcile the rhetoric of a homogeneous, Christian society with the reality of large numbers of Moriscos and the powerful cultural legacies of the past[1].

The transformations of the late fifteenth and early sixteenth centuries followed roughly two hundred years of relative social stability on the frontier, a circumstance remarkable when one considers the significant internal and external pressures that frontier residents faced. In particular, the combination of hostility and cultural exchange fostered, in Old Christians, deep-seated anxieties about the proper boundaries between members of different religious groups and the nature of their society. These anxieties, moreover, played out in the context of the real or imagined specter of invasion from nearby Muslim polities. Ironically, the constant threat of physical attack often helped permit these composite societies to thrive despite discourses of religious intolerance. The need for collective responses to shared challenges and the regular, peaceful interactions coexistence required meant that ideologies of exclusion always competed with practical concerns that could not be ignored. Amiable enmity was thus a source of stability.

Public spectacles of various kinds permitted the articulation of these social incongruities through theatrics that could function in a variety of ways. They were distractions from pressing concerns, but they were also reminders of past glories, attacks on vulnerable groups, or alternate worldviews that emphasized the cooperative nature of society. Elites controlled the messages but circumstances often required them to invite the active participation of the audience or to craft their pageants in particular ways. Elites, in other words, could not use spectacle to freely impose their viewpoints on the populace. Instead, they attempted to nudge the people toward a policy while seeming to tell them what they wanted to hear. The content of these performances, therefore, acts as a window into often-elusive popular sentiment. We cannot know for certain how individual audience members understood or received a performance, but we can assess how the elite sponsors of that performance, who were far closer to late medieval popular culture than we can be, expected people to react. We can also measure the effectiveness of particular performances from their real social effects; we can, in other words, judge what people thought based on our knowledge of what they did.

The final decades of the fifteenth century in Iberia saw the gradual disintegration of traditional modes of frontier life or, as it has often been described, the breakdown of *convivencia*. The causes of this shift have long been debated, and scholars have pointed to, among other explanations, ecological challenges, the misrule of Enrique IV, the extension of monarchical power, and new ideas of *limpieza de sangre*. On the frontier, the ramifications of this shift from relative openness to a society defined as exclusively Christian can be traced through public spectacles as leaders attempted to harness changes in popular sentiment for their own ends. Miguel Lucas's attempt to break patterns of inaction through a decisive military campaign illustrates that "traditional" attitudes toward Granada were still largely in place in the 1460s; he appealed to the people by showing them that Christian victory would not disrupt existing relations with the people of Granada. A decade later, the Marquis of Villena could predict that the Old Christians of Córdoba would reject their *converso* neighbors and that Alonso de Aguilar would attempt to protect them, thus putting Aguilar at odds with the majority of his subjects. By the 1480s, successive victories in the war against Granada meant that Jews and Muslims were no longer seen as dangerous enemies. The Murcian *concejo* confirmed this by forcing them into roles in the Corpus Christi festivals and victory galas that portrayed them simply as outsiders, defeated enemies who had no place in the new order. These public representations of Jews and Muslims were particularly effective on the frontier because they were familiar, having long been a fundamental means of addressing issues arising from religious pluralism.

This was more than a Spanish phenomenon. Late medieval frontier societies across the Mediterranean world shared, despite significant contextual differences, several key concerns. Similar patterns can be discerned, though there is not space here to detail all of them, in the kingdom of Sicily, the crusader principalities, the Balkans, Lusignan Cyprus, Venice, and various locations in North Africa. In all these cases, internal religious tensions combined with physical insecurity to produce particular social, cultural, and religious attitudes. Whether the prominent role played by public spectacles in suppressing or mobilizing extant discourses of openness and rejection in fifteenth-century Spain was replicated elsewhere is a topic for further study. It is, however, a relevant question. An understanding of the ways popular sentiments regarding religious minorities, or elite perceptions of those sentiments, conditioned the content of civic pageants can offer insights into other instances of breakdowns in convivial relationships.

For just one example of how such processes played out in other contexts, we might look at fourteenth-century Cyprus. At the time, this island was

ruled by a Latin Christian enclave while the majority of the population followed the Greek Orthodox rite. There were also smaller communities that
adhered to a number of other confessional identities. Just as in Castile, then,
the population of late medieval Cyprus comprised a multitude of religious
communities, whose relations were colored by ambivalent attitudes and so
ranged from partnership to uneasy coexistence to open hostility. Foreigners
visiting Cyprus were often taken aback by the degree of religious convergence, and so papal ambassadors grumbled that Latin women preferred to
hear mass in Greek churches while visiting Orthodox monks wondered why
their Cypriot coreligionists wanted so much to join the Latins' holiday
processions.

These concerns came to a crisis of sorts with the arrival, in 1360, of papal
legate Peter Thomas. Peter had a dual mandate on Cyprus: to bring the
Orthodox under more direct Roman control and to facilitate the crusading
ambitions of King Peter I. Peter Thomas had an inauspicious beginning to
his sojourn in Cyprus. In addressing the first of his duties, he harangued the
Orthodox hierarchy in the cathedral of Nicosia, almost starting a riot in the
process. This was of particular significance given the proposed crusade, which
materialized as the Alexandria Crusade. The king's plans required stripping
the island of most of its military forces, thus removing a check on Greek
insurrection at a moment when revolts against Latin rule were occurring on
other islands, notably Venetian-dominated Crete. A crusade, moreover,
meant an increased tax burden on the Greek peasantry and an enhanced risk
of Mamluk invasion. In other words, cordial Greek-Latin relations were a
sine qua non for the crusade.

The outbreak of plague on Cyprus in 1362 posed yet another challenge
to dreams of crusade. But Peter Thomas was able to turn this tragedy into an
ecumenical moment by leading processions in which all the people of Nicosia
and Famagusta, regardless of rank or rite, would fast on bread and water
and march barefoot to beg God's forgiveness. According to Peter Thomas's
hagiographer, "Greeks, Armenians, Nestorians, Jacobites, Georgians, Nubi-
ans, Indians, Ethiopians, and many other Christians" joined the processions
while "many infidel Turks, Saracens, and Jews . . . burst into tears and walked
with bare feet and great devotion in the Christian procession."[2] While we
need to read this account with care, there is no reason to doubt that Peter
Thomas deliberately opened his penitential processions to Cypriots of all rites
and faiths. The legate, in other words, found an effective means of negotiating the complex religious landscape of Lusignan Cyprus that won qualified

approval from enough of the Greek hierarchy and people that the Alexandria Crusade went forward without fear of rebellion.[3]

While there were dramatic contextual differences between fourteenth-century Cyprus and fifteenth-century Castile, there was also a set of shared challenges. Both had a long period of stability in which members of multiple confessional groups lived in close proximity as well as fears of foreign invasion and internal rebellion and social anxieties over proper interfaith boundaries. In both cases, moreover, outsiders decried what they saw as a slow drift toward a common religious practice on the frontier. In times of transition or crisis, these factors induced elites to engage in a kind of identity politics, using public spectacles of various sorts to nudge the broader populace toward the attitudes they desired. In order to do so most effectively, temporal and ecclesiastic authorities relied on their own perceptions of popular sentiment, aiming to tell the people what they thought the people wanted to hear. This led to a cycle of reflexive feedback that reflected real attitudes while also changing them.

But why would Castile and Cyprus, with their very different histories, share anything? There are two potential answers. The first is that they were both Mediterranean societies. The second is that they were both frontier societies. For the former, a number of historians have long argued that the Mediterranean region has particular geographic, topographic, and/or social features that have made it an interconnected, unified system. Whether through a shared set of environmental challenges or via regular contact with outsiders, Mediterranean societies therefore have a number of common features, despite significant local variation. The precise definition of a Mediterranean society has been hotly debated, and some scholars have challenged the entire notion, making it difficult and potentially misleading to label the amiable enmity of Castile, Cyprus, or, for that matter, any other locale as a result of its "Mediterraneanness."[4]

At the same time, the Mediterranean region was also the central point of contact for the three Abrahamic religions, as well as for various Christian sects. Cities and polities situated near the Mediterranean therefore were far more likely to host religiously diverse populations than were comparable areas in northern or western Europe or in the central lands of the Islamic world. In the period under study, in other words, there were relatively few places outside of the Mediterranean region where significant populations lived under the rule of members of a different faith or rite. One can characterize the challenges of the composite societies in Castile and Cyprus that led to forms of amiable enmity as particular to the Mediterranean.

Perhaps more useful, however, is to consider these locations from the perspective of frontier studies. As described in the introduction, Castile was both a "frontier zone," a meeting point between different civilizations, as well as a "frontier society" that encompassed two or more religious or cultural groups within one political entity. Cyprus, though an island that would not at first seem to constitute a frontier in the sense we usually use the term, met these definitions as well.[5] Because of the broad set of encounters between Christianity and Islam in the late medieval Mediterranean world, so did a number of other societies in and around the inland sea.

Pageantry had long been a primary means for the expression of power and thus an essential tool of governance. It was particularly effective in frontier contexts where, by functioning as a way of negotiating and articulating the boundaries between religious communities, it was used to address unsettling inconsistencies between ideology and reality. Such boundary making bore the potential for violence but was not in itself an instrument either of tolerance or of aggression. Rulers could, through public spectacles, mobilize a range of ideas about religious others in order to stabilize confessional identities or transform them. The frequency with which they turned to the theme of interfaith relations highlighted the social importance of those relations and the ambivalent attitudes that characterized Mediterranean frontiers. The fifteenth-century Castilian experience that is the subject of this book, then, must be considered not in isolation but in the context of both a long tradition of such spectacles and their use in a wide range of situations. Such an approach can give greater insight in the complex politics of religious identity in Iberia and in other composite late medieval and early modern communities.

Nor are these completely separate from later events. While there is much in this book that is particular to Castilian or Mediterranean frontiers of the late Middle Ages and therefore does not apply to other contexts, the social processes described here—the conditions that led to amiable enmity, elite perceptions of popular mind-sets, and the expression of social concerns through spectacle—are not inevitably tied to that moment in time. Although the role of spectacle as a tool of governance has shifted in many ways since the fall of Granada, it has only grown in importance. Indeed, the transference of many forms of spectacle from in-person experiences to mass media has extended their reach and influence. Scholars examining modern instances in which there has been a significant shift in the status of a minority group therefore might fruitfully consider whether social dynamics similar to those examined in this book played a role and, if so, how they interacted with local contexts.

Of course, the events described in this book *did* have a direct influence on the later development of Spanish society. I opened this chapter with Constantine Cavafy's 1898 poem "Waiting for the Barbarians." This poem's setting, an indeterminate imperial capital paralyzed at the potential approach of barbarians, at first glance seems to have little relation to late medieval interfaith relations. But its central question—how does a society respond when the encounter to which it has dedicated itself is no longer relevant—reminds us of the significance of the end of the Granadan frontier for Castilian society. The aristocracy had committed itself to the project of reconquest and the realization of this objective posed a real danger to its self-identity. To remedy this, of course, the nobles soon moved on to new frontiers in the Americas and in North Africa, where the experience of the Granadan frontier conditioned their responses to other peoples.

In Spain itself, the effects of the extended encounter with Islam in Iberia were long lasting. Notably, recent work has shown that the complex attitudes toward other religious groups held by many in the fifteenth century did not simply disappear. In the century after the fall of Granada, Spanish authorities moved to convert their Muslim subjects, through education, economic coercion, or force. At the same time, ironically, Christians could once again openly express their admiration for Islamic culture and dally with Muslim manners and dress in a way similar to that which had helped to doom the reign of Enrique IV.[6] This was not simply a superficial interest in exotic customs, however. The fluid notions of religious identity that had characterized the frontier survived as well. As Stuart Schwartz has shown, members of all strata of society held relativistic views of religion throughout the sixteenth century.[7]

The sixteenth century also saw a flowering of theatrics and civic spectacles, many of which drew on the frontier past. Mock battles between Christians and "Muslims" akin to Miguel Lucas's Christmas tournament became commonplace in Spain and in its American colonies only after Christian victory in Granada. In Spain, the prevalence of these festivals as well as other instances of "playing the Moor" indicated deeply felt insecurities about Christian identities that led people to symbolically and repeatedly defeat Muslim incursions while proudly displaying evidence of cultural hybridity.[8] In the New World, these *danzas de moros y cristianos* also contained what Max Harris has called a "hidden transcript" of dissent and resistance.[9]

Although Golden Age Spaniards openly addressed their conflicted notions regarding the Muslim past, later generations sought to downplay or even erase the role played by Muslims in their history. This was in part due to fears that the long Muslim presence in Iberia had somehow pushed Spain from the historical paths traveled by other European nations, a sentiment concisely articulated by W. H. Auden, who referred to "that arid square, that fragment nipped off from hot / Africa, soldered so crudely to inventive Europe."[10] In response, they have struggled to understand the role played by the centuries of Muslim rule on the development of modern Spain. In a well-known debate, two of the most influential twentieth-century Spanish historians—Américo Castro and Claudio Sánchez-Albornoz—proposed conflicting interpretations that highlight still unresolved tensions. Castro's understanding of a creative *convivencia* has proved triumphant, at least in scholarly circles, over Sánchez-Albornoz's idea of a fundamental, eternal Spanish national character.

Yet the "Moor" continues to represent otherness and danger, and the role of Muslim influence on modern Spain remains an open and important question, with the nation's self-image at stake. Is Spain a cosmopolitan society that has inherited an ideal of tolerance and *convivencia* from the historic and open medieval encounter between cultures and religions? Or is it an unabashedly Roman Catholic nation, forged in eight centuries of struggle against the infidel invaders? Such questions, though never far below the surface, have emerged anew in the last couple of decades, fueled by increased immigration from North Africa and by fears of terrorism. Modern Spanish anxieties and ambivalent attitudes toward Islam reflect, in many ways, those of their medieval forebears. This may help us understand why Spanish civic and religious spectacles are, even today, heavily draped in the trappings of overt Christianity while the Muslims are, each year, defeated anew on dozens of town plazas throughout Spain.

NOTES

INTRODUCTION

1. Diego Ortiz de Zúñiga, *Anales eclesiásticos y seculares de la ciudad de Sevilla*, 4 vols. (Madrid, 1795), 2: 144 (año 1356); Cynthia L. Chamberlin, "'Unless the Pen Writes as It Should': The Proto-Cult of Saint Fernando III in Sevilla in the Thirteenth and Fourteenth Centuries," in *Sevilla 1248: Congreso Internacional Conmemorativo del 750 Aniversario de la Conquista de la Ciudad de Sevilla por Fernando III, Rey de Castilla y León*, ed. Manuel Jiménez González (Seville, 2000), 389–418; Manuel González Jiménez, *Fernando III El Santo* (Seville, 2006), 291–92. For a description of the sword, see María Isabel Herráez Martín, "La espada de Fernando III, El Santo," *Laboratorio del Arte* 15 (2002): 335–48. Fernando, later known as "de Antequera" after capturing that city from Granada in 1410, became King Fernando I of Aragón in 1412. All translations of original sources are by the author unless otherwise noted.

2. *Crónica de Juan II de Castilla*, ed. Juan de Mata Carriazo (Madrid, 1982), 130.

3. Ibid., 130–31: "caualleros, condes, e ricos omes."

4. Angus MacKay, "Religion, Culture, and Ideology on the Late Medieval Castilian-Granadan Frontier," in *Medieval Frontier Societies*, ed. Robert Bartlett and Angus MacKay (Oxford, 1989), 233–39.

5. *Historia de los hechos del Marqués de Cádiz*, ed. Juan Luis Carriazo Rubio (Granada, 2003), 142.

6. Angus MacKay, "Ferdinand of Antequera and the Virgin Mary," in Ian Macpherson and Angus MacKay, *Love, Religion and Politics in Fifteenth Century Spain* (Leiden, 1998), 132–39; Juan Torres Fontes, "Don Fernando de Antequera y la romántica caballeresca," *MMM* 5 (1980): 83–120.

7. Teofilo Ruiz, "The Symbolic Meaning of Sword and Palio in Late Medieval and Early Modern Ritual Entries: The Case of Seville," *Memoria y Civilización* 12 (2009): 18ff.; Ruiz, *A King Travels: Festive Traditions in Late Medieval and Early Modern Spain* (Princeton, N.J., 2012), 78–84, 115.

8. Archivio Segreto Vaticano, Reg. Vat. 389, fols. 136r–137r. Published in Shlomo Simonsohn, *The Apostolic See and the Jews: Documents, 1394–1464* (Toronto, 1988), 930–32,

no. 773; Yitzhak Baer, *Die Juden im Christlichen Spanien*, vol. 1, *Urkunden und Regesten*, pt. 2, *Kastilien/Inquisitionsakten* (Berlin, 1936), 302, 315.

9. For examples, see Baer, *Die Juden*, 162, 520, 523–24; Ángel Luis Molina Molina, "Sermones, procesiones y romerías en la Murcia bajomedieval," *MMM* 19–20 (1995–1996): 229–32.

10. Teofilo Ruiz, "Elite and Popular Culture in Late Fifteenth-Century Castilian Festivals: The Case of Jaén," in *City and Spectacle in Medieval Europe*, ed. Barbara Hanawalt and Kathryn Reyerson (Minneapolis, 1994), 296–318; Ronald Surtz, *The Birth of a Theater: Dramatic Convention in the Spanish Theater from Juan del Encina to Lope de Vega* (Madrid, 1979), 81–82; Charlotte Stern, "Christmas Performances in Jaén in the 1460s," in *Studies in Honor of Bruce W. Wardropper*, ed. Dian Fox, Harry Sieber, and Robert Ter Horst (Newark, Del., 1989), 326; Lucien Clare, "Fêtes, jeux et divertissements à la cour du connétable de Castille, Miguel Lucas de Iranzo (1460–1470): Les exercices physiques," in *Frontières andalouses: La vie a' Jae'n entre 1460 et 1471, d'apre's "Los hechos del condestable Miguel Lucas de Iranzo"*, ed. Jacques Heers (Paris, 1996), 15–34; Angus MacKay, "Religion, Culture, and Ideology," 217–44.

11. Alfonso de Palencia, *Crónica de Enrique IV*, ed. Antonio Paz y Melia, BAE 257, 258, 267 (Madrid, 1973–1975), 2: 86; Charlotte Stern, *The Medieval Theater in Castile* (Binghamton, N.Y., 1996), 117.

12. The term was coined by Julián Juderías, in his *La leyenda negra y la verdad histórica: Contribución al estudio del concepto de España en Europa, de las causas de este concepto y de la tolerancia política y religiosa en los países civilizados* (Madrid, 1914).

13. David Nirenberg, *Communities of Violence: Persecution of Minorities in the Middle Ages* (Princeton, N.J., 1996).

14. Mark Meyerson, *A Jewish Renaissance in Fifteenth-Century Spain* (Princeton, N.J., 2004); Barbara Fuchs, *Exotic Nation: Maurophilia and the Construction of Early Modern Spain* (Philadelphia, 2009); Stuart Schwartz, *All Can Be Saved: Religious Tolerance and Salvation in the Iberian Atlantic World* (New Haven, Conn., 2008).

15. Frederick Jackson Turner, "The Significance of the Frontier in American History," in *The Frontier in American History* (New York, 1920), 1–3.

16. The term "reconquest" is contested, with many scholars suggesting that it is a later invention and employing it only with qualifications. It is not, however, an artificial concept but one that reflects, although imperfectly, medieval realities, at least from the eleventh century on. As Miguel Angel Ladero Quesada notes, "Actualmente, muchos consideran espúreo el término reconquista para describir la realidad histórica de aquellos siglos, y prefieren hablar simplemente de conquista y sustitución de una sociedad y una cultura, la andalusí, por otra, la cristiano-occidental; pero aunque esto fue así, también lo es que el concepto de reconquista nació en los siglos medievales y pertenece a su realidad en cuanto que sirvió para justificar ideológicamente muchos aspectos de aquel proceso" ("¿Es todavía España un enigma histórico? Releyendo a Sánchez-Albornoz," in *Lecturas sobre la España historica* [Madrid, 1998], 334). Accordingly, "reconquest" is used in this book as shorthand for a loose ensemble of ideas and beliefs about the legitimacy of Castilian expansion at the expense of Muslim-ruled Granada. For a discussion of work on this

issue, see Manuel González Jiménez, "Sobre la ideología de la reconquista: Realidades y tópicos," in *Memoria, mito y realidad en la historia medieval: XIII Semana de Estudios Medievales, Nájera, del 29 de julio al 2 de agosto de 2002*, ed. José Ignacio de la Iglesia Duarte and José Luis Martín Rodríguez (Logroño, 2003), 151–70; Francisco García Fitz, "La Reconquista: Un estado de la cuestión," *Clio y Crimen* 6 (2009): 142–215; and García Fitz, *La Reconquista* (Granada, 2010).

17. For examples, see Juan de Mata Carriazo, "Un alcalde entre los cristianos y los moros, en la frontera de Granada," in *Homenaje al profesor Carriazo*, vol. 1, *En la frontera de Granada* (Seville, 1971), 85–142; José Enrique López de Coca-Castañer, "Institutions on the Castilian-Granadan Frontier, 1369–1482," in *Medieval Frontier Societies*, ed. Robert Bartlett and Angus MacKay (Oxford, 1989), 127–50; Robert I. Burns, "The Parish as a Frontier Institution in Thirteenth Century Valencia," *Speculum* 37 (1962): 244–51; Nora Berend, "Medievalists and the Notion of Frontier," *MHJ* 2 (1999): 61.

18. For overviews of the historiography, see Robert I. Burns, "The Significance of the Frontier in the Middle Ages," in *Medieval Frontier Societies*, ed. Robert Bartlett and Angus MacKay (Oxford, 1989), 307–17; Berend, "Medievalists and the Notion of Frontier," 55–72; and Edward Peters, "*Omnia permixta sunt*: Where's the Border?" *MHJ* 4 (2001): 109–27.

19. Gabriel Jackson, *The Making of Medieval Spain* (New York, 1972), 36–37; Claudio Sánchez-Albornoz, "The Frontier and Castilian Liberties," in *The New World Looks at Its History: Proceedings of the Second International Congress of Historians of the United States and Mexico*, ed. Archibald R. Lewis and Thomas McGann (Austin, Tex., 1963), 27–46; and Charles Julian Bishko, "The Castilian as Plainsman: The Medieval Ranching Frontier in La Mancha and Extremadura," in *The New World Looks at Its History*, 47–69. Some scholars have kept aspects of the Turnerian argument, while taking it in new directions. See Lawrence McCrank, "The Cistercians of Poblet as Medieval Frontiersmen," in *Estudios en homenaje a don Claudio Sánchez Albornoz en sus 90 años: Anexos de Cuadernos de historia de España* (Buenos Aires, 1983), 2:313–60; Heath Dillard, *Daughters of the Reconquest: Women in Castilian Town Society, 1100–1300* (Cambridge, 1984); and Burns, "The Significance of the Frontier in the Middle Ages." For a broader discussion of the role of frontiers in the Spanish-speaking world, see the essays in Benita Sampedro Vizcaya and Simon Doubleday, eds., *Border Interrogations: Questioning Spanish Frontiers* (New York, 2008).

20. Thomas Glick, *From Muslim Fortress to Christian Castle: Social and Cultural Change in Medieval Spain* (Manchester, 1995). See also his earlier *Islamic and Christian Spain in the Early Middle Ages: Comparative Perspectives on Social and Cultural Formation* (Princeton, N.J., 1979)

21. Homi K. Bhabha, *The Location of Culture* (London, 1994); Bhabha, "Culture's In-Between," in *Questions of Cultural Identity*, ed. Stuart Hall and Paul Du Gay (London, 1996), 53–60; Jonathan Rutherford, "The Third Space: Interview with Homi Bhabha," in *Identity, Community, Culture, Difference*, ed. Rutherford (London, 1990), 207–21; and José Rodríguez Molina, *La vida de moros y cristianos en la frontera* (Jaén, 2007).

22. The term "borderland" has become increasingly common in American scholarship as distinct from "frontier," which continues to bear Turnerian overtones. I prefer the latter term, however, as the one used by medieval Castilians and in much of the relevant historical literature.

23. This concept is similar in some respects to what Christopher MacEvitt has described as "rough tolerance" in *The Crusades and the Christian World of the East: Rough Tolerance* (Philadelphia, 2008). The essential distinction is that MacEvitt describes relations between Christian groups, in which there was much common religious ground. In Iberia, the gaps between Christianity and Islam and Judaism led to a different dynamic. Américo Castro, *España en su historia (Cristianos, moros y judíos)* (Barcelona, 1983), 565.

24. Peter Linehan, "At the Spanish Frontier," in *The Medieval World*, ed. Peter Linehan and Janet L. Nelson (London, 2001), 53 (italics in original).

25. On this castle, see Juan Antonio López Cordero, "El Castillo de Chincoya en la bibliografía," *Elucidario* 1 (2006): 237–48.

26. Alfonso X el Sabio, *Cantigas de Santa María*, ed. Walter Mettmann, 3 vols (Madrid, 1986–1989), 2: 204–7, no. 185 (hereafter *CSM*).

27. *CSM*, 2: 204–7, no. 185.

28. Ibid.

29. MacKay, "Religion, Culture, and Ideology," 217, 222, 232–38.

30. *Hechos del condestable don Miguel Lucas de Iranzo*, ed. Juan de Mata Carriazo, CCE 3 (Madrid, 1940), 474.

31. Ibid., 471, 474–75.

32. *Historia de los hechos del Marqués*, 159.

33. *Hechos del condestable*, 417–18.

34. *Historia de los hechos del Marqués*, 265–66.

35. AMM, *AC* 1434–1435, fol. 49v.

36. *Hechos del condestable*, 417.

37. *Historia de los hechos del Marqués*, 264.

38. As Juan de Mata Carriazo has argued, "peace was never lasting nor a complete cessation of all forms of warfare. Nor were truces complete: at best, they resulted in a state of diminished warfare" ("Un alcalde," 139). Cf. Rodríguez Molina, who argues that peace and war were markedly different states on the frontier, *La vida de moros y cristianos*, esp. chap. 3, "La guerra y la paz: Dos tiempos de la frontera," 95–114.

39. The text of the 1475 truce has been lost while that of the later agreement is published in *El Tumbo de los Reyes Católicos del concejo de Sevilla*, ed. Ramón Carande and Juan de Mata Carriazo (Seville, 1929–1968), 1: 122–23. A slightly different version is preserved in AMJ, *AC* 1476, fols. 29r–30r. A transcription of this text is available in Manuel González Jiménez, "Peace and War on the Frontier of Granada: Jaén and the Truce of 1476," in *Medieval Spain: Culture, Conflict, and Coexistence: Studies in Honor of Angus MacKay*, ed. Roger Collins and Anthony Goodman (Basingstoke, 2002), 168–70.

40. AMJ, *AC* 1476, fols. 14v, 20r.

41. AMJ, *AC* 1476, fol. 57v: "avía fecho muchas sinrazones a los moros de Guadix tomando y mandando tomar moros furtados e çiertas acémilas y yeguas estando asentada la paz."

42. AMJ, *AC* 1476, fols. 112v–114r, 191r: "porque no se sabe qué farán los moros."

43. AMJ, *AC* 1476, fol. 185r: "vino nueva como el rey de Granada avía corrido e entrado en tierra de cristianos a faser mal e daño, luego los dichos señores mandaron apercibir la gente desta çibdad, caualleros e peones."

44. AMJ, *AC* 1476, fol. 177r: "los caualleros de contia desta çibdad esta muy amenguada e non ay caualleros como solía, de lo qual viene grand daño a la çibdad e deserviçio a los reyes nuestros señores." González Jiménez, "Peace and War," 166–68, provides a detailed account of the *concejo's* attempts to ready the city's military forces.

45. AMJ, *AC* 1476, fol. 9r. No *actas capitulares* for Jaén prior to 1476 are extant.

46. AMJ, *AC* 1479, fols. 68v, 115r.

47. AMJ, *AC* 1476, fols. 114r, 179v.

48. Carriazo, "Un alcalde," 140–42.

49. Philippe Buc, *The Dangers of Ritual: Between Early Medieval Texts and Social Scientific Theory* (Princeton, N.J., 2001).

50. Catherine Bell, *Ritual Theory, Ritual Practice* (Oxford, 1990); Geoffrey Koziol, *Begging Pardon and Favor: Ritual and Political Order in Early Medieval France* (Ithaca, N.Y., 1992).

51. Janice Mann, *Romanesque Architecture and Its Sculptural Decoration in Christian Spain, 1000–1120: Exploring Frontiers and Defining Identities* (Toronto, 2009).

CHAPTER I. THE ANATOMY OF A SPECTACLE

1. Palencia, *Crónica de Enrique IV*, 1:168; Diego de Valera, *Memorial de diversas hazañas: Crónica de Enrique IV*, ed. Juan de Mata Carriazo, CCE 4 (Madrid, 1941), 99; Diego Enríquez del Castillo, *Crónica del rey don Enrique el cuarto de este nombre*, ed. Cayetano Rosell, BAE 70 (Madrid, 1953), 144–45.

2. Ruiz, "Elite and Popular Culture," 309.

3. Claire Sponsler, "The Culture of the Spectator: Conformity and Resistance to Medieval Performances," *Theatre Journal* 44 (1992): 15–29.

4. See Teofilo Ruiz, "Festivités, couleurs, et symboles du pouvoir en Castille au XVe siècle," *Annales: Économies, Sociétés, Civilisations* 3 (1991): 521–46.

5. Angus MacKay, "Ritual and Propaganda in Fifteenth-Century Castile," *Past and Present* 107 (1985): 3–43.

6. For magical interpretations of the Farce of Ávila, see Jean Lucas-Dubreton, *El rey huraño: Enrique IV de Castilla y su época* (Madrid, 1945), 135–46; Jocelyn N. Hillgarth, *The Spanish Kingdoms, 1250–1516*, 2 vols. (Oxford, 1976–1978), 2:334.

7. Thus the king may die but the crown does not. See Ernst Kantorowicz, *The King's Two Bodies: A Study in Medieval Political Theology* (Princeton, N.J., 1957).

8. MacKay, "Ritual and Propaganda," 18–20.

9. Palencia, *Crónica de Enrique IV*, 1:168. Diego de Valera, *Memorial de diversas hazañas*, 99, described the scene in similar terms: "y a todo esto gimian y lloraban la gente que lo veyan." Enríquez del Castillo, the other key chronicler who gave an account of the ritual (*Crónica del rey don Enrique*, 144–45), does not mention the lament.

10. MacKay, "Ritual and Propaganda," 23–24.

11. Palencia, *Crónica de Enrique IV*, 1:167.

12. Ibid.

13. For a more detailed study of this issue, see Thomas Devaney, "Representing the Medieval Festivals of Jaén Through Text, Enactment and Image," in *Re-Presenting the Past: Archaeology Through Image and Text*, ed. Sheila Bonde and Stephen Houston (Oakville, Conn., 2013), chap. 8.

14. For instance, Ruiz, "Elite and Popular Culture," 305, 315.

15. *Partidas*, 1:256–57, tit. 23, law 1.

16. Sponsler, "Culture of the Spectator," 19–21.

17. For an overview of this literature, see Jesús Rodríguez Velasco, *El debate sobre la caballería en el siglo XV: La tratadística caballeresca castellana en su marco europeo* (Valladolid, 1996).

18. Gema Palomo Fernández and José Luis Senra Gabriel y Galán, "La ciudad y la fiesta en la historiografía castellana de la baja edad media: Escenografía lúdico-festiva," *Hispania* 54/1 (1994): 5–36; MacKay, "Ritual and Propaganda," 22–23.

19. John Edwards, *Christian Córdoba: The City and Its Region in the Late Middle Ages* (Cambridge, 1982), 63–64, 131–33, 144–47. For reasons of simplicity and clarity, the term *caballero* is employed throughout this discussion as contemporaries generally used it: to refer to military professionals, those who trained as knights and made a career in military and administrative service, whether or not they were members of a hereditary lineage (*linaje*). Urban knights who received their privileges by attaining a minimum wealth qualification or through occasional service are described as *caballeros de cuantía*.

20. Teofilo Ruiz, *Spain's Centuries of Crisis, 1300–1474* (Oxford, 2007), 81–82.

21. The duties and privileges of *caballeros* crystallized in the thirteenth century, as the *Partidas* detailed both a way of life and a set of legal responsibilities; see *Partidas*, 2:417–32, tit. 21. See also the sources collected in Carlos Heusch and Jesús Rodríguez Velasco, eds., *La caballería castellana en la Baja Edad Media: Textos y contextos* (Montpellier, 2000), 53–80, which include treatises on knighthood contemporary with the *Partidas*. For the early development of Castilian knighthood, see Rodríguez Velasco, *El debate*, 17–25; and Josef Fleckenstein, *La caballería y el mundo caballeresco* (Madrid, 2006). For a detailed and comprehensive study of fifteenth-century *caballero* literature, see Rodríguez Velasco, *El debate*.

22. Valera, *Espejo de verdedera nobleza*, in *Prosistas castellanos del siglo XV*, ed. Mario Penna, BAE 116 (Madrid, 1959), 106.

23. Rodrigo Sánchez de Arévalo, *Suma de la política*, in *Prosistas castellanos del siglo XV*, ed. Mario Penna, BAE 116 (Madrid, 1959), 277: "deve ser todo cavallero bien armado y mal vestido."

24. Johan Huizinga, *The Autumn of the Middle Ages*, trans. Rodney J. Payton and Ulrich Mammitzsch (Chicago, 1996), 119–20.

25. Rosana de Andrés Díaz, "Las fiestas de caballería en la Castilla de los Trastámara," *En la España Medieval* 5 (1986): 82.

26. Rodrigo Sánchez de Arévalo, *Vergel de los príncipes*, in *Prosistas castellanos del siglo XV*, ed. Mario Penna, BAE 116 (Madrid, 1959), 326.

27. On the culture of Castilian knights-errant in the fifteenth century, see Martín de Riquer, *Caballeros andantes españoles* (Madrid, 1967); Víctor Gibello Bravo, "La violencia convertida en espectáculo: Las fiestas caballerescas medievales," in *Fiestas, juegos y espectáculos en la España medieval: Actas del VII Curso de Cultura Medieval, celebrado en Aguilar de Campoo (Palencia) del 18 al 21 de septiembre de 1995* (Aguilar de Campoo, 1999), 157–72.

28. See, for instance, Pedro Rodríguez de Lena, *El passo honroso de Suero de Quiñones*, ed. Amancio Labandeira Fernández (Madrid, 1977); Pedro Carrillo de Huete, *Crónica del halconero de Juan II*, ed. Juan de Mata Carriazo, CCE 8 (Madrid, 1946), 20–22; Lope de Barrientos, *Refundación de la Crónica del halconero*, ed. Juan de Mata Carriazo, CCE 9 (Madrid, 1946), 59–62; Fernán Pérez de Guzmán, *Crónica del príncipe don Juan Segundo*, ed. Cayetano Rosell. BAE 70 (Madrid, 1953), chap. 16; Enríquez de Castillo, *Crónica del rey don Enrique*, chaps. 23–24; Riquer, *Caballeros andantes*, 59; Francisco Rico, "Unas coplas de Jorge Manrique y las fiestas de Valladolid en 1428," *Anuario de Estudios Medievales* 2 (1965): 517–24; Ruiz, "Festivités, couleurs, et symboles du pouvoir"; Andrés Díaz, "Las fiestas de caballería," 94–95.

29. Andrés Díaz, "Las fiestas de caballería," 89–91, describes the presentation of tournaments in several of the most popular romances, including *Curial y Güelfa* and *Tirant lo Blanc*.

30. Ibid., 95. The novelizing of one's life was not unusual. Mary Carruthers, *The Book of Memory: A Study of Memory in Medieval Culture* (Cambridge, 1990), 179–80, in describing how Heloise quoted Cornelia's lament as means of making sense of her entry into a convent, argues that "a modern woman would be very uncomfortable to think she was facing the world with a 'self' constructed out of bits and pieces of great authors of the past, yet I think in large part that is exactly what a medieval self or 'character' was."

31. Huizinga, *Autumn of the Middle Ages*, 85: "Sports retain at all times such a dramatic and erotic element; today's rowing or soccer contests contain much more of the emotional qualities of a medieval tournament than athletes and spectators themselves are perhaps conscious of. But while modern sports have returned to a natural, almost Greek, simplicity and beauty, medieval, or at least late medieval, tournaments were a sport overladen with embellishments and heavily elaborated, in which the dramatic and romantic element was so deliberately worked out that it virtually came to serve the function of drama itself."

32. Carrillo de Huete, *Crónica del halconero*, 20–22; Barrientos, *Refundación*, 59–62; Andrés Díaz, 82–83 n. 4, 91 n. 43; Palomo Fernández and Senra Gabriel y Galán, "La ciudad y la fiesta," 33–34.

33. Ian Macpherson, "The Game of Courtly Love," in Macpherson and MacKay, *Love, Religion and Politics*, 241–43.

34. Carrillo de Huete, *Crónica del halconero*, 228. Only a few months later, the royals returned to Luna's palace for a similar event (231).

35. *Crónica de don Alvaro de Luna, condestable de Castilla, maestre de Santiago*, ed. Juan de Mata Carriazo, CCE 2 (Madrid, 1946), 207. Macpherson explains the wordplay in some examples of *invenciones* from the *Crónica del halconero* in "Game of Courtly Love," 243–44.

36. Carrillo de Huete, *Crónica del halconero*, 154–60.

37. Ibid., 25.

38. Huizinga, *Autumn of the Middle Ages*, 118–19.

39. Francisco Flores Arroyuelo, *El caballero: Hombre y prototipo* (Murcia, 1979), 11–12; Ángel Luis Molina Molina, "Estampas medievales murcianas: Desde la romántica caballeresca, caza y fiesta, a la predicación, procesión y romería," in *Fiestas, juegos y espectáculos en la España medieval: Actas del VII Curso de Cultura Medieval, celebrado en Aguilar de Campoo (Palencia) del 18 al 21 de septiembre de 1995* (Aguilar de Campoo, 1999), 33–34; Torres Fontes, "Don Fernando de Antequera."

40. See, for instance, Thomas Head and Richard Landes, eds., *The Peace of God: Social Violence and Religious Response in France Around the Year 1000* (Ithaca, N.Y., 1992); Bernard of Clairvaux, "In Praise of the New Knighthood," trans. Conrad Greenia, in *The Works of Bernard of Clairvaux*, vol. 7, *Treatises III*, Cistercian Fathers Series 19 (Kalamazoo, Mich., 1977), 127–67; Gregory IX, *Decretalium D. Gregorii Papæ IX*, in *Corpus Iuris Canonici*, ed. Emil Ludwig Richter and Emil Friedberg, 2 vols. (Graz, 1959), 2:804, book 5, tit. 13, "De torneamentis"; John XXII, *Extravagantes tum viginti D. Ioannis Papæ XXII tum communes suæ integritati restitutæ*, in *Corpus Iuris Canonici*, ed. Richter and Friedberg, 2:1215, tit. 9, "De torneamentis"; and Richard W. Kaeuper, *Chivalry and Violence in Medieval Europe* (Oxford, 1999), 80ff.

41. Alfonso de Cartagena, *The Chivalric Vision of Alfonso de Cartagena: Study and Edition of the "Doctrinal de los caualleros"*, ed. Noel Fallows (Newark, Del., 1995), 255 (hereafter, Cartagena, *Doctrinal*). On his career, see Luciano Serrano, *Los conversos D. Pablo de Santa María y D. Alfonso de Cartagena, obispos de Burgos, gobernantes, diplomáticos y escritores* (Madrid, 1942); Luis Fernández Gallardo, *Alfonso de Cartagena, 1385–1456: Una biografía política en la Castilla del siglo XV* (Valladolid, 2002). See also Mario Penna's introductory essay in *Prosistas españoles del siglo XV*, BAE 116 (Madrid, 1959), xxxvii–lxx.

42. Alfonso de Cartagena, *Un tratado de Alonso de Cartagena sobre la educación y los estudios literarios*, ed. Jeremy N. H. Lawrance (Barcelona, 1979), 54: "nullius utilitatis."

43. Iñigo López de Mendoza and Alfonso de Cartagena, "Qüestion fecha por el marqués de Santillana al muy sabio e noble perlado don Alfonso de Cartagena y su respuesta," in *Iñigo López de Mendoza, Marqués de Santillana: Obras completas*, ed. Ángel Gómez Moreno and Maximilian P. A. M. Kerkhof (Barcelona, 1988), 420–22 (previously published in Gómez Moreno, "La qüestion del marqués de Santillana a don Alfonso de Cartagena," *El Crotalón* 2 (1985): 335–63).

44. Cartagena, *Doctrinal*, 255.

45. Ibid., 178.

46. See Noel Fallows, "Introduction," in Cartagena, *Doctrinal*, 29–34; and Fallows, "Just Say No? Alfonso de Cartagena, the *Doctrinal de los caballeros*, and Spain's Most Noble Pastime," in *Studies on Medieval Spanish Literature in Honor of Charles F. Fraker*, ed. Mercedes Vaquero and Alan Deyermond (Madison, Wis., 1995), 129–41.

47. Cartagena, *Doctrinal*, 255. He refers here, and again on 291–92, to the conclusions of the Fourth Lateran Council in 1215, which not only banned tournaments but also linked them to private warfare and general disorder. Fourth Lateran Council, Canon 71, in Henry Joseph Schroeder, *Disciplinary Decrees of the General Councils: Text, Translation and Commentary* (St. Louis, 1937), 236–96. The Latin text of this canon is published in *Constitutiones Concilii Quarti Lateranensis una cum commentariis glossatorum*, ed. Antonio García y García. Monumenta Iuris Canonici, Ser. A: Corpus Glossatorum 2 (Vatican City, 1981), 167–70. Despite this censure, tournaments may not have actually obstructed crusade preparations. Maurice Keen, for instance, has argued that they provided an unparalleled opportunity for advertising the Crusades and recruiting knights, *Chivalry* (New Haven, Conn., 1984), 97ff. See also Fallows's comment in *Doctrinal*, 255 n. 5.

48. On the Order of the Band, see D'Arcy Jonathan Dacre Boulton, *The Knights of the Crown: The Monarchical Orders of Knighthood in Later Medieval Europe, 1325–1520* (New York, 1987), 46–95.

49. Cartagena, *Doctrinal*, 291–302.

50. Sánchez de Arévalo, *Vergel*, 324; Palomo Fernández and Senra Gabriel y Galán, "La ciudad y la fiesta," 9. On his life and works, see Teodoro Toni, "Don Rodrigo Sánchez de Arévalo: Su personalidad y actividades," *Anuario de historia del derecho español* 12 (1935): 97–360; Richard H. Trame, *Rodrigo Sánchez de Arévalo, 1404–1470: Spanish Diplomat and Champion of the Papacy* (Washington, D.C., 1958); Robert B. Tate, "Rodrigo Sánchez de Arévalo (1404–1470) and His *Compendiosa Historia Hispanica*," *Nottingham Medieval Studies* 4 (1960): 58–80; Juan María Laboa, *Rodrigo Sánchez de Arévalo, alcaide de Sant'-Angelo* (Madrid, 1973); and Lorenzo Velázquez Campo, "Rodrigo Sánchez de Arévalo," in *La filosofía española en Castilla y León: De los orígenes al Siglo de Oro*, ed. Maximiliano Fartos Martínez (Valladolid, 1997), 121–36.

51. Sánchez de Arévalo, *Vergel*, 313.

52. Ibid., 314.

53. Ibid., 322–23.

54. Ibid., 323.

55. Cited in Marcellin Defourneaux, *La vida cotidiana en la España del Siglo de Oro* (Barcelona, 1983), 111.

56. Ferrer's journey to Castile is detailed in José María Garganta and Vicente Forcada, *Biografía y escritos de San Vicente Ferrer* (Madrid, 1956); Pedro Manuel Cátedra García, *Sermón, sociedad y literatura en la Edad Media: San Vicente Ferrer en Castilla (1411–1412)* (Salamanca, 1994); Molina Molina, "Estampas medievales murcianas," 52–59;

and Juan Torres Fontes, "Moros, judíos y conversos en la regencia de don Fernando de Antequera," *CHE* 31–32 (1960): 84–85.

57. AMC, *AC* 1434, fol. 48r, and *AC* 1471, fol. 56r; María de los Llanos Martínez Carrillo, "Fiestas ciudadanas: Componentes religiosos y profanos de un cuadro bajamedieval Murcia," *MMM* 16 (1990–1991): 13.

58. Molina Molina, "Estampas medievales murcianas," 53.

59. Ibid., 56–57; Torres Fontes, "Moros, judíos y conversos," 85.

60. *Partidas*, 1:76–77, tit. 5, law 57.

61. Ana Arranz Guzmán provides a detailed study of both synodal records and inspection reports in "Fiestas, juegos y diversiones prohibidas al clero en la Castilla Bajomedieval," *CHE* 78 (2003–2004): 9–33; idem, "Las visitas pastorales a las parroquias de la Corona de Castilla durante la Baja Edad Media: Un primer inventario de obispos visitadores," *En la España Medieval* 26 (2003): 295–339; and Bonifacio Bartolomé Herrero, "Una visita pastoral a la diócesis de Segovia durante los años 1446 y 1447," *En la España Medieval* 18 (1995): 303–49. Antonio García y García summarizes synodal restrictions by category in "Religiosidad popular y festividades en el occidente peninsular (siglos XIII–XIV)," in *Fiestas y Liturgia: Actas del coloquio celebrado en la Casa de Velásquez* (Madrid, 1988), 38ff.

62. The literature on urban festivities is too extensive to be summarized here. Relevant work on the relationship between popular dramatic activities and church or civil authorities on the Castilian frontier includes Pierre Córdoba and Jean-Pierre Etienvre, eds., *La fiesta, la ceremonia, el rito* (Granada, 1990); María Marcela Mantel, "Carácter socioeconómico de los juegos y entretenimientos en Castilla: Siglos XIII al XV," *Estudios de Historia de España* 3 (1990): 51–116; Raquel Homet, "Sobre el espacio de las fiestas en la sociedad medieval," *Temas Medievales* 1 (1991): 143–61; Pedro Gómez García, ed., *Fiestas y religión en la cultura popular andaluza* (Granada, 1992); María de los Llanos Martínez Carrillo, "Elitismo y participación popular en las fiestas medievales," *MMM* 18 (1993–1994): 95–107; Juan José Capel Sánchez, "Murcia como espacio lúdico urbano en la Baja Edad Media," *MMM* 25–26 (2001–2002): 9–22; and Mariana Valeria Parma, "Fiesta y revuelta: La teatralidad política en Valencia a principios de la modernidad," *CHE* 77 (2001–2002): 145–64.

63. Martínez Carrillo, "Fiestas ciudadanas," 17–23, 26.

64. Fernando Lázaro Carreter, *Teatro medieval* (Madrid, 1981), 22. See also his "El drama litúrgico, los 'juegos de escarnio' y el 'Auto de los Reyes Magos'," in *Historia y crítica de la literatura española*, vol. 1, *Edad media*, ed. Alan Deyermond (Barcelona, 1979), 461–65; and "Juegos de escarnio," in *Dictionary of the Literature of the Iberian Peninsula*, ed. Germán Bleiberg, Maureen Ihrie, and Janet Pérez (Westport, Conn., 1993), 897.

65. Palomo Fernández and Senra Gabriel y Galán, "La ciudad y la fiesta," 9–11; Lázaro Carreter, *Teatro medieval*, 24–25.

66. Carrillo de Huete, *Crónica del halconero*, 158.

67. For overviews of these issues, see Angus MacKay, "Popular Movements and Pogroms in Fifteenth-Century Castile," *Past and Present* 55 (1972): 33–67; MacKay,

Money, Prices, and Politics in Fifteenth-Century Castile (London, 1981); Pablo Sánchez León, "Changing Patterns of Urban Conflict in Late Medieval Castile," *Past and Present* 195, supp. 2 (2007): 217–32.

68. See, for instance, Molina Molina, "Estampas medievales murcianas," 59–63.

CHAPTER 2. THE MEANINGS OF CIVIC SPACE

1. *Hechos del condestable*, 376–80; Ruiz comments briefly on these spectacles in "Elite and Popular Culture," 312–13.

2. *Hechos del condestable*, 380.

3. Cf. the hierarchical description of eighteenth-century Montpellier analyzed by Robert Darnton in "A Bourgeois Puts His World in Order: The City as a Text," in *The Great Cat Massacre and Other Episodes in French Cultural History* (New York, 1999), 107–43.

4. Jean-Charles Payen, "Théâtre médiéval et culture urbaine," *Revue d'Histoire du Théâtre* 35 (1983): 233.

5. *Partidas*, 7:1473, tit. 33, law 6, and 2:332, tit. 10, law 1. The literature on urban life in medieval Castile is vast. For an introduction to the historiography of the topic, see Fermín Miranda García, "La ciudad medieval hispana: Una aproximación bibliográfica," in *Las sociedades urbanas en la España medieval: XXIX Semana de Estudios Medievales, Estella, 15 a 19 de julio de 2002* (Pamplona, 2003), 591–626; and María Asenjo González, "Las ciudades medievales castellanas. Balance y perspectivas de su desarrollo historiográfico (1990–2004)," *En la España Medieval* 28 (2005): 415–53. General studies include Manuel Fernando Ladero Quesada, "Consideraciones metodológicas sobre el estudio de los núcleos urbanos en la Castilla bajomedieval: Notas para un modelo teórico de análisis," *Espacio, Tiempo y Forma*, ser. 3, *Historia Medieval* 4 (1991): 353–66; Ángel Luis Molina Molina, *Urbanismo medieval: La región de Murcia* (Murcia, 1992); Teófilo Ruiz, *Crisis and Continuity: Land and Town in Late Medieval Castile* (Philadelphia, 1994); Juan Gelabert, "Cities, Towns and Small Towns in Castile, 1500–1800," in *Small Towns in Early Modern Europe*, ed. Peter Clark (Cambridge, 1995), 271–94; the articles in Juan Antonio Bonachía Hernando, ed., *La ciudad medieval: Aspectos de la vida urbana en la Castilla Bajomedieval* (Valladolid, 1996); and Pablo Sánchez León, "Town and Country in Castile, 1400–1650," in *Town and Country in Europe, 1300–1800*, ed. S. R. Epstein (Cambridge, 2001), 272–91.

6. Brian Robert Tate offers a brief background on the medieval urban *descriptio* genre as it relates to Iberian authors in "*Laus Urbium*: Praise of Two Andalusian Cities in the Mid-Fifteenth Century," in *Medieval Spain: Culture, Conflict, and Coexistence; Studies in Honor of Angus MacKay*, ed. Roger Collins and Anthony Goodman (Basingstoke, 2002), 148–52. Antonio Antelo Iglesias examines Arévalo's classical and medieval sources in "La ciudad ideal según fray Francesc Eiximenis y Rodrigo Sánchez de Arévalo," *En la España Medieval* 6 (1985): 19–50.

7. Sánchez de Arévalo, *Suma de la política*, 264.

8. Ibid., 278.

9. Ibid., 266.

10. For Golden Age treatises on cities, which developed ideas first articulated in the fifteenth century, see Santiago Quesada, *La idea de ciudad en la cultura hispana de la edad moderna* (Barcelona, 1992), especially chaps. 2 and 3; Richard Kagan, "*Urbs* and *Civitas* in Sixteenth- and Seventeenth-Century Spain," in *Envisioning the City: Six Studies in Urban Cartography*, ed. David Buisseret (Chicago, 1998), 75–108; Richard Kagan and Fernando Marías, *Urban images of the Hispanic world, 1493–1793* (New Haven, Conn.2000), 19–44; and Andrea Mariana Navarro, "Pasado y antigüedad clásica en los discursos sobre ciudades: Las *Laudes* en la historiografía andaluza" *Temas Medievales* 16 (2008).

11. Jerónimo of Córdoba, *Córdoba en el siglo XV*, ed. and trans. Manuel Nieto Cumplido (Córdoba, 1973), 43.

12. Ibid., 49.

13. Alfonso de Palencia, *Epístolas latinas*, ed. Robert B. Tate and Rafael Alemany Ferrer (Barcelona, 1982), letter 2,"De laudibus Ispalis," pp. 37–39; Robert Brian Tate, "The Civic Humanism of Alfonso de Palencia," *Renaissance and Modern Studies* 23 (1979): 38.

14. Palencia, *Epístolas*, pp. 36–37.

15. Ibid., 37.

16. Tate, "*Laus Urbium*," 156–57; Alfonso de Palencia, *De perfectione militaris triumphi: La perfeçión del triunfo*, ed. Javier Durán Barceló (Salamanca, 1996), 161–62.

17. Palencia, *Epístolas*, letter 7, "Sapientissimo viro patrique ornatus ac utilis . . . ," 60; for Palencia's other comments on fifteenth-century Rome, see Tate, "Civic Humanism," 30–32.

18. Palencia, *Epístolas*, p. 37; Tate similarly contrasts the river descriptions of Palencia and Jerónimo in "*Laus Urbium*," 154.

19. Palencia, *Epístolas*, 38–39; the population figure is certainly exaggerated, and Tate, "*Laus Urbium*," 154, suggests that sixty thousand would be more likely.

20. Palencia, *Epístolas*, p. 39. See *PCG*, 2:769, chap. 1128.

21. Palencia, *De perfectione militaris*, 140; Tate, "Civic Humanism," 39.

22. Palencia, *Epístolas*, 39.

23. Tate, "Civic Humanism," 34–35.

24. Jerónimo, *Córdoba en el siglo XV*, 44.

25. Ibid., 51–52. Although the Italian community in Córdoba, which Jerónimo never mentions, was far smaller than that of Seville, it was still significant in terms of both numbers and influence. See Manuel Nieto Cumplido, *Historia de Córdoba: Islam y cristianismo* (Córdoba, 1984), 285–86; and Nieto Cumplido, *Córdoba 1492: Ambiente artístico y cultural* (Córdoba, 1992), 57–58.

26. Jerónimo, *Córdoba en el siglo XV*, 50.

27. Ibid.

28. Ibid., 51.

29. Mario Penna, in his introduction to *Prosistas españoles del siglo XV*, suggests that Arévalo chose Castilian in order to better honor Don Pedro de Acuña, to whom the work was dedicated and who did not read Latin, . lxxv–lxxvi.

30. We do not know how long Jerónimo lived in Italy, but the opening line of his *Descriptio* underscores the personal importance of that visit: "Córdoba gave birth to me, Italy made me an adult." Jerónimo, *Córdoba en el siglo XV*, 43.

31. Tate, *"Laus Urbium,"* 158. On humanist influences on Palencia's writings, see Robert Brian Tate and Anscari Mundó, "The *Compendiolum* of Alfonso de Palencia: A Humanist Treatise on the Geography of the Iberian Península," *Journal of Medieval and Renaissance Studies* 5 (1975): 253–78; Ottavio Di Camillo, *El humanismo castellano del siglo XV* (Valencia, 1976), 180ff.; and Antonio Antelo Iglesias, "Alfonso de Palencia: Historiografía y humanismo en la Castilla de siglo XV," *Espacio, Tiempo y Forma* ser. 3, *Historia Medieval* 3 (1990): 21–40.

32. Di Camillo, *El humanismo*, esp. chap. 1; José Rodríguez Molina, *La vida de la ciudad de Jaén en tiempos del condestable Iranzo* (Jaén, 1996), 289.

33. Francisco Delicado, *La Lozana andaluza*, ed. Jacques Joset and Folke Gernert (Barcelona, 2007). The text has been edited a number of times; other recent editions include *La Lozana andaluza*, ed. Bruno M. Damiani (Madrid, 1982); and *Retrato de la Lozana andaluza*, ed. Claude Allaigre (Madrid, 1985). It has also been translated into English and French in *Portrait of Lozana: The Lusty Andalusian Woman*, trans. Bruno M. Damiani, Scripta Humanistica 34 (Potomac, Md., 1987); and *Portrait de la Gaillarde andalouse: Roman*, trans. Claude Bleton (Paris, 1993). All subsequent references are to the Joset and Gernert edition.

34. Delicado, *La Lozana*, 9–10. For what little is known of his life, see Angus MacKay, "Women on the Margins," in Macpherson and MacKay, *Love, Religion and Politics*, 28–29; MacKay, "The Whores of Babylon," in Macpherson and MacKay, *Love, Religion and Politics*, 179. See also Augusta Foley, *La Lozana andaluza*, Critical Guides to Spanish Texts 18 (London, 1977), 25–27; John Edwards, "Conversion in Córdoba and Rome: Francisco Delicado's *La Lozana Andaluza*," in *Medieval Spain: Culture, Conflict, and Coexistence*, ed. Collins and Goodman, 205; and idem, "The Culture of the Street: The Calle de la Feria in Córdoba, 1470–1520," in *Mediterranean Urban Culture, 1400–1700*, ed. Alexander Cowan (Exeter, 2000), 69–70.

35. Delicado, *La Lozana*, 14–15.

36. Edwards, "Culture of the Street," 71–5; idem, "Conversion in Córdoba and Rome," 207–8. On the Calle de la Feria and the surrounding streets, see José Manuel Escobar Camacho, *La vida urbana cordobesa: El Potro y su entorno en la Baja Edad Media* (Córdoba, 1985), 36–40, 56–63; idem, *Córdoba en la Baja Edad Media: Evolución urbana de la ciudad* (Córdoba, 1989), 134–48. Regulations for wool merchants are enumerated in the "Ordenanzas del concejo de Córdoba (1435)," ed. Manuel González Jiménez, *HID* 2 (1975): 194–95, 202, 244.

37. Delicado, *La Lozana*, 14.

38. Ibid., 26.

39. Ibid., 27.

40. Edwards, "Culture of the Street," 75–78, and "Conversion in Córdoba and Rome," 208; "Ordenanzas," ed. González Jiménez, 270; Escobar Camacho, *La vida urbana cordobesa*, 34–35, 65–66.

41. Miguel de Cervantes Saavedra, *El ingenioso hidalgo don Quijote de la Mancha*, ed. Tom Lathrop (Newark, Del., 1997), I.3, p. 32, and I.17, p. 122; "Ordenanzas," ed. González Jiménez, 237; Escobar Camacho, *La vida urbana cordobesa*, 28–32. On the topography and economics of the Potro area, see Jesús Padilla González and José Manuel Escobar Camacho, "La mancebía de Córdoba en la Baja Edad Media," in *La sociedad medieval andaluza, grupos no privilegiados: Actas del III Coloquio de Historia Medieval Andaluza* (Jaén, 1984), 279–92.

42. Ricardo Molina, *Córdoba en sus plazas* (Córdoba, 1962), 16–17.

43. Teodomiro Ramírez de Arellano y Gutiérrez, *Paseos por Córdoba, o sea Apuntes para su historia* (León, 1973), 225–29.

44. Miguel Ángel Ortí Belmonte, *Córdoba monumental, artística e histórica* (Córdoba, 1980), 164–70; Escobar Camacho, *Córdoba en la Baja Edad Media*, 218–19.

45. ACC, caja Z, nos. 52 (1 January 1428) and 296 (30 September 1456); Escobar Camacho, *Córdoba en la Baja Edad Media*, 219.

46. Delicado, *La Lozana*, 70–71.

47. Marcelino Menéndez y Pelayo, *Edición nacional de las obras completas de Menéndez Pelayo* (Madrid, 1940–1959), 25:449–51. The *Cantar* reads in part:

> Al comienzo malo—de mis amores
> convidó Fernando—los Comendadores
> a buenas gallinas—capones mejores . . .
> Jueves era, jueves,—día de mercado,
> y en Sancta Marina—hacían rebato,
> que Fernando dicen —el que es veinticuatro,
> había muerto a Jorge—y a su hermano,
> y a la sin ventura—Doña Beatriz.

This was not the only literary rendition of these events. For the contemporary version penned by the *converso* poet Antón de Montoro, see his "Coplas que fizo Antón de Montoro de Córdoba por la muerte de los dos hermanos comendadores Jorge e Fernando de Córdoba, que mataron un día," in *Cancionero*, ed. Marcella Ciceri and Julio Rodríguez-Puértolas (Salamanca, 1990), 249–54. The theme remained popular in the sixteenth century with renditions by, among others, Juan Gutiérrez Rufo and Lope de Vega. For citations to these, see *Cancionero*, 249.

48. For an in-depth study of these events, see José Manuel Escobar Camacho and Antonio Varo Pineda, *El veinticuatro Fernán Alonso y los comendadores de Córdoba: Historia, literatura y leyenda* (Córdoba, 1999).

49. Delicado, *La Lozana*, 47–48.

50. On his career, see Adelaida Sagarra Gamazo, *Juan Rodríguez de Fonseca, un toresano en dos mundos* (Zamora, 2006).

51. Delicado, *La Lozana*, 242.

52. Martha C. Howell, "The Spaces of Late Medieval Urbanity," in *Shaping Urban Identity in Late Medieval Europe,* ed. Marc Boone and Peter Stabel (Leuven, 2000), 8–9, 14–16.

53. For brief description of each type of element, see Kevin Lynch, *The Image of the City* (Cambridge, 1960), 46–48.

54. The situation and Iranzo's response are described in *Hechos del condestable*, 424–31. Angus MacKay treats these events briefly in the context of ballads and stories as arbiters of communal memory in "Religion, Culture, and Ideology," 235–36.

55. *Hechos del condestable*, 425.

56. Ibid., 426–27.

57. The only other marker to receive a name was dubbed "Buena Vista" (ibid., 428–29).

58. Ibid., 430.

59. Ibid.

60. Mann, *Romanesque Architecture*, esp. chap. 4, "Shaping the Christian Presence in Aragon: The Frontier Fortress-Monasteries of King Sancho Ramírez (r. 1064–94)," 101–31.

61. Ibid., 123–27. Cf. the defensive use of Mary's image at Chincoya described in the introduction to the present book.

62. Cited in Mann, *Romanesque Architecture*, 128.

63. Joaquín Yarza Luazes, *Los Reyes Católicos: Paisaje artístico de una monarquía* (Madrid, 1993), 70; María Estrella Cela Esteban, *Elementos simbólicos en el arte castellano de los Reyes Católicos: El poder real y el patronato regio* (Madrid, 2001), 358–68.

64. On the transformation of fortified urban castles into palaces designed chiefly for political and recreational purposes, see Palomo Fernández and Senra Gabriel y Galán, "La ciudad y la fiesta," 10–15.

65. *Hechos del condestable*, 45–46. A nineteenth-century description of the palace by Valentín Carderera can be found in *Relación de los hechos del muy magnífico e más virtuoso señor, el señor don Miguel Lucas, muy digno condestable de Castilla*, ed. Pascual de Gayango, Memorial histórico español: Colección de documentos, opúsculos, y antigüedades 8 (Madrid, 1855), Appendix D, "Sobre las casas del Condestable en Jaén," 512–17. While the *sala*'s original Mudéjar ceiling and door remain intact, the palace has since been renovated and its exterior façade as well as several of the interior halls date from the 1920s. Tess Knighton discusses both the decoration of the *sala* and its social functions, with an emphasis on musical performances, in "Spaces and Contexts for Listening in 15th-Century Castile: The Case of the Constable's Palace in Jaén," *Early Music* 25 (1997): 661–77.

66. Knighton, "Spaces and Contexts," 669.

67. I use the term "Moorish" in the sense proposed by Barbara Fuchs, as a means to refer to practices that reflected the cultural legacy of al-Andalus. This term better reflects that of the sources—*moro*—than does "Islamicate." Fuchs, *Exotic Nation*, 6.

68. Ruiz, "Elite and Popular Culture," 311–13; Knighton, "Spaces and Contexts," 663, 666; Rodríguez Molina, *La vida de la ciudad*, 293.

69. See, for instance, recent work on access analysis such as Sheila Bonde and Clark Maines,"*Ne aliquis extraneus claustrum intret*: Entry and Access at the Augustinian Abbey of Saint-Jean-des-Vignes, Soissons," in *Perspectives for an Architecture of Solitude: Essays on Cistercians, Art and Architecture in Honour of Peter Fergusson*, ed. Terryl N. Kinder, Medieval Church Studies 11, Studia et Documenta 13 (Turnhout, 2004), 173–86; and Amanda Richardson, "Corridors of Power: A Case Study in Access Analysis from Medieval England," *Antiquities* 77 (2003): 373–84.

70. Capel Sánchez, "Murcia como espacio lúdico urbano," 10–11; José Damián González Arce and Francisco José García Pérez, "Ritual, jerarquías y símbolos en las exequias reales de Murcia (siglo XV)," *MMM* 19–20 (1995–1996): 129–38; Parma, "Fiesta y revuelta,"145–64. Teofilo Ruiz offers a thorough analysis of how such symbolic representations of power were deployed during a series of spectacles sponsored by Juan II at Valladolid in 1428 in his "Festivités, couleurs, et symboles du pouvoir," 521–46.

71. *Hechos del condestable*, 54.

72. Luis Rubio García has painstakingly reconstructed fifteenth-century preparations for Corpus Christi in Murcia in *La procesión de Corpus en el siglo XV en Murcia* (Murcia, 1987).

73. AMM, *AC* 1469–1470, 6 June 1470, fol. 121v: "Por quanto los días del Cuerpo de Dios los regidores e ofiçiales del dicho Conçejo que van aconpannar el Cuerpo de Nuestro Sennor Jhesu Xpristo estan muy apretados entre la gentre que alli andan quando pasan los entremeses que van en la prosysión en tal manera que los regidores e ofiçiales del dicho Conçejo buenamente nos puden asy bien mirar los dichos entremeses por toda rason los dichos sennores conçejo ordenaron e mandaron a Juan Nunnes de Astudillo su mayordomo que faga faser un cadafalgo de madera para que esten los dichos regidores e ofiçiales del dicho Conçejo para mirar desde alli la dicha prosysyon."

74. AMM, *AC* 1479–1480, 27 May 1480, fol. 222v.

75. AMM, *AC* 1480–1481, 16 June 1481, fol. 170. "Otrosy dieron cargo a Antonio Hurtado jurado para los cadalsos que se ovieron de faser en la Traperia . . . e mandaron que ninguno non faga cadalso en la dicha calle de la Traperia el dia del Corpus Xpristi syn el dicho Antonio Hurtado so pena de quinientos maravedis la terçia parte para el acusador e las dos terçias partes para la hermandad." A similar resolution had been passed several years earlier; see AMM, *AC* 1474–1475, 30 July 1474, fol. 59. The Santa Hermandad, or Holy Brotherhood, was a national militia force established in 1476 as an extension of local *hermandades*.

76. AMM, *AC* 1480–1481, 19 June 1481, fol. 171.

77. AMM, *AC* 1481–1482, 1 June 1482, fol. 255; a similar arrangement is documented in AMM, *AC* 1483–1484, 12 June 1484, fol. 60r.

78. Capel Sánchez, "Murcia como espacio lúdico urbano," 18.

CHAPTER 3. KNIGHTS, MAGI, AND MUSLIMS

1. *Ordenanzas de la muy noble, famosa y muy leal ciudad de Jaén, guarda y defendimiento de los reinos de Castilla*, ed. Pedro A. Porras Arboledas (Granada, 1993), 74. The full title was "La muy noble, famosa y muy leal ciudad de Jaén, guarda y defendimiento de los reinos de Castilla." See José Rodríguez Molina, "Jaén: Organización de sus tierras y hombres (siglos XIII–XVI)," in *Historia de Jaén* (Jaén, 1982), 216–17; idem, "La frontera entre Granada y Jaén: Fuente de engrandecimiento para la nobleza," in *Relaciones exteriores del Reino de Granada: IV Coloquio de historia medieval andaluza*, ed. Cristina Segura Graíño (Almería, 1988), 237–50;

2. José Martínez de Mazas, *Retrato al natural de la ciudad y términos de Jaén*, ed. José Rodríguez Molina (Barcelona, 1978); Rafael Machado Santiago and Emilio Arroyo López, "El territorio y el hombre (análisis geográfico): Jaén," in *Historia de Jaén* (Jaén, 1982), 15–48.

3. José Rodríguez Molina emphatically argues for the centrality of peaceful transfrontier relations among nonelite members of society. See his *La vida de la ciudad*, 103–32; and *La vida de moros y cristianos*, 11–19. Several other scholars have advocated similar readings of the *actas capitulares*. See Juan de Mata Carriazo, "Relaciones fronterizas entre Jaén y Granada: El año 1479," in *En la frontera de Granada*, 237–64; Carriazo, "Los moros de Granada en las actas del concejo de Jaén de 1479," *En la frontera de Granada*, 265–310; Juan Carlos Garrido Aguilera, "Relaciones fronterizas con el reino de Granada en las Capitulares del Archivo Histórico Municipal de Jaén," in *Relaciones exteriores del Reino de Granada: IV Coloquio de historia medieval andaluza*, ed. Cristina Segura Graíño (Almería, 1988), 161–72; Pedro A. Porras Arboledas, "Las relaciones entre la ciudad de Jaén y el reino de Granada: La paz y la guerra según el libros de Actas de 1480 y 1488," *Al-Qantara* 9, fasc. 1 (1988): 29–46; idem, "El comercio entre Jaén y Granada en 1480," *Al-Qantara* 9, fasc. 2 (1988): 519–24; and idem, "La frontera del Reino de Granada a través del Libro de Actas del Cabildo de Jaén de 1476," *Al-Qantara* 14, fasc. 1 (1993): 127–62. Other relevant works on frontier relations in Jaén include José Rodríguez Molina, "Banda territorial común entre Granada y Jaén: Siglo XV," in *Estudios sobre Málaga y el Reino de Granada en el V Centenario de la Conquista* (Málaga, 1987), 113–30; and Carmen Argente del Castillo Ocaña, "Los cautivos en la frontera entre Jaén y Granada," in *Relaciones exteriores del Reino de Granada: IV Coloquio de historia medieval andaluza*, ed. Cristina Segura Graíño (Almería, 1988), 211–26.

4. On his early life, see Lorenzo Galíndez de Carvajal, "Adiciones genealógicas a los Claros varones de Fernán Pérez de Guzmán, señor de Batres," in Colección de documentos inéditos para la historia de España, vol. 18 (Madrid, 1851), 453. Many additional details are found in Pascual de Gayangos y Arce's appendixes to his edition of the *Hechos, Relación de los fechos del mui magnífico e mas virtuosos señor, el señor don Miguel Lucas, mui digno Condestable de Castilla*. Memorial histórico español: Colección de documentos, opúsculos, y antigüedades 8 (Madrid, 1855). These were compiled from notes in the Salazar manuscript (Real Academia de la Historia, D-117) and from a "libro viejo de Cabildo del

Archivo de Baeza." See also Rodríguez Molina, *La vida de la ciudad*, 231–32; and Palencia, *Crónica de Enrique IV*, 1:82; Miguel Lucas is described as "natural nascido en la villa de Belmonte" in his patent of nobility, in "Cédula del rey don Enrique haciendo noble a Miguel Lucas de Iranzo con señalamiento de las armas que debía traer en el escudo: En el real sobre Granada 12 de junio de 1455," in *Memorias de don Enrique IV de Castilla*, Colección diplomática de Enrique IV (Madrid, 1913), 2:141. Cf. the introduction to Carriazo's edition of the *Hechos del condestable*, xxxviii–xxxix.

5. *Crónica anónima de Enrique IV de Castilla, 1454–1474*, ed. Maria Pilar Sánchez-Parra García (Madrid, 1991), 13; Enrique Toral Peñaranda, *Jaén y el condestable Miguel Lucas de Iranzo* (Jaén, 1987), 13–14. On the ambiguous role of a *criado* in a noble household, see Angus MacKay, "Religion, Culture, and Ideology," 233.

6. *Crónica anónima de Enrique IV*, 16; Toral Peñaranda, *Jaén y el condestable*, 14–18; Rodríguez Molina, *La vida de la ciudad*, 237. The *halconero mayor*'s access to the monarch and all aspects of courtly life is exemplified by Miguel Lucas's predecessor Pedro Carrillo de Huete, who wrote a detailed account of events from 1435 to 1454. Carrillo's chronicle was reworked by the influential bishop Lope de Barrientos, who likely had a hand in Miguel Lucas's entry to court. See Carrillo de Huete, *Crónica del halconero*; and Barrientos, *Refundición*.

7. Enríquez del Castillo, *Crónica del rey don Enrique*, 149–58.

8. Valera, *Memorial de diversas hazañas*, 22–23. A nearly identical account is found in the *Crónica anónima de Enrique IV*, 40–41.

9. Palencia, *Crónica de Enrique IV*, 1:71. Palencia thought this habit indicative of Enrique's vicious nature and disgraceful attitude toward his office and the good men of the realm.

10. Diego de Valera, *Memorial de diversas hazañas*, 23; *Crónica anónima de Enrique IV*, 41; "Cédula del rey don Enrique," 141, 143; María del Pilar Carcaller Cerviño, "El ascenso político de Miguel Lucas de Iranzo: Ennoblecimiento y caballería al servicio de la monarquía," *BIEG* 176 (2000): 18–19.

11. "Cédula del rey don Enrique," 142–43.

12. Valera, *Memorial de diversas hazañas*, 48. The ceremony is described in detail in *Hechos del condestable*, 6–11.

13. *Hechos del condestable*, 10.

14. A number of historians have referred to the years 1457–1463 as the time of "Villena's government of Castile." See Nancy F. Marino, *Don Juan Pacheco: Wealth and Power in Late Medieval Spain* (Tempe, Ariz., 2006), 67–90. On the rivalry between Iranzo and Villena, see Lucien Clare and Michel García, "La guerre entre factions ou clientèles dans la crónica de Miguel Lucas de Iranzo," in *Frontières andalouses: La vie a' Jae'n entre 1460 et 1471, d'après "Los hechos del condestable Miguel Lucas de Iranzo"*, ed. Jacques Heers (Paris, 1996), 137–39.

15. Palencia, *Crónica de Enrique IV*, 1:62–63.

16. When Enrique did choose a master, it was, ironically, another young aspirant pushed to the fore by Villena in order to supplant Miguel Lucas. Beltrán de la Cueva held

the office from 1463 to 1467, at which time Villena finally secured the appointment and was master until his death in 1474. Villena's complaints are also ironic in that he too was an *hombre nuevo*, whose rise under Juan II was similar to that of Miguel Lucas.

17. *Hechos del condestable*, 18–19.

18. Ibid., 27.

19. Ibid., 30–31.

20. The authorship of the *Hechos del condestable* has been the subject of much debate. Carriazo and many others agree that Pedro de Escavias, *alcaide* of Andújar and the constable's friend and ally, is the most likely candidate. See, for instance, *Hechos del condestable*, xxv; Juan Bautista Avalle-Arce, *El cronista Pedro de Escavias: Una vida del siglo XV* (Chapel Hill, N.C., 1972), 20–22; and Michel García, "A propos de la chronique du connètable Miguel Lucas de Iranzo," *Bulletin hispanique* 75 (1973): 5–39. Rodríguez Molina, however, argues in favor of Diego Fernández de Iranzo, in *La vida de la ciudad*, 429–92. In any case, the chronicle was almost certainly by a contemporary who greatly admired the constable and had regular and intimate access to him, suggesting that the work reflects the attitudes of those in Miguel Lucas's circle and perhaps of the constable himself.

21. *Crónica anónima de Enrique IV*, 85. A nearly identical account was appended to the Salazar manuscript of the *Hechos del condestable*, and published as "Appendix A" in Gayango's edition of that text, 495–96. Palencia commented on this as well in *Crónica de Enrique IV*, 1:106–7.

22. Marino, *Don Juan Pacheco*, 75–76; Townsend Miller, *Henry IV of Castile, 1425–1474* (Philadelphia, 1972), 103–7.

23. Palencia, *Crónica de Enrique IV*, 1:105–6.

24. Juan Torres Fontes, for instance, has argued that "Miguel Lucas de Iranzo, lacking the political genius and ambitions of don Alvaro Luna, did not want to fight to defend the position which the king had assigned him. Without grand aspirations and prudent in the face of the scant security that Enrique's personality offered, he was attracted by the more tranquil and bourgeois life possible in Jaén and chose to remove himself from the intrigues and conspiracies. There he could build a strong military force to consolidate his territories and secure his sector of the frontier with Granada" ("Los condestables de Castilla en la Edad Media," *Anuario de historia del derecho español* 41 [1971]: 89).

25. Enrique Toral Peñaranda describes the betrothal arrangements in *Jaén y el condestable*, 14–15. On the Torres family, see Rodríguez Molina, *La vida de la ciudad*, 223–31. On Teresa de Torres, see María del Consuelo Díez Bedmar, *Teresa de Torres (ca. 1442–1521): Condesa de Castilla* (Madrid, 2004).

26. Iranzo's military campaigns are described in detail in the *Hechos del condestable* and receive numerous mentions in Palencia's *Crónica de Enrique IV*. For syntheses, see Rodríguez Molina, *La vida de la ciudad*, 75–103; and Mateo Antonio Páez García, "El condestable Iranzo y la frontera con Granada: Un itinerario de sus actividades militares," in *Andalucía entre Oriente y Occidente (1236–1492): Actas del V Coloquio Internacional de Historia Medieval de Andalucía*, ed. Emilio Cabrera (Córdoba, 1988), 385–98.

27. Palencia, *Crónica de Enrique IV*, 1:183.

28. *Hechos del condestable*, 65–66.

29. José Rodríguez Molina, *El reino de Jaén en la baja Edad Media: Aspectos demográficos y económicos* (Granada, 1978), 54–56.

30. *Hechos del condestable*, 66.

31. Ibid., 89.

32. The clearest statement of this is a letter Iranzo wrote to Pope Sixtus IV on 15 October 1471 in which he pledged that he and his followers would devote "all our possessions, our wives, our children, our freedom, our homeland, and in the end, our lives" to the "holy exercise" (*santo exerçiçio*) of fighting Granada (*Hechos del condestable*, 471, 474–75).

33. *Hechos del condestable*, 164.

34. Ibid., 63–64, 123, 166; Lucien Clare, "Les formes dramatiques primitives du théâtre espagnol d'après 'Los hechos del condestable don Miguel Lucas de Iranzo' (1460–1470)," in *Frontières andalouses*, ed. Heers, 85–86; Rodríguez Molina, *La vida de la ciudad*, 300–301; Francis Very, "A Fifteenth-Century Spanish Easter Egg Combat and Some Parallels," *Romance Notes* 4 (1962): 66–69.

35. *Hechos del Condestable*, 52.

36. Miguel Lucas's campaign of 1462 is described in *Hechos del condestable*, 76–94; and summarized in Rodríguez Molina, *La vida de la ciudad*, 81–85; and Paéz García, "El condestable Iranzo y la frontera."

37. *Hechos del condestable*, 95–96.

38. Ibid., 98.

39. Ibid., 99.

40. Surtz, *Birth of a Theatre*, 81–2; MacKay, "Religion, Culture, and Ideology, 227; Stern, "Christmas Performances in Jaén in the 1460s," 326.

41. Lucien Clare, "Fêtes, jeux et divertissements," 25–9.

42. MacKay, "Religion, Culture, and Ideology," 235, 239.

43. *Hechos del condestable*, 47–48.

44. AMJ, *AC* 1476, fols. 27v, 37v–38r, and 198r; AMJ, *AC* 1480, 80r–84v; AMJ, *Ordenanzas de Jaén*, fols. 105v, 160r, 161v; Rodríguez Molina, *La vida de la ciudad*, 104–17; Garrido Aguilera, "Relaciones fronterizas," 166; Porras Arboledas, "Las relaciones entre la ciudad de Jaén y el reino de Granada"; and idem, "El comercio entre Jaén y Granada."

45. Ruiz, "Elite and Popular Culture," 298; Rodríguez Molina, *La vida de la ciudad*, 16–20. For other examples of popular unrest in contemporary Castile, see Sánchez León, "Changing Patterns of Urban Conflict," 217–32; Emilio Cabrera Muñoz and Andrés Moros, *Fuenteovejuna: La violencia antiseñorial en el siglo XV* (Barcelona, 1991), esp. 137, 142, 150; and Julio Valdeón, *Los conflictos sociales en el reino de Castilla en los siglos XIV y XV* (Madrid, 1975).

46. Ruiz, "Elite and Popular Culture," 309, 315.

47. On the popularity of Muslim styles of dress, see Carmen Bernis, "Modas moriscas en la sociedad cristiana española del siglo XV y principios del XVI," *Boletín de la Real*

Academia de la Historia 144 (1959): 199–228. On the context for the Mudéjar features of Iranzo's palace, see above, Chapter 2.

48. Max Harris, *Aztecs, Moors, and Christians: Festivals of Reconquest in Mexico and Spain* (Austin, Tex., 2000), 58–59.

49. For a discussion of dialogues between communities and authority in another context, see Cristina Jular Pérez-Alfaro, "The King's Face on the Territory: Royal Officers, Discourse, and Legitimating Practices in Thirteenth- and Fourteenth-Century Castile," in *Building Legitimacy: Political Discourses and Forms of Legitimation in Medieval Societies*, ed. Isabel Alfonso, Hugh Kennedy, and Julio Escalona (Leiden, 2004), 107–38.

50. *Hechos del condestable*, 152–53.

51. Ibid., 70.

52. Ibid., 71; Stern, "Christmas Performances," 328.

53. *Hechos del condestable*, 102. Ruiz, "Elite and Popular Culture," 297, claims that this "fool" was meant to represent "a sworn enemy of the constable," presumably Villena. But the mastership remained in Enrique's custody at this time and would only be given to Cueva in the following year. Villena did not become master of Santiago until 1467. Given Miguel Lucas's own past flirtation with the office, perhaps this character was intended to personify the foolishness of the cutthroat struggles for position at court.

54. *Hechos del condestable*, 102.

55. Ibid., 101.

56. Ibid., 103–9; Rodríguez Molina, *La vida de la ciudad*, 85–86.

57. *Hechos del condestable*, 110.

58. Ibid.

59. Ibid., 111–12.

60. Ibid., 112.

61. Harris, *Aztecs, Moors, and Christians*, 55.

62. *Hechos del condestable*, 187–95. Harris sees this as an attempt to present the Muslims as feminine and childish; see his *Aztecs, Moors, and Christians*, 56–57. See also Ruiz, "Elite and Popular Culture," 304–5.

63. For these examples, see *Hechos del condestable*, 95, 116–17, 132, 169–72, 257–59. Rodríguez Molina offers an overview of tournaments involving Muslim attire in *La vida de la ciudad*, 299–300. See also Angustias Contreras Villar, "La Corte de Condestable Iranzo: La ciudad y la fiesta," *En la España Medieval* 10 (1987): 305–22.

64. Luis Coronas Tejada, *Conversos and Inquisition in Jaén* (Jerusalem, 1998), 11–22; and idem, *Los judíos en Jaén* (Jaén, 2008), 27–50.

65. *Hechos del condestable*, 372–73 (emphasis added).

66. Ibid., 374–75.

67. On the spread of anti-*converso* riots from Córdoba to Jaén, see Rodríguez Molina, *La vida de la ciudad*, 385–93.

68. Michel García, "Una carta inédita del condestable Miguel Lucas de Iranzo," *BIEG* 53 (1967): 15–22; Toral Peñaranda, *Jaén y el condestable*, 110–11; Rodríguez Molina, *La vida de la ciudad*, 392–93.

69. Palencia, *Crónica de Enrique IV*, 2:88. Diego de Valera's account of the uprising is similar in nearly all the details, in *Memorial de diversas hazañas*, 243–44.

70. Palencia, *Crónica de Enrique IV*, 2:89.

71. Ibid.

72. Ibid. Miguel Lucas's death is also recorded in Pedro de Escavias, *Repertorio de principes de España y obra poética del alcaide Pedro de Escavias*, ed. Michel García (Jaén, 1972), 368. For the attack on the *converso* community, see Luis Coronas Tejada, "El motín antijudio de 1473 en Jaén," in *Proceedings of the Seventh World Congress of Jewish Studies*, ed. Israel Gutman, 2 vols. (Jerusalem, 1981), 2:141–77.

73. AMJ, *AC* 1476, fols. 5r–5v; José Rodríguez Molina, *Colección diplomática del Archivo histórico municipal de Jaén: Siglos XIV y XV* (Jaén, 1985), doc. xii.

74. Coronas Tejada, *Conversos and Inquisition*, 23–24.

CHAPTER 4. A "CHANCE ACT"

1. Palencia, *Crónica de Enrique IV*, 2:86. See also the less detailed but fundamentally similar account by Valera in his *Memorial de diversas hazañas*, 240–42. The events here are given scholarly treatment in Manuel Nieto Cumplido, "La revuelta contra los conversos de Córdoba en 1473," in *Homenaje de Antón de Montoro en el V centenario de su muerte* (Montoro, 1977), 29–49; Margarita Cabrera Sánchez, "El problema converso en Córdoba: El incidente de la Cruz del Rastro," in *La Península Ibérica en la era de los descubrimientos, 1391–1492: Actas de las III Jornadas Hispano-Portuguesas de Historia Medieval*, 2 vols. (Seville, 1997), 1:331–39; and John Edwards, "The 'Massacre' of Jewish Christians in Córdoba, 1473–1474," in *The Massacre in History*, ed. Mark Levene and Penny Roberts (New York, 1999), 55–68.

2. Palencia, *Crónica de Enrique IV*, 2:86; Valera, *Memorial de diversas hazañas*, 241.

3. Palencia, *Crónica de Enrique IV*, 2:86.

4. Ibid., 87.

5. Ibid.

6. Ibid.

7. Ibid. Valera's description, *Memorial de diversas hazañas*, 242, reads as a summary of Palencia's, only leaving out some of the details: "And so the *converso* homes, and some belonging to Old Christians, were burned and robbed, and many were killed, and many virgins defiled and matrons dishonored, and some killed. There was no kind of cruelty that was not practiced that day by the looters."

8. Palencia, *Crónica de Enrique IV*, 2:87–88, 128–30; Valera, *Memorial de diversas hazañas*, 243.

9. This is according to Palencia's dating. Valera states that the disturbances took place in April, with the culminating attack on 17 April, or Holy Saturday. Evidence from the cathedral archives, however, confirms Palencia's report that they occurred in March,

as does Escavias, *Repertorio*, 230. Enríquez del Castillo gave no date in his brief mention of the violence, *Crónica del rey don Enrique*, 214.

10. Antón de Montoro, "A don Alonso de Aguilar, quando la destruición de los conversos de Córdoba," in *Cancionero*, 294–95.

11. Ibid., 291.

12. See, for instance, Anton van den Wyngaerde's 1567 depiction of Córdoba, in Richard Kagan, ed., *Spanish Cities of the Golden Age: The Views of Anton van den Wyngaerde* (Berkeley, Calif., 1989), 257–60; or the anonymous sixteenth-century drawing of Córdoba published in Jerónimo, *Córdoba en el siglo XV*, 73. Howell, "Spaces of Late Medieval Urbanity," 20–23, describes a series of similar representations.

13. Margarita Cabrera Sánchez, "Los corregidores de Córdoba en el siglo XV," *Meridies: Revista de Historia Medieval* 2 (1995): 95–108; eadem, "Los regidores de Córdoba en 1480: Aproximación prosopográfica," *Meridies: Revista de Historia Medieval* 3 (1996): 61–88.

14. For a detailed description of municipal government in Córdoba, see Edwards, *Christian Córdoba*, 24–57.

15. Escobar Camacho, *Córdoba en la Baja Edad Media*, 287–88; Edwards, *Christian Córdoba*, 133, 139–43; María Concepción Quintanilla Raso, "Estructuras sociales y familiares y papel político de la nobleza cordobesa (siglos XIV y XV)," *En la España Medieval* 3 (1982): 331–52; Marie-Claude Gerbet, "La population noble dans la royaume de Castille vers 1500: La répartition géographique de ses différentes composantes," *Anales de Historia Antigua y Medieval* 20 (1977–1979): 78–99. For the general condition of the Cordoban elite, see Margarita Cabrera Sánchez, *Nobleza, oligarquía y poder en Córdoba al final de la Edad Media* (Córdoba, 1998).

16. John Edwards, "Nobleza y religión: Don Alonso de Aguilar (1447–1501)," *Ámbitos: Revista de Estudios de Ciencias Sociales y Humanidades de Córdoba* 3 (2000): 9–19; Edwards, *Christian Córdoba*, 131–63; María Concepción Quintanilla Raso, *Nobleza y señoríos en el reino de Córdoba: La casa de Aguilar (siglos XIV–XV)* (Córdoba, 1979); eadem, "El dominio de las ciudades por la nobleza: El caso de Córdoba en la segunda mitad del siglo XV," *En la España Medieval* 10 (1987): 109–24; eadem, "Estructura y función de los bandos nobiliarios en Córdoba a fines de la Edad Media," in *Bandos y querellas dinásticas en España al final de la Edad Media* (Paris, 1991), 135–55; eadem, "La caballería cordobesa a finales de la Edad Media: Análisis de un conflicto social urbano," in *Villes et sociétés urbaines au Moyen Âge*, ed. Pierre Desportes (Paris, 1994), 121–32; and José Luis del Pino García, "El concejo de Córdoba a finales de la Edad Media: Estructura interna y política municipal," *HID* 20 (1993): 355–402.

17. On the status of *hidalgos* in fifteenth- and sixteenth-century Castile more generally, see Michael Crawford, *The Fight for Status and Privilege in Late Medieval and Early Modern Castile, 1465–1598* (University Park, Pa., 2014).

18. John Edwards, "A Society Organized for War? Córdoba in the Time of Ferdinand and Isabella," in *Jews, Muslims and Christians in and Around the Crown of Aragon: Essays in Honour of Professor Elena Lourie*, ed. Harvey J. Hames (Leiden, 2004), 92–96.

On the traditional urban liberties of the frontier the *caballeros* professed to defend, see Sánchez-Albornoz, "The Frontier and Castilian Liberties," 27–46.

19. Escobar Camacho, *Córdoba en la Baja Edad Media*, 292–314; idem, *La vida urbana cordobesa*, 105.

20. On fourteenth- and early fifteenth-century strife, see Emilio Mitre Fernández, "Córdoba y su campiña: Una comarca fronteriza al comenzar el siglo XV," *Cuadernos de Estudios Medievales* 1 (1973): 9–32; Manuel Nieto Cumplido, "Luchas nobiliarias y movimientos populares en Córdoba a fines del siglo XIV," in *Tres estudios de historia medieval andaluza*, ed. Manuel Riu Riu, Cristóbal Torres, and Manuel Nieto Cumplido (Córdoba, 1977), 11–65; and Fernando Maza Romero, "Tensiones sociales en el municipio cordobés en la primera mitad del siglo XV," in *Actas del I Congreso de Historia de Andalucía*, 8 vols. (Córdoba, 1978), 2:85–112.

21. Escobar Camacho, *Córdoba en la Baja Edad Media*, 293.

22. Ibid., 191–23, 303, 307, 311; Escobar Camacho, *La vida urbana cordobesa*, 105; Josefa Leva Cuevas, "Escribanos y notarios en la Castilla Bajomedieval: Su ejercicio en la Córdoba de la época," *Ambitos: Revista de Estudios de Ciencias Sociales y Humanidades* 21 (2009): 63–93. The extant data permit classification by occupation only and not by wealth. These broad categories thus do not distinguish between, for instance, the wealthy merchant and the humble shopkeeper. Nor do they take into account social capital by outlining the distribution of those who claimed *hidalgo* or *caballero* status.

23. See Margarita Cabrera Sánchez, "La vivienda noble en Córdoba durante el siglo XV," in *Córdoba en la Historia: La construcción de la urbe*, ed. Francisco R. García Verdugo and Francisco Acosta Ramírez (Córdoba, 1999), 263–70.

24. Escobar Camacho, *Córdoba en la Baja Edad Media*, 123–48, 307; Josefa Leva Cuevas, "Una elite en el mundo artesanal de la Córdoba de los siglos XV y XVI: Plateros, joyeros y esmaltadores," *Ámbitos: Revista de Estudios de Ciencias Sociales y Humanidades* 16 (2006): 99–115; Margarita Cabrera Sánchez, "Oligarquía urbana y negocio inmobiliario en Córdoba en la segunda mitad del siglo XV," *HID* 20 (1993): 107–26; Edwards, *Christian Córdoba*, 166–67.

25. Richard Kagan, *Lawsuits and Litigants in Castile, 1500–1700* (Chapel Hill, N.C., 1981), 18–19.

26. Edwards, *Christian Córdoba*, 127–30.

27. Manuel Nieto Cumplido, "Religiosidad popular andaluza: La regla medieval de la Cofradía de Animas de Castro del Río (Córdoba)," *Revista del Centro de Estudios Históricos de Granada y su Reino* 16 (2004): 257–82.

28. While the dearth of detailed sources means that no systematic study of the confraternities of medieval Córdoba has been attempted, such work is available for several other Iberian cities. See, for instance, Marie-Claude Gerbet, "Les confréries religieuses à Cáceres de 1467 à 1523," *MCV* 7 (1971): 75–114; Rafael Ángel Martínez González, *Las cofradías Penitenciales de Palencia* (Palencia, 1979); Maureen Flynn, *Sacred Charity: Confraternities and Social Welfare in Spain, 1400–1700* (Ithaca, N.Y., 1989) (where the focus is on Zamora); Antonio Gil Albarracín, *Cofradías y hermandades en la Almería moderna (historia y documentos)* (Barcelona, 1997); Susan Verdi Webster, *Art and Ritual in Golden-Age Spain:*

Sevillian Confraternities and the Processional Sculpture of Holy Week (Princeton, N.J., 1998); and Manuel Benítez Bolorinos, *Las cofradías medievales en el Reino de Valencia, 1329–1458* (Alicante, 1998). There is a vast literature on European confraternities that explores both their devotional and social aspects. Useful introductions include André Vauchez, *The Laity in the Middle Ages: Religious Beliefs and Devotional Practices* (South Bend, Ind., 1993); Catherine Vincent, *Les confréries médiévales dans le Royaume de France, XIII–XVe siècle* (Paris, 1994); Katherine A. Lynch, *Individuals, Families and Communities in Europe, 1200– 1800* (Cambridge, 2003), esp. 87–102 and 111ff.; and the articles in Bernard Dompnier and Paola Vismara, eds., *Confréries et dévotions dans la catholicité moderne (mi-XVe–début XIXe siècle)*, Collection de l'École Française de Rome, 393 (Rome, 2008). For the number of confraternities in Córdoba, see Ramírez de Arellano, *Paseos por Córdoba*, 41, 137, 207.

29. Miguel Ángel Ladero Quesada, "Producción y renta cerealeras en el reino de Córdoba a finales del siglo XV," in *Actas del I Congreso de Historia de Andalucía* (Córdoba, 1978), 1:387–88; Iluminado Sanz Sancho, "El poder episcopal en Córdoba en la Baja Edad Media," *En la España Medieval* 13 (1990): 163–206; Edwards, *Christian Córdoba*, 164–70.

30. Miguel Ángel Ladero Quesada, *Los mudéjares de Castilla en tiempos de Isabel I* (Valladolid, 1969), 91–92; Escobar Camacho, *Córdoba en la Baja Edad Media*, 110–12, 291; Juan Aranda Doncel, *Los moriscos en tierras de Córdoba* (Córdoba, 1984), 41–45; Edwards, *Christian Córdoba*, 177–79. There are no works in English on the general condition of the *mudéjares* in Castile to match those centered on Aragón such as John Boswell's *The Royal Treasure: Muslim Communities Under the Crown of Aragon in the Fourteenth Century* (New Haven, Conn., 1977); and Brian Catlos's *The Victors and the Vanquished: Christians and Muslims in Catalonia and Aragon, 1050–1300* (Cambridge, 2001). A useful introduction to relatively recent work on this topic, however, can be found in Manuel González Jiménez and Isabel Montes Romero-Camacho, "Los mudéjares andaluces (siglos XIII–XV) aproximación al estado de la cuestión y propuesta de un modelo teórico," in *Los mudéjares valencianos y peninsulares*, ed Manuel Ruzafa (Valencia, 2004), 47–78.

31. Yitzhak Baer, *A history of the Jews in Christian Spain*, trans. Louis Schoffman. 2 vols. (Philadelphia, 1961–1966), 2:95–169; Philippe Wolff, "The 1391 Pogrom in Spain: Social Crisis or Not?" *Past and Present* 50 (1971): 4–18; Nieto Cumplido, "Luchas nobiliarias," 43–46. Angus MacKay has focused particularly on the economic contexts of anti-Semitic violence in Castile. See his "The Hispanic-*Converso* Predicament," *Transactions of the Royal Historical Society*, 5th ser., 35 (1985): 159–79; idem, "Popular Movements;" and idem, "Climate and Popular Unrest in Late Medieval Castile," in *Climate and History: Studies in Past Climates and Their Impact on Man*, ed. Thomas M. L. Wigley, Martin J. Ingram, and G. Farmer (Cambridge, 1981), 356–76. Mark Meyerson's study of the Jewish community in Morvedre, a small town in Valencia, has recently challenged the accepted view of an overall decline in Jewish fortunes after 1391. See his *A Jewish Renaissance in Fifteenth-Century Spain*.

32. Escobar Camacho, *Córdoba en la Baja Edad Media*, 108–9.

33. Margarita Cabrera Sánchez, through extensive research in surviving notarial documents, has developed a detailed study of one prominant *converso* family, in "Los conversos de Córdoba en el siglo XV: La familia del jurado Martín Alonso," *Anuario de Estudios Medievales* 35 (2005): 185–232.

34. MacKay, "Hispanic-*Converso* Predicament," 163; and "Popular Movements," 46–48. The *conversos'* visibility and the success of their entry into the highest ranks in the realm is attested by the proportion of authors mentioned in this study who either had themselves converted or had *converso* relatives, including Alfonso de Palencia, Diego de Valera, Hernando del Pulgar, Alfonso de Cartagena, Íñigo López de Mendoza, and Antón de Montoro. On the concept of *limpieza de sangre*, see David Nirenberg, "Was There Race Before Modernity? The Example of 'Jewish' Blood in Late Medieval Spain," in *The Origins of Racism in the West*, ed. Miriam Eliav-Feldon, Benjamin Isaac, and Joseph Ziegler (Cambridge, 2009), 232–64; and the articles in Max S. Hering Torres, María Elena Martínez, and David Nirenberg, eds., *Race and Blood in the Iberian World* (Berlin, 2012).

35. Antón de Montoro, "A la reina doña Isabel," *Cancionero*, 75. Montoro was popularly known by the sobriquet of "Ropero," or cloth merchant. Yirmiyahu Yovel, "Converso Dualities in the First Generation: The 'Cancioneros,'" *Jewish Social Studies* n.s. 4 (1998): 5–6, suggests that the "guilt" to which Montoro referred was that of Jewish complicity in Christ's death, which conversion could never, in the eyes of the Old Christians, erase. On the ways in which Montoro used his poetry to better understand his *converso* identity and position in society, see Ana M. Gómez-Bravo, "Ser social y poética material en la obra de Antón de Montoro, mediano converso," *Hispanic Review* 78 (2010): 145–67.

36. Rafael Carrasco, *Inquisición y represión sexual en Valencia: Historia de los sodomitas (1565–1785)* (Barcelona, 1985), 27, as quoted in Barbara Weissberger, "'¡A tierra, puto!' Alfonso de Palencia's Discourse of Effeminacy," in *Queer Iberia: Sexualities, Cultures, and Crossings from the Middle Ages to the Renaissance*, ed. Josiah Blackmore and Gregory S. Hutcheson (Durham, N.C., 1999), 294 n. 14; and idem, *Isabel Rules: Constructing Queenship, Wielding Power* (Minneapolis, 2004), 74.

37. MacKay, "Popular Movements."

38. Francisco Márquez Villanueva, "Conversos y cargos concejiles en el siglo XV," *Revista de archivos, bibliotecas y museos* 58 (1957): 503–40; MacKay, "Popular Movements," 43–52.

39. The historiography of the Inquisition is vast, but useful introductions include Baer, *A history of the Jews in Christian Spain* (Philadelphia, 1966), 2:324–423; Haim Beinart, *Conversos on Trial: The Inquisition in Ciudad Real* (Jerusalem, 1981); Henry Kamen, *The Spanish Inquisition: A Historical Revision* (New Haven, Conn., 1998); John Edwards, *The Spanish Inquisition* (Stroud, 1999); Gretchen D. Starr-LeBeau, *In the Shadow of the Virgin: Inquisitors, Friars, and* Conversos *in Guadalupe, Spain* (Princeton, N.J., 2003); Joseph Pérez, *The Spanish Inquisition: A History*, trans. Janet Lloyd (New Haven, Conn., 2005); and Helen Rawlings, *The Spanish Inquisition* (Malden, Mass., 2006).

40. As quoted in MacKay, "Whores of Babylon," 182–84. See also his "Women on the Margins," 41–42. Pulgar went on to note that to burn the uninformed was not only cruel but "even difficult to do, because they would flee in desperation to places where there would never be any hope of ever correcting them."

41. Lucero's career and fall are described in John Edwards, "Trial of an Inquisitor: The Dismissal of Diego Rodríguez Lucero, Inquisitor of Córdoba, in 1508," *Journal of*

Ecclesiastical History 37 (1986): 240–57; and Edwards, "The *Judeoconversos* in the Urban Life of Córdoba, 1450–1520," in *Villes et sociétés urbaines au Moyen Âge*, ed. Pierre Desportes (Paris, 1994), 287–99.

42. Palencia, *Crónica de Enrique IV*, 2:87.

43. Nieto Cumplido, "La revuelta," 35–36; Edwards, "Massacre," 65.

44. On the layout and history of the monastery, see Escobar Camacho, *La vida urbana cordobesa*, 87–94.

45. APC, Protocolos notoriales, 13666P, fols. 58r, 201r; 13667P, fols. 418v, 435v, 446v, 508r, 520v, 532r, 555v, 559v; AMC, *AC* 1503; Edwards, *Christian Córdoba*, 169–70; and Escobar Camacho, *La vida urbana cordobesa*, 96–97. The brotherhood was refounded in 1940 and still conducts processions through the Cruz del Rastro and along the Calle de la Feria. Its members maintain a website at http://www.hermandaddelacaridad.org/princi pal.html.

46. Palencia, *Crónica de Enrique IV*, 2:85: "cierta reciprocidad de servicios entre ellos y D. Alonso de Aguilar."

47. For an overview of the political situation at this time, see Hillgarth, *The Spanish Kingdoms*, 2:330–65.

48. Valera, *Memorial de diversas hazañas*, 240.

49. Palencia, *Crónica de Enrique IV*, 2:85. Rodrigo Girón had succeeded his father Pedro Girón as master of Calatrava; see Manuel Ciudad Ruiz, "El maestrazgo de Don Rodrigo Téllez Girón," *En la España Medieval* 23 (2000): 321–65.

50. Palencia, *Crónica de Enrique IV*, 2:86. Palencia is incorrect in stating that the confraternity was founded at this time; it may, however, have greatly expanded its membership in the late 1460s and early 1470s.

51. Valera, *Memorial de diversas hazañas*, 240.

52. Palencia, *Crónica de Enrique IV*, 2:86.

53. MacKay, "Hispanic-*Converso* Predicament," 171.

54. Maureen Flynn, "The Spectacle of Suffering in Spanish Streets," in *City and Spectacle in Medieval Europe*, ed. Barbara Hanawalt and Kathryn Reyerson (Minneapolis, 1994), 153–68.

55. Nirenberg, *Communities of Violence*, 201. On what he describes as the "systematic violence" of the Easter season, particularly Holy Week, see the same work, 200–230.

56. Vulgate, Matthew 27:25. John Edwards, "Massacre," 56, speculates that Aguilar used a lance because a commoner was unworthy of death by a sword. Christ's wounding by a Roman soldier is described in John 19:34. Pilate plays a role in all four Gospels; Matthew 27:13–25 is the most emphatic regarding Pilate's unwillingness to take responsibility for Christ's death.

57. Palencia, *Crónica de Enrique IV*, 2:88. Despite his expressed disdain for such "imaginings," Palencia diligently followed up on reports of this whale sighting to provide a detailed description of its miraculous appearance.

58. For another example of *converso* attempts to prove their Christian worth by attacking other *conversos*, see Yovel, "Converso Dualities," 3.

59. On millenarian impulses at this time, see above, Introduction; Angus MacKay, "Andalucía y la guerra del fin del mundo," in *Andalucía entre Oriente y Occidente (1236–1492): Actas del V Coloquio Internacional de Historia Medieval de Andalucía*, ed. Emilio Cabrera (Córdoba, 1988), 329–42; and John Edwards, "Elijah and the Inquisition: Messianic Prophecy Among *Conversos* in Spain, c. 1500," *Nottingham Medieval Studies* 28 (1984): 79–94.

60. These examples are cited in Kamen, *Spanish Inquisition*, 42; and Benzion Netanyahu, *The Origins of the Inquisition in Fifteenth-Century Spain* (New York, 1995), 995–96.

61. Palencia, *Crónica de Enrique IV*, 2:93.

62. Kamen, *Spanish Inquisition*, 42–43; Netanyahu, *Origins of the Inquisition*, 997ff.

63. David Nirenberg, "Conversion, Sex, and Segregation: Jews and Christians in Medieval Spain," *American Historical Review* 107 (2002): 1065–93; and idem, *Communities of Violence*, 127–65.

64. Antón de Montoro, "Otra suya a su mujer," in *Cancionero*, 60.

65. Valera, *Memorial de diversas hazañas*, 242. See above, note 7.

66. Palencia, *Crónica de Enrique IV*, 2:87; Valeria, *Memorial de diversas hazañas*, 242: "muchos vinieron a robar"; Nieto Cumplido, "La revuelta," 47; Emilio Cabrera Muñoz, "Violencia urbana y crisis política en Andalucía en el siglo XV," in *Violencia y conflictividad en la sociedad de la España bajomedieval*, ed. Muñoz (Zaragoza, 1995), 22–24; Edwards, "Massacre," 61–63.

67. Edwards, *Christian Córdoba*, 197–98; MacKay, "Popular Movements," 66–67.

68. Palencia, *Crónica de Enrique IV*, 2:87–88.

69. Nieto Cumplido, "La revuelta," 43–44, 47, 49; Edwards, "Massacre," 59.

70. See, for instance, MacKay, "Hispanic-*Converso* Predicament," 169–71; John Edwards, "Religious Belief and Social Conformity: The 'Converso' Problem in Late-Medieval Córdoba," *Transactions of the Royal Historical Society* 5th ser. 31 (1981), 126–27.

71. Palencia, *Crónica de Enrique IV*, 2:93–94.

72. John Edwards, "Politics and Ideology in Late-Medieval Córdoba," *En la España Medieval* 4 (1984), 302–3.

73. Antón de Montoro, "A don Alonso de Aguilar," in *Cancionero*, 294.

74. Cf. Natalie Z. Davis, "The Rites of Violence: Religious Riot in Sixteenth-Century France," *Past and Present* 59 (1975): 51–90.

CHAPTER 5. MURCIA AND THE BODY OF CHRIST TRIUMPANT

1. For the early years of Fernando and Isabel's reign and their efforts to consolidate their rule, see John Edwards, *The Spain of the Catholic Monarchs, 1474–1520* (Oxford, 2000), esp. 1–67. William Phillips argues persuasively that many of the reforms typically viewed as Isabelline were actually begun under Enrique in *Enrique IV and the Crisis of Fifteenth-Century Castile, 1425–1480* (Cambridge, Mass., 1978).

2. On the start of the war, see Alfonso de Palencia, *Historia de la guerra de Granada*, ed. Antonio Paz y Melia, BAE 267 (Madrid, 1975), 88ff.; and Fernando del Pulgar, *Crónica de los reyes Católicos*, ed. Juan de Mata Carriazo, CCE 5–6, 2 vols. (Madrid, 1943), 2:3–5. There are a number of scholarly accounts of the Granadan war. See especially Miguel Ángel Ladero Quesada, *Castilla y la conquista de Granada* (Valladolid, 1967); and Luis Suárez Fernández, *Los Reyes Católicos: El tiempo de la guerra de Granada* (Madrid, 1989). Summaries of the war's progress can be found in Edwards, *Spain of the Catholic Monarchs*, 101–40; and Hillgarth, *The Spanish Kingdoms*, 2:367–93.

3. Juan Torres Fontes, "La guerra de Granada: La documentación de los archivos murcianos," in idem., *La frontera murciano-granadina* (Murcia, 2003), 489–90.

4. The structure and functioning of the Murcian *concejo* has been more extensively studied than that of Córdoba or Jaén, due to the extent of the surviving *actas capitulares*. For overviews, see Juan Torres Fontes, "El concepto concejil murciano de limosna en el siglo XV," in *A pobreza e a assistência aos pobres na Peni'nsula Ibe'rica durante a Idade Me'dia: Actas das 1ᵃˢ Jornadas Luso-Espanholas de Histo'ria Medieval, 25–30 de setembro de 1972* (Lisbon, 1973), 2:839–72; Juan Abellán Pérez, "El concejo murciano de junio de 1429 a junio de 1430: Su estructura," *MMM* 5 (1980): 121–58; Francisco Veas Arteseros, "Dinámica del concejo de Murcia (1420–1440): Los regidores," *MMM* 9 (1982): 87–117; and María Belén Piqueras García, "Funcionamiento del concejo murciano (1462–1474)," *MMM* 14 (1987–1988): 9–47. On the transition to crown control of municipal authority, see Denis Menjot, *Murcie castillane: Une ville au temps de la frontière (1243–milieu du XVᵉ s.)*, 2 vols. (Madrid, 2002), 2:937–77.

5. Juan Manuel Moyano Martínez, "Familia y poder político en la Murcia bajomedieval (siglos XIV y XV)," *MMM* 17 (1992): 9–41; Juan Torres Fontes, "Los Fajardo en los siglos XIV y XV," *MMM* 4 (1978): 108–76; idem, "Murcia y Don Juan Manuel: Tensiones y conflictos," in *Don Juan Manuel: VII centenario* (Murcia, 1982), 353–83; idem, *Fajardo el Bravo* (Murcia, 2001); María de los Llanos Martínez Carrillo, *Manueles y Fajardos: La crisis bajomedieval en Murcia* (Murcia, 1985); and Menjot, *Murcie castillane*, 2:984–1011.

6. AMM, CR 1478–1488, fol. 491-v, 14 November 1479; also published in Andrea Moratalla Collado, *Documentos de los Reyes Católicos: 1475–1491*, Colección de documentos para la historia del reino de Murcia 19 (Murcia, 2003), doc. 172, 354–55.

7. AMM, CR 1453–1478, fols. 223r-v, 15 March 1475; 223r, 26 March 1475; and 223v–224r, 14 March 1475: "tan çercana a los moros enemigos de nuestra santa fe católica." The requirement that Jews and Muslims maintain horses and arms dated from 1473; see AMM, *AC* 1473–1474, fol. 110r, 15 March 1474; and Juan Francisco Jiménez Alcázar, "El hombre y la frontera: Murcia y Granada en época de Enrique IV," *MMM* 17 (1992): 77–96. The town of Lorca acted as Murcia's first line of defense, as Priego did for Córdoba. See Francisco Veas Arteseros, "Lorca, base militar murciana frente a Granada en el reinado de Juan II (1406–1454)," *MMM* 5 (1980): 159–88; and Juan Torres Fontes, *Xiquena, castillo de la frontera* (Murcia, 1960). See also Torres Fontes, "La incorporación a la caballería de los judíos murcianos en el s. XV," *Murgetana* 27 (1967): 5–14, esp. doc. 2, 13–14.

8. Menjot, *Murcie castillane*, 1:171–76, 584–605; 2:731–33, 763–76. Juan Torres Fontes, *Instituciones y sociedad en la frontera murciano-granadina* (Murcia, 2004); José García Antón, "La tolerancia religiosa en la frontera de Murcia y Granada en los últimos tiempos del reino nazarí," *Murgetana* 57 (1980): 133–43; Moratalla Collado, *Documentos de los Reyes Católicos*, doc. 55, 99–100.

9. On the Murcian economy, see Menjot, *Murcie castillane*, 1:484–644; Juan Torres Fontes, "Los cultivos murcianos en el siglo XV," *Murgetana* 37 (1971): 89–96; idem, *El Regadío murciano en la primera mitad del siglo XIV* (Murcia, 1975); Ángel Luis Molina Molina, *El campo de Murcia en el siglo XV* (Murcia, 1989); Isabel García Díaz, *La huerta de Murcia en el siglo XIV (propiedad y producción)* (Murcia, 1990); María Martínez Martínez, *La industria del vestido en Murcia: Siglos XIII–XV* (Murcia, 1988); and eadem, *La cultura del aceite en Murcia: Siglos XIII–XV* (Murcia, 1995).

10. Ángel Luis Molina Molina, "Mercaderes genoveses en Murcia durante la época de los Reyes Católicos (1475–1516)," *MMM* 2 (1976): 277–312; Juan Torres Fontes, "Relaciones comerciales entre los reinos de Mallorca y Murcia en el siglo XIV," *Murgetana* 36 (1971): 5–20. Interior cities, notably Córdoba but also Jaén, hosted communities of Italian merchants, but these were much smaller than that of Murcia.

11. On the position of the Mudéjares in Murcian society, see María del Carmen Veas Arteseros, *Mudéjares murcianos: Un modelo de crisis social (s. XIII–XV)* (Cartagena, 1992), 29–41; as well as Ángel Luis Molina Molina, "Datos sobre sociodemografía Murciana a fines de la Edad Media (1475–1515)," *Anales de la Universidad de Murcia: Filosofía y letras* 36 (1977–1978): 176–82; idem, *La sociedad murciana en el tránsito de la edad media a la moderna* (Murcia, 1996), 65–84; Juan Torres Fontes, "La puerta de la traición," *Murgetana* 37 (1971): 83–88; idem, "Los mudéjares murcianos: Economía y sociedad," in *IV Simposio Internacional de Mudejarismo: Economía* (Teruel, 1993), 365–94; and idem, "Los mudéjares murcianos en la Edad Media," in *III Simposio Internacional de Mudejarismo: Economía* (Teruel, 1986), 55–66.

12. AMM, CR 1453–1478, fol. 264v, 25 June 1477 (also published in Moratalla Collado, *Documentos de los Reyes Católicos*, doc. 124, 267–68); AMM, CR 1478–1488, fols. 107v–108r, 29 May 1483 (also published in Ródolfo Bosque Carceller, *Murcia y los Reyes Católicos* [Murcia, 1994], doc. 8, 217).

13. Molina Molina, *La sociedad murciana*, 54; Menjot, *Murcie castillane*, 1:331–33, 345–47. Much has been written on Murcia's Jews. For overviews with extensive bibliographic notes, see the documents collected in Luis Rubio García, *Los judíos de Murcia en la baja Edad Media (1350–1500): Colección documental*, 3 vols. (Murcia, 1992–1994); as well as Francisco Veas Arteseros, *Los judíos de Lorca en la Baja Edad Media* (Murcia, 1992). On the particular period during and after the 1391 pogroms, see Juan Torres Fontes, "Los judíos murcianos a fines del siglo XIV y comienzos del XV," *MMM* 8 (1981): 55–117.

14. AMM, CR, 1453–1478, fols. 255v–256r, 18 April 1476; Moratalla Collado, *Documentos de los Reyes Católicos*, doc. 82, pp. 148–50.

15. AMM, CR 1453–1478, fols. 233v–234v, 258v–259r, 260v–261r, 262r–v. See also Moratalla Collado, *Documentos de los Reyes Católicos*, docs. 21, 38, 83, 85, 95, 117, 119, 143, 151, 176, 194, 204, 206, 215, 230, 286, 288, 293, 421, 425, and 426.

16. Jiménez Alcázar, "El hombre y la frontera," 85–87; Rubio García, *Los judíos de Murcia*, 1:15–32.

17. AMM, CR 1478–1488; fols. 55r–56r, 24 April 1481 (also published in Juan Torres Fontes, *Don Pedro Fajardo: adelantado mayor del reino de Navarra* [Murcia, 1953], 301–4); and fols. 64v–65r, 27 August 1481. See also Juan Torres Fontes, "Los judíos murcianos en el siglo XIII," *Murgetana* 16 (1962): 5–20; and Torres Fontes, "La judería murciana en la época de los Reyes Católicos," *Espacio, Tiempo y Forma*, ser. 3, *Historia Medieval* 6 (1993): 177–228.

18. AMM, *AC* 1473–1474, fol. 75r, 20 November 1473: "cosa fea . . . mal ejenplo"; AMM, *AC* 1474–1475, fol. 167r, 20 March 1473. On relations between church authorities and the Jewish community, see Francisco Reyes Marsilla de Pascua, "Los judíos y el cabildo catedralicio de Murcia en el siglo XV," *MMM* 15 (1989): 55–84.

19. AMM, *AC* 1410–1411, fols. 146v–147v, 24 March 1411; Ángel Luis Molina Molina, "Estampas medievales murcianas," 55–56; idem, *Estudios sobre la vida cotidiana (ss. XIII–XVI)* (Murcia, 2003), 133–34.

20. On the origins and early adoption of the feast, the urban contexts of the Eucharistic veneration in which it originated, and its significance to medieval audiences, see Miri Rubin, *Corpus Christi: The Eucharist in Late Medieval Culture* (Cambridge, 1991), 164–212; eadem, "The Eucharist and the Construction of Christian Identities," in *Culture and History, 1350–1600*, ed. David Aers (Detroit, 1992), 43–63; and Barbara R. Walters, Vincent Corrigan, and Peter T. Ricketts, *The Feast of Corpus Christi* (University Park, Pa., 2006), xv–54.

21. The first documentary mention of Corpus processions in Murcia in 1406 suggests an ongoing, rather than completely new, festival. From that point on, mentions of the procession in the *actas capitulares* occur nearly every year. Juan Barceló Jiménez, *Historia del teatro en Murcia* (Murcia, 1980), 15 n. 24: "Item, que ningún clérigo ni sacristán que non preste vestimenta alguna que sea de la Iglesia para ningunos, salvo sinon fuesen juegos de la Iglesia o a la procesión de Corpus Cristi e otras procesiones semejantes." See also María Martínez Martínez, "Gastos del concejo lorquino para el Corpus de 1472," *Estudios Románicos* 6 (1989): 1688. For an example of Corpus festivities elsewhere in Castile, see Antonio Romero Abao, "La fiesta del Corpus Christi en Sevilla en el siglo XV," in *La religiosidad popular*, ed. María Jesús Buxó i Rey, Salvador Rodríguez Becerra, and León Carlos Álvarez y Santaló, 3 vols. (Seville, 1989), 3:19–30.

22. For the spatial arrangement of spectators, see Chapter 1.

23. AMM, *AC* 1419–1420, fol. 76v, 1 June 1420; Rubio García, *La procesión*, 101–7; Juan José Capel Sánchez, *La vida lúdica en la Murcia bajomedieval* (Murcia, 2000), 94–95.

24. AMM, *AC* 1461–1462, fol. 80v, 1 June 1462; 1464–1465, fol. 122v, 8 May 1464; 1468–1469, fol. 108r, 20 May 1469; 1495–1496, fol. 179r, 26 May 1496; Rubio García, *La procesión*, 109–10, 127–28. Inflation during this period explains some, but not all, of the increases in expenses.

25. AMM, *AC* 1468–1469, fol. 108r, 20 May 1469.

26. AMM, *AC* 1470–1471, fol. 122v, 25 May 1471; Rubio García, *La procesión*, 111–12.

27. AMM, *AC* 1470–1471, fol. 131r, 18 June 1471; Rubio García, *La procesión*, 111–12. For comparative purposes, see Martínez Martínez, "Gastos del concejo lorquino," 1690–96, in which the author has compiled the dozens of separate expenses involved in the 1472 Corpus festival in the smaller city of Lorca and calculated the total cost at 6,462 *mrs*; see also Menjot, *Murcie castillane*, 2:1053.

28. AMM, *AC* 1479–1480, fols. 211v, 5 May 1480, and 222v, 27 May 1480; Rubio García, *La procesión*, 116–17.

29. AMM, *AC* 1482–1483, fol. 167r, 27 May 1483: "E los dichos sennores Conçejo ordenaron e mandaron que ningunas personas onbres nin mugeres non vayan a Orihuela esta fiesta del Cuerpo de Dios porque cunple asy a serviçio del Rey e Reyna nuestros sennores." Rubio García, *La procesión*, 120–21.

30. AMM, *AC* 1483–1484, fol. 154r, 29 May 1484; Rubio García, *La procesión*, 72, 121–22. See also Martínez Carrillo, "Fiestas ciudadanas," 9–15.

31. AMM, *AC* 1483–1484, fol. 154v, 1 June 1484; fol. 155r, 3 June, 1484; Rubio García, *La procesión*, 161–62.

32. AMM, *AC* 1483–1484, fols. 156–157v, 5 June 1484: "porque son fechos mas para solazar e deleytar la gente que no para trahella a devoçion. . . . E asy presentado el dicho escripto luego los dichos sennores Conçejo dixeron que syn embargo de lo en el estando mandavan e mandaron que se fisiesen los dichos juegos este dicho presente anno." Rubio García, *La procesión*, 172–75; Capel Sánchez, *La vida lúdica*, 87–88.

33. ACM, *Libro viejo de acuerdos*, 1455–1494, fols. 62–63; AMM, *AC* 1461–1462, fol. 41r–v, 7 July 1461; Capel Sánchez, *La vida lúdica*, 101; Rubio García, *La procesión*, 57, 62–63, 151–52. On Murcia's banner, or *pendón*, see Juan Torres Fontes, "Estampas de la vida murciana en la época de los reyes católicos: El pendón de la ciudad," *Murgetana* 13 (1960): 47–72.

34. Capel Sánchez, *La vida lúdica*, 101–2; Rubio García, *La procesión*, 28–34, and on the guild representatives and musicians who participated in the procession, 63–68, 88–99.

35. On the construction, maintenance, and ownership of the *carros*, see Rubio García, *La procesión*, 70–75.

36. AMM, *AC* 1469–1470, fol. 126v, 19 June 1470: "Otrosy ordenaron e mandaron que la representaçion de los misterios del dia del Cuerpo de Dios se faga en esta manera, el primer delante el Corpus, el segundo donde estovieren los sennores adelantado e dona Leonor, el terçero al canton de Alfonso de Vallybrera, el quarto al canton del Cabeçon, el quinto a las casas de Rodrigo de Soto e el otro a San Llorençio, e el otro en par de la plaça de Almenara, el otro a las casas de Diego Tomas, e el otro a las casas de Alfonso Carles, regidor." Rubio García, *La procesión*, 78.

37. AMM, *AC* 1446–1447, fol. 55v, 30 May 1447.

38. AMM, *AC* 1470–1471, fol. 122v, 25 May 1471; *AC* 1471–1472, fol. 16r, 2 July 1471; *AC* 1479–1480, fol. 211v–212r, 5 May 1480; *AC* 1493–1494, fol. 33v, 15 October 1493; Rubio García, *La procesión*, 81–85; Capel Sánchez, *La vida lúdica*, 116–23.

39. For an overview of the few surviving fragments, see Stern, *Medieval Theater*, 18–20, 116–21.

40. Capel Sánchez, *La vida lúdica*, 119–22; Rubio García, *La procesión*, 86–87.

41. Vicente Lleó Cañal, *Fiesta grande: El Corpus Christi en la historia de Sevilla* (Seville, 1980); Stern, *Medieval Theater*, 118–19. For the development of Corpus pageants in the Crown of Aragón, see Hermenegildo Corbató, *Los misterios del Corpus de Valencia* (Berkeley, 1932); and *Llibre de les solemnitats de Barcelona*, vol. 1, *1424–1546*, ed. A. Duran i Sanpere and Josep Sanabre (Barcelona, 1930).

42. Carmen Torroja Menéndez and María Rivas Palá, *Teatro en Toledo en el siglo XV: 'Auto de la Pasión' de Alonso del Campo* (Madrid, 1977), 181–84; Stern, *Medieval Theater*, 119–20.

43. Torroja Menéndez and Rivas Palá, *Teatro en Toledo*; Josep Lluís Sirera Turo, "La construcción del *Auto de la Pasión* y el teatro medieval castellano," in *Actas del III Congreso de la Asociación Hispánica de Literatura Medieval*, ed. María Isabel Toro Pascua (Salamanca, 1994), 2:1011–20; Stern, *Medieval Theater*, 124–25.

44. Stern, *Medieval Theater*, 20–24.

45. Rubin, *Corpus Christi*, 271–87 and 302–11; Flynn, "The Spectacle of Suffering," 153–68; Claire Sponsler, *Drama and Resistance: Bodies, Goods, and Theatricality in Late Medieval England* (Minneapolis, 1997), esp. chap. 6, "Violated Bodies: The Spectacle of Suffering in Corpus Christi Pageants," 136–60; Caroline Walker Bynum, "The Female Body and Religious Practice in the Later Middle Ages," in *Fragmentation and Redemption: Essays on Gender and the Human Body in Medieval Religion* (New York, 1991), 181–238; Nirenberg, *Communities of Violence*, esp. 200–230.

46. Sponsler, *Drama and Resistance*, 137, 147.

47. John Gatton, "'There Must Be Blood': Mutilation and Martyrdom on the Medieval Stage," in *Violence in Drama*, ed. James Redmond (Cambridge, 1991), 80.

48. Sponsler, *Drama and Resistance*, 149–60.

49. On Host desecration, see Miri Rubin, *Gentile Tales: The Narrative Assault on Late Medieval Jews* (Philadelphia, 2004). On ritual murder accusations, see Ronnie Po-Chia Hsia, *The Myth of Ritual Murder: Jews and Magic in Reformation Germany* (New Haven, Conn., 1988).

50. Lester K. Little, "The Jews in Christian Europe," in *Essential Papers on Judaism and Christianity in Conflict: From Late Antiquity to the Reformation*, ed. Jeremy Cohen (New York, 1991), 287; Hsia, *Myth of Ritual Murder*.

51. Flynn, "The Spectacle of Suffering."

52. Rubio García, *La procesión*, 13, 16. Cf. Molina Molina who paraphrases Rubio's claims, "Estampas medievales," 228.

53. Stern, *Medieval Theater*, 117; Gabriel Llompart, "La fiesta del Corpus y representaciones religiosas en Zaragoza y Mallorca (siglos XIV–XVI)," *Analecta Sacra Tarraconensia: Revista de ciencias historioeclesiásticas* 42 (1969): 181–209.

54. Stern, *Medieval Theater*, 123.

55. AMM, *AC* 1424–1425, fol. 95v, 2 June 1425: "mandaron al dicho Juan Ferrandes de Canpo mayordomo sobre dicho que enbie a todas estas morerias para que vengan los mas juglares que pudieren ser ávidos para la dicha fiesta e que faga la dicha fiesta onrrada mente segund que de cada anno se acostumbra." Rubio García, *La procesión*, 89–90.

56. Veas Arteseros, *Mudéjares murcianos*, 65–66.

57. Capel Sánchez, *La vida lúdica*, 110.

58. AMM, *AC* 1479–1480, fol. 223r, 27 May 1480: "despues que esta çibdad se gano de los moros e los moros destas morerías quedaron aqui syenpre acostunbraron vestir e traer aljubas de seda morisca . . . e nunca en otros vedamientos generales gelos quitaron . . . tienen suplicado a la junta general entre tanto que los dichos diputados generales les provean ordenaron que los dichos moros puedan vestir aljubas e cubertores de cabeça de seda esto el dia del Cuerpo de Dios e non mas syn pena alguna." Rubio García, *La procesión*, 131–32.

59. AMM, *AC* 1479–1480, fol. 227r, 30 May 1480: "que para el dia del Cuerpo de Dios que por onrra de la fiesta todas e qualesquier presonas asy xpristianos como judios e moros puedan traher e vestir aquel dia todas las ropas e cosas defendidas a vedadas por la ley de la hermandad syn pena alguna."

60. AMM, *AC* 1467–1468, fol. 115r, 20 April 1468: "Otrosi que los judios e moros que estudiesen en la calle quando llevaren el Cuerpo de Dios o quando fisieren proçesiones generales por la çibdad, sean tenidos de se apartar de la calle o de se esconder o que finquen los ynojos." Rubio García, *La procesión*, 130, 176–77.

61. ACM, *Libro viejo de acuerdos* 1455–1494, fols. 62–63, 7 June 1482.

62. AMM, caja 80, 1472, 29 May 1472; AMM, *AC* 1471–1472, fols. 85v–86v, 30 May 1472; Rubio García, *La procesión*, 113–14, 166–67; Rubio García, *Los judíos de Murcia*, 37–39.

63. AMM, *AC* 1484–1485, fol. 150v, 31 May 1485: "agarrochen en la Traperia el domingo delante del dia del Corpus Cristi por las alegrías de la toma de la çibdad de Ronda e de los otros lugares e villas quel Rey nuestro sennor a tomado en el reyno de Granada." Rubio García, *La procesión*, 19, 45, 133–34.

64. AMM, *AC* 1494–1495, fol. 134r–v, 24 March 1495.

65. For the seige and fall of Málaga, see Hillgarth, *Spanish Kingdoms*, 2:382–84. The announcement of the city's capture came immediately to Murcia in a royal missive, AMM, CR 1478–1488, fol. 202r, 18 August 1487.

66. AMM, *AC* 1487–1488, fol. 32r, 4 September 1487: "e que ellos tengan cargo mandando de fazer todo lo que sera menester para que se fagan los dichos juegos."

67. AMM, *AC* 1487–1488, fol. 33r, 11 September 1487.

68. Joseph F. O'Callaghan, *Reconquest and Crusade in Medieval Spain* (Philadelphia, 2003), 194.

69. AMM, *AC* 1487–1488, 39r, 27 September 1487: "Los dichos sennores mandaron . . . sabado en la tarde que baylen los judios y los moros"; "segund se faze las carnestolendas."

70. AMM, *AC* 1487–1488, fol. 39r–v, 27 September 1487.

71. AMM, *AC* 1487–1488, fol. 113, 5 April 1488: "que sean tales que den plazer."

72. AMM, *AC* 1491–1492, fol. 96v, 9 January 1492: "Que en estos tres dias todos los ofyçiales y labradores y mugeres que non fagan faziendo en estos tres dias sy non que los

guarden como el dia de domingo so pena de dozientos maravedis a cada uno que lo contrario fiziese para los dichos gastos de las dichas albriçias."

73. *CSM*, 2:172–74, no. 169; see also Joseph F. O'Callaghan, *Alfonso X and the Cantigas de Santa Maria: A Poetic Biography* (Leiden, 1998), 121–25; and Amy G. Remensnyder, "Marian Monarchy in Thirteenth-Century Castile," in *The Experience of Power in Medieval Europe, 950–1350*, ed. Robert F. Berkhoper III, Alan Cooper, and Adam Kosto (Aldershot, 2005), 204–5.

74. AMM, *AC* 1491–1492, fol. 97r, 9 January 1492.

75. AMM, *AC* 1491–1492, fol. 101v, 14 January 1492: "todos los tronpetas e otros menestriles e juglares e moros e xpristianos de qualquier calidad y condiçion."

76. AMM, *AC* 1491–1492, fols. 97v–98r, 9 January 1492; Molina Molina, *La sociedad murciana*, 25.

77. AMM, *AC* 1491–1492, fol. 97r, 9 January 1492: "fablen con los judios e les manden que paguen de oy en tres dias cinquenta mill maravedis que les cupieron del repartimiento de la guerra, fueles notificada e dixeron que non heran obligados."

78. On Murcia's Hermandad taxes, see Lope Pascual Martínez, "Las hermandades en Murcia durante la baja Edad Media," *MMM* 3 (1977): 206–9.

79. AMM, CR 1488–1495, 19 July 1490: "sobre las biudas e huerfanos e otras miserables personas." Antonio Gomariz Marín, *Documentos de los Reyes Católicos: 1492–1504*. Colección de documentos para la historia del reino de Murcia 20 (Murcia, 2000), doc. 429.

80. AMM, pergamino 151, 14 October 1487, "Carta de privilegio y confirmación de los Reyes Católicos a la aljama de moros en Murcia de los privilegios otorgados por los reyes anteriores," fols. 1v–2r: "por razón de las guerras e de los otros males que son acaesçidos en tierra de Murçia e la mayor parte de los moros son muertos e los otros fuydos, por las tales cosas la tierra es muy despoblada e menguada . . . los moros que son fuera de la mi tierra, ayan favor de venir e que todos sean ricos e bien andantes e que nos puedan mejor servir."

81. AMM, *AC* 1491–1492, fol. 97r, 9 January 1492: "para el sueldo de la guerra de Granada . . . e para las alegrias e albriçias que en esta çibdad se han de fazer y por el entrego de la dicha çibdad de Granada."

82. AMM, *AC* 1491–1492, fol. 97v, 9 January 1492.

83. The Castilian version of the edict is published in Luis Suárez Fernández, *Documentos acerca de la expulsión de los judíos* (Valladolid, 1964), 391–95. The translation above is from Edward Peters, "Jewish History and Gentile Memory: The Expulsion of 1492," *Jewish History* 9 (1995): 23–28.

84. All relevant documents are published in Rubio García, *Los judíos de Murcia*, 2:336ff.

85. Stern, *Medieval Theater*, 117.

86. AMM, *AC* 1491–1492, fol. 98v, 9 January 1492: "por honra de la dicha fiesta ninguno non traya luto."

CONCLUSION

Epigraph: Constantine P. Cavafy, "Waiting for the Barbarians," in *C. P. Cavafy: Collected Poems*, trans. Edmund Keeley and Philip Sherrard, rev. ed. (Princeton, N.J., 1992), 18–19.

1. Fuchs, *Exotic Nation*, passim.

2. Philippe de Mézières, *The Life of Saint Peter Thomas*, ed. Joachim Smet, Textus and Studia Carmelitana 2 (Rome, 1954), 100.

3. For a full discussion of these events, see Thomas Devaney, "Spectacle, Community, and Holy War in Fourteenth-Century Cyprus," *Medieval Encounters* 19 (2013): 300–341.

4. On recent definitions of Mediterranean connectivity and unity, see Peregrine Horden and Nicholas Purcell, *The Corrupting Sea: A Study of Mediterranean History* (Oxford, 2000); Gadi Algazi, "Diversity Rules." *Mediterranean Historical Review* 20 (2005): 227–45; Molly Greene, *Catholic Pirates and Greek Merchants: A Maritime History of the Mediterranean* (Princeton, N.J., 2010); and Eric Dursteler, *Renegade Women: Gender, Identity, and Boundaries in the Early Modern Mediterranean* (Baltimore, 2011). See also the many essays included in W. V. Harris, ed., *Rethinking the Mediterranean* (Oxford, 2005); and Adnan K. Husain and K. E. Fleming, eds., *A Faithful Sea: The Religious Cultures of the Mediterranean, 1200–1700* (Oxford, 2007).

5. For a discussion of how medieval Cyprus fits modern scholarly concepts of frontier, see Peter Edbury, "Latins and Greeks on Crusader Cyprus," in *Medieval Frontiers: Concepts and Practices*, ed. David Abulafia and Nora Berend (Aldershot, 2002), 133–42.

6. Fuchs, *Exotic Nation*.

7. Schwartz, *All Can Be Saved*.

8. Fuchs, *Exotic Nation*, 88ff.; Marlene Alpert-Llorca and José Antonio González Alcantud, *Moros y cristianos: Representaciones del otro en las fiestas del Mediterráneo occidental* (Toulouse, 2003); and Demetrio E. Brisset Martín, "Fiestas hispanas de moros y cristianos: Historia y significados," *Gazeta de Antropología* 17 (2001).

9. Harris, *Aztecs, Moors, and Christians*.

10. W. H. Auden, *Spain* (London, 1937).

GLOSSARY OF SPANISH TERMS

Many Spanish words in the text are explained when first used. The list below consists of a selection of the most commonly used terms.

(*Cabildo* and *concejo* both mean "council" and were used interchangeably to refer to civic, ecclesiastic, and other councils. For clarity, I have limited *cabildo* to cathedral chapters, and *concejo* to municipal councils.)

actas capitulares. City council minutes.
adelantado. Military governor.
alcaide. Garrison commander.
alcalde. Judge.
alfaqueque. Professional ransomer.
aljama. The Muslim (or sometimes Jewish) community in a city.
almogávar. Raider.
bando. Network of relatives, clients, and vassals, usually headed by a noble patron.
caballero villano (or *de premia* or *de cuantía*). Nonnoble urban knight.
cabildo. Cathedral chapter.
cadalhalso. Viewing platform.
catafalco. Viewing platform.
comendador. Commander.
concejo. City council.
converso. A convert (usually from Judaism to Christianity).
corregidor. Royally appointed civic administrator.
entremés. Short skit performed during intermissions, such as between courses at a banquet or contests at a tournament.
hidalgo. Hereditary noble.
invención. Word game or riddle.
judería. Jewish quarter of a city.

jurado. Neighborhood representative.

letrado. University graduate trained in canon or civil law

limpieza de sangre. Blood purity.

linaje. Family lineage.

maravedí (*mrs.*) Monetary unit of account whose value fluctuated widely in the late fifteenth century.

mirador. Viewing platform.

morería. Muslim quarter of a city.

peon. Foot soldier.

regidor. Member of city council.

señorío. Lordship.

vecino. Citizen.

veinticuatro. Member of city council.

BIBLIOGRAPHY

MANUSCRIPT SOURCES

Archivo Catedralicio de Murcia (ACM)
  Libro viejo de acuerdos, 1455–1494
Archivo de la Catedral de Córdoba (ACC)
  Caja Z.
Archivo Histórico Provincial de Córdoba (APC)
  Protocolos notoriales
Archivo Municipal de Córdoba (AMC)
  Libros de Actas Capitulares (AC), 1434, 1471, 1479, 1495, 1503
Archivo Municipal de Jaén (AMJ)
  Leg. 1, Cuadro 3
  Libros de Actas Capitulares (AC), 1476, 1479, 1480, 1521
  Ordenanzas de Jaén
Archivo Municipal de Murcia (AMM)
  Caja 80
  Cartas reales (CR), 1453–1478, 1478–1488, 1488–1495
  Libros de Actas Capitulares (AC), 1410–1411, 1419–1420, 1424–1425, 1429–1430, 1434–1435, 1446–1447, 1460–1461, 1461–1462, 1464–1465, 1467–1468, 1468–1469, 1469–1470, 1470–1471, 1471–1472, 1473–1474, 1474–1475, 1479–1480, 1480–1481, 1481–1482, 1482–1483, 1483–1484, 1484–1485, 1487–1488, 1488–1489, 1491–1492, 1493–1494, 1494–1495, 1495–1496
  Pergamino 151

PUBLISHED DOCUMENTARY SOURCES

Baer, Yitzhak. *Die Juden im Christlichen Spanien*. Vol. 1, *Urkunden und Regesten*, pt. 2 *Kastilien/Inquisitionsakten*. Berlin, 1936.
Bosque Carceller, Ródolfo. *Murcia y los Reyes Católicos*. Murcia, 1994.
———. *A history of the Jews in Christian Spain*. Trans. Louis Schoffman. 2 vols. Philadelphia, 1961–1966.

"Cédula del rey don Enrique haciendo noble a Miguel Lucas de Iranzo con señalamiento de las armas que debía traer en el escudo: En el real sobre Granada 12 de junio de 1455." In *Memorias de don Enrique IV de Castilla*, Colección diplomática de Enrique IV, 2. vols., 2:139–141. Madrid, 1913.

Constitutiones Concilii Quarti Lateranensis una cum commentariis glossatorum. Ed. Antonio García y García. Monumenta Iuris Canonici, Ser. A: Corpus Glossatorum 2. Vatican City, 1981.

Galíndez de Carvajal, Lorenzo. *Adiciones genealógicas a los Claros varones de Fernán Pérez de Guzmán, señor de Batres*. In Colección de documentos inéditos para la historia de España 17:423–536. Madrid, 1851.

García, Michel. "Una carta inédita del condestable Miguel Lucas de Iranzo." *BIEG* 53 (1967): 15–22.

Gomariz Marín, Antonio. *Documentos de los Reyes Católicos: 1492–1504*. Colección de documentos para la historia del reino de Murcia 20. Murcia, 2000.

Gregory IX, *Decretalium D. Gregorii Papæ IX*. In *Corpus Iuris Canonici*. Ed. Emil Ludwig Richter and Emil Friedberg. 2 vols. 2:1–1070. Graz, 1959.

Heusch, Carlos, and Jesús Rodríguez Velasco, eds. *La caballería castellana en la Baja Edad Media: Textos y contextos*. Montpellier, 2000.

John XXII. *Extravagantes tum viginti D. Ioannis Papæ XXII tum communes suæ integritati restitutæ*. In *Corpus Iuris Canonici*, ed. Emil Ludwig Richter and Emil Friedberg. 2 vols. 2: 1201–38. Graz, 1959.

Llibre de les solemnitats de Barcelona. Vol. 1, *1424–1546*. Ed. A. Duran i Sanpere and Josep Sanabre. Barcelona, 1930.

Moratalla Collado, Andrea. *Documentos de los Reyes Católicos: 1475–1491*. Colección de documentos para la historia del reino de Murcia 19. Murcia, 2003.

Ordenanzas de la muy noble, famosa y muy leal ciudad de Jaén, guarda y defendimiento de los reinos de Castilla. Ed. Pedro A. Porras Arboledas. Granada, 1993.

"Ordenanzas del concejo de Córdoba (1435)." Ed. Manuel González Jiménez. *HID* 2 (1975): 189–316.

Rodríguez Molina, José. *Colección diplomática del Archivo histórico municipal de Jaén: Siglos XIV y XV*. Jaén, 1985.

Rubio García, Luis. *Los judíos de Murcia en la baja Edad Media (1350–1500): Colección documental*. 3 vols. Murcia, 1992–1994.

Schroeder, Henry Joseph. *Disciplinary Decrees of the General Councils: Text, Translation and Commentary*. St. Louis, 1937.

Las Siete Partidas. Ed. Robert I. Burns, trans. Samuel Parsons Scott. 5 vols. Philadelphia, 2000–2001.

Simonsohn, Shlomo. *The Apostolic See and the Jews: Documents, 1394–1464*. Toronto, 1988.

Suárez Fernández, Luis. *Documentos acerca de la expulsión de los judíos*. Valladolid, 1964.

El Tumbo de los Reyes Católicos del concejo de Sevilla. Ed. Ramón Carande and Juan de Mata Carriazo. Seville, 1929–1968.

PUBLISHED NARRATIVE SOURCES

Alfonso X, el Sabio. *Cantigas de Santa María.* Ed. Walter Mettmann. 3 vols. Madrid, 1986–1989.

———. *Cantigas de Santa María: Edición facsímil del Códice T.I.1 de la Biblioteca de San Lorenzo el Real de El Escorial, siglo XIII.* Madrid, 1979.

Alfonso de Cartagena. *The Chivalric Vision of Alfonso de Cartagena: Study and Edition of the "Doctrinal de los caualleros."* Ed. Noel Fallows. Newark, Del., 1995.

———. *Un tratado de Alonso de Cartagena sobre la educación y los estudios literarios.* Ed. Jeremy N. H. Lawrance. Barcelona, 1979.

Antón de Montoro, *Cancionero.* Ed. Marcella Ciceri and Julio Rodríguez-Puértolas. Salamanca, 1990.

———. "Cantar de los Comendadores de Córdoba." In Marcelino Menéndez y Pelayo, *Edición nacional de las obras completas de Menéndez Pelayo,* 65 vols., 25:449–51. Madrid, 1940–1959.

Barrientos, Lope de. *Refundación de la Crónica del halconero.* Ed. Juan de Mata Carriazo. CCE 9. Madrid, 1946.

Bernard of Clairvaux. "In Praise of the New Knighthood." Trans. Conrad Greenia. In *The Works of Bernard of Clairvaux,* vol. 7, *Treatises III,* 127–67. Cistercian Fathers Series 19. Kalamazoo, Mich., 1977.

Carrillo de Huete, Pedro. *Crónica del halconero de Juan II.* Ed. Juan de Mata Carriazo. CCE 8. Madrid, 1946.

Cervantes Saavedra, Miguel de. *El ingenioso hidalgo don Quijote de la Mancha.* Ed. Tom Lathrop. Newark, Del., 1997.

Crónica anónima de Enrique IV de Castilla, 1454–1474. Ed. Maria Pilar Sánchez-Parra García. Madrid, 1991.

Crónica de Alfonso III. Ed. Antonio Ubieto Arteta. Textos Medievales 3. Valencia, 1971.

Crónica de don Alvaro de Luna, condestable de Castilla, maestre de Santiago. Ed. Juan de Mata Carriazo. CCE 2. Madrid, 1946.

Crónica de Juan II de Castilla. Ed. Juan de Mata Carriazo. Madrid, 1982.

Delicado, Francisco. *La Lozana andaluza.* Ed. Bruno M. Damiani. Madrid, 1982.

———. *La Lozana andaluza.* Ed. Jacques Joset and Folke Gernert. Barcelona, 2007.

———. *Portrait de la Gaillarde andalouse: Roman.* Trans. Claude Bleton. Paris, 1993.

———. *Portrait of Lozana: The Lusty Andalusian Woman.* Trans. Bruno M. Damiani. Scripta Humanistica 34. Potomac, Md., 1987.

———. *Retrato de la Lozana andaluza.* Ed. Claude Allaigre. Madrid, 1985.

Enríquez del Castillo, Diego. *Crónica del rey Don Enrique el cuarto de este nombre.* Ed. Cayetano Rosell. BAE 70. Madrid, 1953.

Escavias, Pedro de. *Repertorio de Príncipes de España y obra poética del alcaide Pedro de Escavias.* Ed. Michel García. Jaén, 1972.

Hechos del condestable don Miguel Lucas de Iranzo (Crónica del siglo XV). Ed. Juan de Mata Carriazo. CCE 3. Madrid, 1940.

Historia de los hechos del Marqués de Cádiz. Ed. Juan Luis Carriazo Rubio. Granada, 2003.

Jerónimo of Córdoba. *Córdoba en el siglo XV*. Ed. and trans. Manuel Nieto Cumplido. Córdoba, 1973.

López de Mendoza, Iñigo, and Alfonso de Cartagena. "Qüestion fecha por el marqués de Santillana al muy sabio e noble perlado don Alonso de Cartagena y su respuesta." In *Iñigo López de Mendoza, Marqués de Santillana: Obras completas*, ed. Ángel Gómez Moreno and Maximilian P. A. M. Kerkhof, 414–34. Barcelona, 1988.

Martínez de Mazas, José. *Retrato al natural de la ciudad y términos de Jaén*. Ed. José Rodríguez Molina. Barcelona, 1978.

Mézières, Philippe de. *The Life of Saint Peter Thomas*. Ed. Joachim Smet. Textus and studia carmelitana 2. Rome, 1954.

Ortiz de Zúñiga, Diego. *Anales eclesiásticos y seculares de la ciudad de Sevilla*. 4 vols. Madrid, 1795.

Palencia, Alfonso de. *Crónica de Enrique IV*. Ed. Antonio Paz y Melia. BAE 257, 258, and 267. Madrid, 1973–1975.

———. *De perfectione militaris triumphi: La perfeçión del triunfo*. Ed. Javier Durán Barceló. Salamanca, 1996.

———. *Epístolas latinas*. Ed. and trans. Robert Brian Tate and Rafael Alemany Ferrer. Barcelona, 1982.

———. *Historia de la guerra de Granada*. Ed. Antonio Paz y Melia. BAE 267. Madrid, 1975.

Pérez de Guzmán, Fernán. *Crónica del príncipe don Juan Segundo*. Ed. Cayetano Rosell. BAE 70. Madrid, 1953.

Primera crónica general de España, ed. Ramón Menéndez Pidal. 2 vols. Madrid, 1977.

Pulgar, Fernando del. *Crónica de los reyes Católicos*. 2 vols. Ed. Juan de Mata Carriazo. CCE 5–6. Madrid, 1943.

Relación de los fechos del mui magnífico e mas virtuosos señor, el señor don Miguel Lucas, mui digno Condestable de Castilla, ed. Pascual de Gayango y Arce. Memorial histórico español: Colección de documentos, opúsculos, y antigüedades 8. Madrid, 1855.

Relación de los hechos del muy magnífico e más virtuoso señor, el señor don Miguel Lucas, muy digno condestable de Castilla. Ed. Juan Cuevas Mata, Juan del Arco Moya, and José del Arco Moya, 249–309. Jae'n, 2001.

Rodríguez de Lena, Pedro. *El passo honroso de Suero de Quiñones*. Ed. Amancio Labandeira Fernández. Madrid, 1977.

Sánchez de Arévalo, Rodrigo. *Suma de la política*. In *Prosistas castellanos del siglo XV*, ed. Mario Penna, 249–309. BAE 116. Madrid, 1959.

———. *Vergel de los príncipes*. In *Prosistas castellanos del siglo XV*, ed. Mario Penna, 311–41. BAE 116. Madrid, 1959.

Valera, Diego de. *Memorial de diversas hazañas: crónica de Enrique IV*. Ed. Juan de Mata Carriazo. CCE 4. Madrid, 1941.

———. *Espejo de verdedera nobleza*, in *Prosistas castellanos del siglo XV*, ed. Mario Penna, 89–116. BAE 116. Madrid, 1959.

SECONDARY SOURCES

Abellán Pérez, Juan. "El concejo murciano de junio de 1429 a junio de 1430: Su estructura." *MMM* 5 (1980): 121–58.

Algazi, Gadi. "Diversity Rules." *Mediterranean Historical Review* 20 (2005): 227–45.

Alpert-Llorca, Marlene, and José Antonio González Alcantud. *Moros y cristianos: Representaciones del otro en las fiestas del Mediterráneo occidental.* Toulouse, 2003.

Andrés Díaz, Rosana de. "Las fiestas de caballería en la Castilla de los Trastámara." *En la España Medieval* 5 (1986): 81–107.

Antelo Iglesias, Antonio. "Alfonso de Palencia: Historiografía y humanismo en la Castilla de siglo XV." *Espacio, Tiempo y Forma* ser. 3, *Historia Medieval* 3 (1990): 21–40.

———. "La ciudad ideal según fray Francesc Eiximenis y Rodrigo Sánchez de Arévalo." *En la España Medieval* 6 (1985): 19–50.

Aranda Doncel, Juan. *Los moriscos en tierras de Córdoba.* Córdoba, 1984.

Argente del Castillo Ocaña, Carmen. "Los cautivos en la frontera entre Jaén y Granada." In *Relaciones exteriores del Reino de Granada: IV Coloquio de historia medieval andaluza*, ed. Cristina Segura Graíño, 211–26. Almería, 1988.

Arranz Guzmán, Ana. "Fiestas, juegos y diversiones prohibidas al clero en la Castilla Bajomedieval." *CHE* 78 (2003–2004): 9–33.

———. "Las visitas pastorales a las parroquias de la Corona de Castilla durante la Baja Edad Media: Un primer inventario de obispos visitadores." *En la España Medieval* 26 (2003): 295–339.

Asenjo González, María. "Las ciudades medievales castellanas: Balance y perspectivas de su desarrollo historiográfico (1990–2004)." *En la España Medieval* 28 (2005): 415–53.

Auden, W. H. *Spain.* London, 1937.

Avalle-Arce, Juan Bautista. *El cronista Pedro de Escavias: Una vida del siglo XV.* Chapel Hill, N.C., 1972.

Baer, Yitzhak. *A history of the Jews in Christian Spain.* Trans. Louis Schoffman. 2 vols. Philadelphia, 1961–1966.

Barceló Jiménez, Juan. *Historia del teatro en Murcia.* Murcia, 1980.

Bartolomé Herrero, Bonifacio. "Una visita pastoral a la diócesis de Segovia durante los años 1446 y 1447." *En la España Medieval* 18 (1995): 303–49.

Beinart, Haim. *Conversos on Trial: The Inquisition in Ciudad Real.* Jerusalem, 1981.

Bell, Catherine. *Ritual Theory, Ritual Practice.* Oxford, 1990.

Benítez Bolorinos, Manuel. *Las cofradías medievales en el Reino de Valencia, 1329–1458.* Alicante, 1998.

Berend, Nora. "Medievalists and the Notion of Frontier." *MHJ* 2 (1999): 55–72.

Bernis, Carmen. "Modas moriscas en la sociedad cristiana española del siglo XV y principios del XVI." *Boletín de la Real Academia de la Historia* 144 (1959): 199–228.

Bhabha, Homi K. "Culture's In-Between." In *Questions of Cultural Identity*, ed. Stuart Hall and Paul Du Gay, 53–60. London, 1996.

———. *The Location of Culture.* London, 1994.

Bishko, Charles Julian. "The Castilian as Plainsman: The Medieval Ranching Frontier in La Mancha and Extremadura." In *The New World Looks at Its History: Proceedings of the Second International Congress of Historians of the United States and Mexico*, ed. Archibald R. Lewis and Thomas McGann, 47–69. Austin, Tex., 1963.

Bonachía Hernando, Juan Antonio, ed. *La ciudad medieval: Aspectos de la vida urbana en la Castilla Bajomedieval*. Valladolid, 1996.

Bonde, Sheila, and Clark Maines. "*Ne aliquis extraneus claustrum intret*: Entry and Access at the Augustinian Abbey of Saint-Jean-des-Vignes, Soissons." In *Perspectives for an Architecture of Solitude: Essays on Cistercians, Art and Architecture in Honour of Peter Fergusson*, ed. Terryl N. Kinder, 173–86. Medieval Church Studies 11, Studia et Documenta 13. Turnhout, 2004.

Boswell, John. *The Royal Treasure: Muslim Communities Under the Crown of Aragon in the Fourteenth Century*. New Haven, Conn., 1977.

Boulton, D'Arcy Jonathan Dacre. *The Knights of the Crown: The Monarchical Orders of Knighthood in Later Medieval Europe, 1325–1520*. New York, 1987.

Brisset Martín, Demetrio E. "Fiestas hispanas de moros y cristianos: Historia y significados." *Gazeta de Antropología* 17 (2001).

Buc, Philippe. *The Dangers of Ritual: Between Early Medieval Texts and Social Scientific Theory*. Princeton, N.J., 2001.

Burns, Robert I. "The Parish as a Frontier Institution in Thirteenth Century Valencia." *Speculum* 37 (1962): 244–51.

———. "The Significance of the Frontier in the Middle Ages." In *Medieval Frontier Societies*, ed. Robert Bartlett and Angus MacKay, 307–30. Oxford, 1989.

Bynum, Caroline Walker. "The Female Body and Religious Practice in the Later Middle Ages." In *Fragmentation and Redemption: Essays on Gender and the Human Body in Medieval Religion*, 181–238. New York, 1991.

Cabrera Muñoz, Emilio. "Renta episcopal y producción agraria en el obispado de Córdoba en 1510." In *Actas del I Congreso de Historia de Andalucía*, 8 vols. 1: 397–412. Córdoba, 1978.

———. "Violencia urbana y crisis política en Andalucía en el siglo XV." In *Violencia y conflictividad en la sociedad de la España bajomedieval*, ed. Cabrera Muñoz, 5–25. Zaragoza, 1995.

Cabrera Muñoz, Emilio, and Andrés Moros, *Fuenteovejuna: La violencia antiseñorial en la siglo XV*. Barcelona, 1991.

Cabrera Sánchez, Margarita. "Los conversos de Córdoba en el siglo XV: La familia del jurado Martín Alonso." *Anuario de Estudios Medievales* 35 (2005): 185–232.

———. "Los corregidores de Córdoba en el siglo XV." *Meridies: Revista de Historia Medieval* 2 (1995): 95–108.

———. *Nobleza, oligarquía y poder en Córdoba al final de la Edad Media*. Córdoba, 1998.

———. "Oligarquía urbana y negocio inmobiliario en Córdoba en la segunda mitad del siglo XV." *HID* 20 (1993): 107–26.

———. "El problema converso en Córdoba: El incidente de la Cruz del Rastro." In *La Península Ibérica en la era de los descubrimientos, 1391–1492: Actas de las III Jornadas Hispano-Portuguesas de Historia Medieval,* 1:331–39. Seville, 1997.

———. "Los regidores de Córdoba en 1480: Aproximación prosopografía." *Meridies: Revista de Historia Medieval* 3 (1996): 61–88.

———. "La vivienda noble en Córdoba durante el siglo XV." In *Córdoba en la Historia: La construcción de la urbe,* ed. Francisco R. García Verdugo and Francisco Acosta Ramírez, 263–70. Córdoba, 1999.

Capel Sánchez, Juan José. "Murcia como espacio lúdico urbano en la Baja Edad Media." *MMM* 25–26 (2001–2002): 9–22.

———. *La vida lúdica en la Murcia bajomedieval.* Murcia, 2000.

Carcaller Cerviño, María del Pilar. "El ascenso político de Miguel Lucas de Iranzo: Ennoblecimiento y caballería al servicio de la monarquía." *BIEG* 176 (2000): 11–30.

Carrasco, Rafael. *Inquisición y represión sexual en Valencia: Historia de los sodomitas (1565–1785).* Barcelona, 1985.

Carriazo, Juan de Mata. "Un alcalde entre los cristianos y los moros, en la frontera de Granada." In *Homenaje al profesor Carriazo,* vol. 1, *En la frontera de Granada,* 85–142. Seville, 1971.

———. "Los moros de Granada en las actas del concejo de Jaén de 1479." In *Homenaje al profesor Carriazo,* vol. 1, *En la frontera de Granada,* 265–310. Seville, 1971.

———. "Relaciones fronterizas entre Jaén y Granada: El año 1479." In *Homenaje al profesor Carriazo,* vol. 1, *En la frontera de Granada,* 237–64. Seville, 1971.

Carruthers, Mary. *The Book of Memory: A Study of Memory in Medieval Culture.* Cambridge, 1990.

Castro, Américo. *España en su historia (Cristianos, moros y judios).* Barcelona, 1983.

Cátedra García, Pedro Manuel. *Sermón, sociedad y literatura en la Edad Media: San Vicente Ferrer en Castilla (1411–1412).* Salamanca, 1994.

Catlos, Brian. *The Victors and the Vanquished: Christians and Muslims in Catalonia and Aragon, 1050–1300.* Cambridge, 2001.

Cavafy, Constantine P. "Waiting for the Barbarians." In *C. P. Cavafy: Collected Poems,* trans. Edmund Keeley and Philip Sherrard, rev. ed., 18–19. Princeton, N.J., 1992.

Cela Esteban, María Estrella. *Elementos simbólicos en el arte castellano de los Reyes Católicos: El poder real y el patronato regio.* Madrid, 2001.

Chamberlin, Cynthia L. " 'Unless the Pen Writes as It Should': The Proto-Cult of Saint Fernando III in Sevilla in the Thirteenth and Fourteenth Centuries." In *Sevilla 1248: Congreso Internacional Conmemorativo del 750 Aniversario de la Conquista de la Ciudad de Sevilla por Fernando III, Rey de Castilla y León,* ed. Manuel Jiménez González, 389–418. Seville, 2000.

Ciudad Ruiz, Manuel. "El maestrazgo de Don Rodrigo Téllez Girón." *En la España Medieval* 23 (2000): 321–65.

Clare, Lucien. "Fêtes, jeux et divertissements à la cour du connétable de Castille, Miguel Lucas de Iranzo (1460–1470): Les exercices physiques." In *Frontières andalouses: La vie aʿ Jaeʾn entre 1460 et 1471, dʾapreʿs "Los hechos del condestable Miguel Lucas de Iranzo,"* ed. Jacques Heers, 15–34. Paris, 1996.

———. "Les formes dramatiques primitives du théâtre espagnol dʾaprès ʿLos hechos del condestable don Miguel Lucas de Iranzoʾ (1460–1470)." In *Frontières andalouses: La vie aʿ Jaeʾn entre 1460 et 1471, dʾapreʿs "Los hechos del condestable Miguel Lucas de Iranzo"*, ed. Jacques Heers, 78–85. Paris, 1996.

Clare, Lucien, and Michel García. "La guerre entre factions ou clientèles dans la crónica de Miguel Lucas de Iranzo." In *Frontières andalouses: La vie aʿ Jaeʾn entre 1460 et 1471, dʾapreʿs "Los hechos del condestable Miguel Lucas de Iranzo"*, ed. Jacques Heers, 135–50. Paris, 1996.

Contreras Villar, Angustias. "La Corte de Condestable Iranzo: La ciudad y la fiesta." *En la España Medieval* 10 (1987): 305–22.

Corbató, Hermenegildo. *Los misterios del Corpus de Valencia*. Berkeley, Calif., 1932.

Córdoba, Pierre, and Jean-Pierre Etienvre, eds. *La fiesta, la ceremonia, el rito*. Granada, 1990.

Coronas Tejada, Luis. *Conversos and Inquisition in Jaén*. Jerusalem, 1998.

———. *Los judíos en Jaén*. Jaén, 2008.

———. "El motín antijudio de 1473 en Jaén." In *Proceedings of the Seventh World Congress of Jewish Studies*, ed. Israel Gutman, 2 vols. 2:141–77. Jerusalem, 1981.

Crawford, Michael. *The Fight for Status and Privilege in Late Medieval and Early Modern Castile, 1465–1598*. University Park, Pa., 2014.

Darnton, Robert. "A Bourgeois Puts His World in Order: The City as a Text." In *The Great Cat Massacre and Other Episodes in French Cultural History*, 107–43. New York, 1999.

Davis, Natalie Z. "The Rites of Violence: Religious Riot in Sixteenth-Century France." *Past and Present* 59 (1975): 51–90.

Defourneaux, Marcellin. *La vida cotidiana en la España del Siglo de Oro*. Barcelona, 1983.

Devaney, Thomas. "Representing the Medieval Festivals of Jaén Through Text, Enactment and Image." In *Re-Presenting the Past: Archaeology Through Image and Text*, ed. Sheila Bonde and Stephen Houston, chap. 8. Oakville, Conn., 2011.

———. "Spectacle, Community, and Holy War in Fourteenth-Century Cyprus." *Medieval Encounters* 19 (2013): 300–341.

Di Camillo, Ottavio. *El humanismo castellano del siglo XV*. Valencia, 1976.

Díez Bedmar, María del Consuelo. *Teresa de Torres (ca. 1442–1521): Condesa de Castilla*. Madrid, 2004.

Dillard, Heath. *Daughters of the Reconquest: Women in Castilian Town Society, 1100–1300*. Cambridge, 1984.

Dompnier, Bernard, and Paola Vismara, eds. *Confréries et dévotions dans la catholicité moderne (mi-XVe–début XIXe siècle)*. Collection de lʾÉcole Française de Rome 393. Rome, 2008.

Dursteler, Eric. *Renegade Women: Gender, Identity, and Boundaries in the Early Modern Mediterranean*. Baltimore, 2011.

Edbury, Peter. "Latins and Greeks on Crusader Cyprus." In *Medieval Frontiers: Concepts and Practices*, ed. David Abulafia and Nora Berend, 133–42. Aldershot, 2002.

Edwards, John. *Christian Córdoba: The City and Its Region in the Late Middle Ages*. Cambridge, 1982.

———. "Conversion in Córdoba and Rome: Francisco Delicado's *La Lozana Andaluza*." In *Medieval Spain: Culture, Conflict, and Coexistence: Studies in Honor of Angus MacKay*, ed. Roger Collins and Anthony Goodman, 202–24. Basingstoke, 2002.

———. "The Culture of the Street: The Calle de la Feria in Córdoba, 1470–1520." In *Mediterranean Urban Culture, 1400–1700*, ed. Alexander Cowan, 69–82, 232–35. Exeter, 2000.

———. "Elijah and the Inquisition: Messianic Prophecy Among *Conversos* in Spain, c. 1500." *Nottingham Medieval Studies* 28 (1984): 79–94.

———. "The *Judeoconversos* in the Urban Life of Córdoba, 1450–1520." In *Villes et sociétés urbaines au Moyen Âge*, ed. Pierre Desportes, 287–99. Paris, 1994.

———. "The 'Massacre' of Jewish Christians in Córdoba, 1473–1474." In *The Massacre in History*, ed. Mark Levene and Penny Roberts, 55–68. New York, 1999.

———. "Nobleza y religión: Don Alfonso de Aguilar (1447–1501)." *Ámbitos: Revista de Estudios de Ciencias Sociales y Humanidades de Córdoba* 3 (2000): 9–19.

———. "Politics and Ideology in Late-Medieval Córdoba," *En la España medieval* 4 (1984): 277–303.

———. "Religious Belief and Social Conformity: The 'Converso' Problem in Late-Medieval Córdoba," *Transactions of the Royal Historical Society* 5th ser. 31 (1981): 115–28.

———. "A Society Organized for War? Córdoba in the Time of Ferdinand and Isabella." In *Jews, Muslims and Christians in and Around the Crown of Aragon: Essays in Honour of Professor Elena Lourie*, ed. Harvey J. Hames, 75–96. Leiden, 2004.

———. *The Spain of the Catholic Monarchs, 1474–1520*. Oxford, 2000.

———. *The Spanish Inquisition*. Stroud, 1999.

———. "Trial of an Inquisitor: The Dismissal of Diego Rodríguez Lucero, Inquisitor of Córdoba, in 1508." *Journal of Ecclesiastical History* 37 (1986): 240–57.

Escobar Camacho, José Manuel. *Córdoba en la Baja Edad Media: Evolución urbana de la ciudad*. Córdoba, 1989.

———. *La vida urbana cordobesa: El Potro y su entorno en la Baja Edad Media*. Córdoba, 1985.

Escobar Camacho, José Manuel, and Antonio Varo Pineda. *El veinticuatro Fernán Alfonso y los comendadores de Córdoba: Historia, literatura y leyenda*. Córdoba, 1999.

Fallows, Noel. "Just Say No? Alfonso de Cartagena, the *Doctrinal de los caballeros*, and Spain's Most Noble Pastime." In *Studies on Medieval Spanish Literature in Honor of Charles F. Fraker*, ed. Mercedes Vaquero and Alan Deyermond, 129–41. Madison, Wis., 1995.

Fernández Gallardo, Luis. *Alfonso de Cartagena, 1385–1456: Una biografía política en la Castilla del siglo XV*. Valladolid, 2002.

Fleckenstein, Josef. *La caballería y el mundo caballeresco*. Madrid, 2006.

Flores Arroyuelo, Francisco. *El caballero: Hombre y prototipo*. Murcia, 1979.

Flynn, Maureen. *Sacred Charity: Confraternities and Social Welfare in Spain, 1400–1700*. Ithaca, N.Y., 1989.

———. "The Spectacle of Suffering in Spanish Streets." In *City and Spectacle in Medieval Europe*, ed. Barbara Hanawalt and Kathryn Reyerson, 153–68. Minneapolis, 1994.

Foley, Augusta. *La Lozana andaluza*. Critical Guides to Spanish Texts 18. London, 1977.

Fuchs, Barbara. *Exotic Nation: Maurophilia and the Construction of Early Modern Spain*. Philadelphia, 2009.

García, Michel. "A propos de la chronique du connètable Miguel Lucas de Iranzo." *Bulletin hispanique* 75 (1973): 5–39.

García Antón, José. "La tolerancia religiosa en la frontera de Murcia y Granada en los últimos tiempos del reino nazarí." *Murgetana* 57 (1980): 133–43.

García Díaz, Isabel. *La huerta de Murcia en el siglo XIV (propiedad y producción)*. Murcia, 1990.

García Fitz, Francisco. *La Reconquista*. Granada, 2010.

———. "La Reconquista: Un estado de la cuestión." *Clio y Crimen* 6 (2009): 142–215.

García y García, Antonio. "Religiosidad popular y festividades en el occidente peninsular (siglos XIII–XIV." In *Fiestas y Liturgia: Actas del coloquio celebrado en la Casa de Velásquez*, 35–51. Madrid, 1988.

Garganta, José María, and Vicente Forcada. *Biografía y escritos de San Vicente Ferrer*. Madrid, 1956.

Garrido Aguilera, Juan Carlos. "Relaciones fronterizas con el reino de Granada en las Capitulares del Archivo Histórico Municipal de Jaén." In *Relaciones exteriores del Reino de Granada: IV Coloquio de historia medieval andaluza*, ed. Cristina Segura Graíño, 161–72. Almería, 1988.

Gatton, John. "'There Must Be Blood': Mutilation and Martyrdom on the Medieval Stage." In *Violence in Drama*, ed. James Redmond, 79–91. Cambridge, 1991.

Gelabert, Juan. "Cities, Towns and Small Towns in Castile, 1500–1800." In *Small Towns in Early Modern Europe*, ed. Peter Clark, 271–94. Cambridge, 1995.

Gerbet, Marie-Claude. "Les confréries religieuses à Cáceres de 1467 à 1523." *MCV* 7 (1971): 75–114.

———. "La population noble dans le royaume de Castille vers 1500: La répartition géographique de ses différentes composantes." *Anales de Historia Antigua y Medieval* 20 (1977–1979): 78–99.

Gibello Bravo, Víctor. "La violencia convertida en espectáculo: Las fiestas caballerescas medievales." In *Fiestas, juegos y espectáculos en la España medieval: Actas del VII Curso de Cultura Medieval, celebrado en Aguilar de Campoo (Palencia) del 18 al 21 de septiembre de 1995*, 157–72. Aguilar de Campoo, 1999.

Gil Albarracín, Antonio. *Cofradías y hermandades en la Almería moderna (historia y documentos)*. Barcelona, 1997.

Glick, Thomas. *From Muslim Fortress to Christian Castle: Social and Cultural Change in Medieval Spain.* Manchester, 1995.

———. *Islamic and Christian Spain in the Early Middle Ages: Comparative Perspectives on Social and Cultural Formation.* Princeton, N.J., 1979.

Gómez-Bravo, Ana M. "Ser social y poética material en la obra de Antón de Montoro, mediano converso." *Hispanic Review* 78 (2010): 145–67.

Gómez García, Pedro, ed. *Fiestas y religión en la cultura popular andaluza.* Granada, 1992.

Gómez Moreno, Ángel. "La qüestion del marqués de Santillana a don Alfonso de Cartagena," *El Crotalón* 2 (1985): 335–63.

González Arce, José Damián, and Francisco José García Pérez. "Ritual, jerarquías y símbolos en las exequias reales de Murcia (siglo XV)." *MMM* 19–20 (1995–1996): 129–38.

González Jiménez, Manuel. *Fernando III El Santo.* Seville, 2006.

———. "Peace and War on the Frontier of Granada: Jaén and the Truce of 1476." In *Medieval Spain: Culture, Conflict, and Coexistence: Studies in Honor of Angus MacKay,* ed. Roger Collins and Anthony Goodman, 160–75. Basingstoke, 2002.

———. "Sobre la ideología de la reconquista: Realidades y tópicos." In *Memoria, mito y realidad en la historia medieval: XIII Semana de Estudios Medievales, Nájera, del 29 de julio al 2 de agosto de 2002,* ed. José Ignacio de la Iglesia Duarte and José Luis Martín Rodríguez, 151–70. Logroño, 2003.

González Jiménez, Manuel, and Isabel Montes Romero-Camacho. "Los mudéjares andaluces (siglos XIII–XV) aproximación al estado de la cuestión y propuesta de un modelo teórico." In *Los mudéjares valencianos y peninsulares,* ed. Manuel Ruzafa, 47–78. Valencia, 2004.

Greene, Molly. *Catholic Pirates and Greek Merchants: A Maritime History of the Mediterranean.* Princeton, N.J., 2010.

Harris, Max. *Aztecs, Moors, and Christians: Festivals of Reconquest in Mexico and Spain.* Austin, Tex., 2000.

Harris, W. V., ed. *Rethinking the Mediterranean.* Oxford, 2005.

Head, Thomas, and Richard Landes, eds. *The Peace of God: Social Violence and Religious Response in France Around the Year 1000.* Ithaca, N.Y., 1992.

Hering Torres, Max S., María Elena Martínez, and David Nirenberg, eds. *Race and Blood in the Iberian World.* Berlin, 2012.

Herráez Martín, María Isabel. "La espada de Fernando III, El Santo." *Laboratorio del Arte* 15 (2002): 335–48.

Hillgarth, Jocelyn N. *The Spanish Kingdoms, 1250–1516.* 2 vols. Oxford, 1976–1978.

Homet, Raquel. "Sobre el espacio de las fiestas en la sociedad medieval." *Temas Medievales* 1 (1991): 143–61.

Horden, Peregrine, and Nicholas Purcell. *The Corrupting Sea: A Study of Mediterranean History.* Oxford, 2000.

Howell, Martha C. "The Spaces of Late Medieval Urbanity." In *Shaping Urban Identity in Late Medieval Europe,* ed. Marc Boone and Peter Stabel, 3–23. Leuven, 2000.

Hsia, Ronnie Po-Chia. *The Myth of Ritual Murder: Jews and Magic in Reformation Germany*. New Haven, Conn., 1988.

Huizinga, Johan. *The Autumn of the Middle Ages*. Trans. Rodney J. Payton and Ulrich Mammitzsch. Chicago, 1996.

Husain, Adnan K., and K. E. Fleming, eds. *A Faithful Sea: The Religious Cultures of the Mediterranean, 1200–1700*. Oxford, 2007.

Jackson, Gabriel. *The Making of Medieval Spain*. New York, 1972.

Jiménez Alcázar, Juan Francisco. "El hombre y la frontera: Murcia y Granada en época de Enrique IV." *MMM* 17 (1992): 77–96.

Juderías, Julián. *La leyenda negra y la verdad histórica: Contribución al estudio del concepto de España en Europa, de las causas de este concepto y de la tolerancia política y religiosa en los países civilizados*. Madrid, 1914.

Jular Pérez-Alfaro, Cristina. "The King's Face on the Territory: Royal Officers, Discourse, and Legitimating Practices in Thirteenth-and Fourteenth-Century Castile." In *Building Legitimacy: Political Discourses and Forms of Legitimation in Medieval Societies*, ed. Isabel Alfonso, Hugh Kennedy, and Julio Escalona, 107–38. Leiden, 2004.

Kaeuper, Richard W. *Chivalry and Violence in Medieval Europe*. Oxford, 1999.

Kagan, Richard. *Lawsuits and Litigants in Castile, 1500–1700*. Chapel Hill, N.C., 1981.

———, ed. *Spanish Cities of the Golden Age: The Views of Anton van den Wyngaerde*. Berkeley, Calif., 1989.

———. "*Urbs* and *Civitas* in Sixteenth- and Seventeenth-Century Spain." In *Envisioning the City: Six Studies in Urban Cartography*, ed. David Buisseret, 75–108. Chicago, 1998.

Kagan, Richard, and Fernando Marías, *Urban Images of the Hispanic World, 1493–1793*. New Haven, Conn., 2000.

Kamen, Henry. *The Spanish Inquisition: A Historical Revision*. New Haven, Conn., 1998.

Kantorowicz, Ernst. *The King's Two Bodies: A Study in Medieval Political Theology*. Princeton, N.J., 1957.

Keen, Maurice. *Chivalry*. New Haven, Conn., 1984.

Knighton, Tess. "Spaces and Contexts for Listening in 15th-Century Castile: The Case of the Constable's Palace in Jaén." *Early Music* 25 (1997): 661–77.

Koziol, Geoffrey. *Begging Pardon and Favor: Ritual and Political Order in Early Medieval France*. Ithaca, N.Y., 1992.

Laboa, Juan María. *Rodrigo Sánchez de Arévalo, alcaide de Sant'Ángelo*. Madrid, 1973.

Ladero Quesada, Miguel Ángel. *Castilla y la conquista de Granada*. Valladolid, 1967.

———. *La hacienda real de Castilla en el siglo XV*. La Laguna, 1973.

———. *Los mudéjares de Castilla en tiempos de Isabel I*. Valladolid, 1969.

———. "Producción y renta cerealeras en el reino de Córdoba a finales del siglo XV." In *Actas del I Congreso de Historia de Andalucía*. 8 vols. 1: 375–96. Córdoba, 1978.

———. "¿Es todavía España un enigma histórico? Releyendo a Sánchez-Albornoz." In *Lecturas sobre la España histórica*, 317–44. Madrid, 1998.

Ladero Quesada, Manuel Fernando. "Consideraciones metodológicas sobre el estudio de los núcleos urbanos en la Castilla bajomedieval: Notas para un modelo teórico de análisis." *Espacio, Tiempo y Forma* ser. 3, *Historia Medieval* 4 (1991): 353–66.

Lázaro Carreter, Fernando. "El drama litúrgico, los 'juegos de escarnio' y el 'Auto de los Reyes Magos'." In *Historia y crítica de la literatura española*, vol. 1, *Edad media*, ed. Alan Deyermond, 461–65. Barcelona, 1979.

———. "Juegos de escarnio." In *Dictionary of the Literature of the Iberian Peninsula*, ed. Germán Bleiberg, Maureen Ihrie, and Janet Pérez, 897. Westport, Conn., 1993.

———. *Teatro medieval*. Madrid, 1981.

Leva Cuevas, Josefa. "Una elite en el mundo artesanal de la Córdoba de los siglos XV y XVI: Plateros, joyeros y esmaltadores." *Ámbitos: Revista de Estudios de Ciencias Sociales y Humanidades* 16 (2006): 99–115.

———. "Escribanos y notarios en la Castilla Bajomedieval: Su ejercicio en la Córdoba de la época." *Ámbitos: Revista de Estudios de Ciencias Sociales y Humanidades* 21 (2009): 63–93.

Linehan, Peter. "At the Spanish Frontier." In *The Medieval World*, ed. Peter Linehan and Janet L. Nelson, 37–59. London, 2001.

Little, Lester K. "The Jews in Christian Europe." In *Essential Papers on Judaism and Christianity in Conflict: From Late Antiquity to the Reformation*, ed. Jeremy Cohen, 276–97. New York, 1991.

Lleó Cañal, Vicente. *Fiesta grande: El Corpus Christi en la historia de Sevilla*. Seville, 1980.

Llompart, Gabriel. "La fiesta del Corpus y representaciones religiosas en Zaragoza y Mallorca (siglos XIV–XVI)." *Analecta Sacra Tarraconensia: Revista de Ciencias Historioeclesiásticas* 42 (1969): 181–209.

López Cordero, Juan Antonio. "El Castillo de Chincoya en la bibliografía." *Elucidario* 1 (2006): 237–48.

López de Coca-Castañer, José Enrique. "Institutions on the Castilian-Granadan Frontier, 1369–1482." In *Medieval Frontier Societies*, ed. Robert Bartlett and Angus MacKay, 127–50. Oxford, 1989.

Lucas-Dubreton, Jean. *El rey huraño: Enrique IV de Castilla y su época*. Madrid, 1945.

Lynch, Katherine A. *Individuals, Families and Communities in Europe, 1200–1800*. Cambridge, 2003.

Lynch, Kevin. *The Image of the City*. Cambridge, 1960.

MacEvitt, Christopher. *The Crusades and the Christian World of the East: Rough Tolerance*. Philadelphia, 2008.

Machado Santiago, Rafael, and Emilio Arroyo López. "El territorio y el hombre (análisis geográfico): Jaén." In *Historia de Jaén*, 15–48. Jaén, 1982.

MacKay, Angus. "Andalucía y la guerra del fin del mundo." In *Andalucía entre oriente y occidente (1236–1492): Actas del V Coloquio internacional de historia medieval de Andalucía*, ed. Emilio Cabrera, 329–42. Córdoba, 1988.

———. "Climate and Popular Unrest in Late Medieval Castile." In *Climate and History: Studies in Past Climates and Their Impact on Man*, ed. Thomas M. L. Wigley, Martin J. Ingram, and G. Farmer, 356–76. Cambridge, 1981.

———. "Ferdinand of Antequera and the Virgin Mary." In Ian Macpherson and Angus MacKay, *Love, Religion and Politics in Fifteenth Century Spain*, 132–39. Leiden, 1998. Previously published as "Don Fernando de Antequera y la Virgen Santa María," in *Homenaje al profesor Juan Torres Fontes*, 2 vols, 2: 949–57. Murcia, 1987.

———. "The Hispanic-*Converso* Predicament." *Transactions of the Royal Historical Society* 5th ser. 35 (1985): 159–79.

———. *Money, Prices, and Politics in Fifteenth-Century Castile*. London, 1981.

———. "Popular Movements and Pogroms in Fifteenth-Century Castile." *Past and Present* 55 (1972): 33–67.

———. "Religion, Culture, and Ideology on the Late Medieval Castilian-Granadan Frontier." In *Medieval Frontier Societies*, ed. Robert Bartlett and Angus MacKay, 217–44. Oxford, 1989.

———. "Ritual and Propaganda in Fifteenth-Century Castile." *Past and Present* 107 (1985): 3–43.

———. "The Whores of Babylon." In Ian Macpherson and Angus MacKay, *Love, Religion and Politics in Fifteenth Century Spain*, 179–87. Leiden, 1998. Previously published in *Prophetic Rome in the High Renaissance Period: Essays*, ed. Marjorie Reeves, 223–32. Oxford, 1992.

———. "Women on the Margins." In Ian Macpherson and Angus MacKay, *Love, Religion and Politics in Fifteenth-Century Spain*, 28–42. Leiden, 1998. Previously published as "Averroistas y marginadas," in *Actas del III Coloquio de Historia Medieval Andaluza: La sociedad medieval andaluza; Grupos no privilegiados*, ed. Manuel González Jiménez and José Rodríguez Molina, 247–61. Jaén, 1984.

Macpherson, Ian. "The Game of Courtly Love." In Ian Macpherson and Angus MacKay, *Love, Religion and Politics in Fifteenth Century Spain*, 236–53. Leiden, 1998.

Macpherson, Ian, and Angus MacKay. *Love, Religion and Politics in Fifteenth Century Spain*. Leiden, 1998.

Mann, Janice. *Romanesque Architecture and Its Sculptural Decoration in Christian Spain, 1000–1120: Exploring Frontiers and Defining Identities*. Toronto, 2009.

Mantel, María Marcela. "Carácter socioeconómico de los juegos y entretenimientos en Castilla: Siglos XIII al XV." *Estudios de Historia de España* 3 (1990): 51–116.

Marsilla de Pascua, Francisco Reyes. "Los judíos y el cabildo catedralicio de Murcia en el siglo XV." *MMM* 15 (1989): 55–84.

Marino, Nancy F. *Don Juan Pacheco: Wealth and Power in Late Medieval Spain*. Tempe, Ariz., 2006.

Márquez Villanueva, Francisco. "Conversos y cargos concejiles en el siglo XV." *Revista de Archivos, Bibliotecas y Museos* 58 (1957): 503–40.

Martínez Carrillo, María de los Llanos. "Elitismo y participación popular en las fiestas medievales." *MMM* 18 (1993–1994): 95–107.

———. "Fiestas ciudadanas: Componentes religiosos y profanos de un cuadro bajamedieval Murcia." *MMM* 16 (1990–1991): 9–50.

———. *Manueles y Fajardos: La crisis bajomedieval en Murcia.* Murcia, 1985.

Martínez González, Rafael Ángel. *Las cofradías Penitenciales de Palencia.* Palencia, 1979.

Martínez Martínez, María. *La cultura del aceite en Murcia: Siglos XIII–XV.* Murcia, 1995.

———. "Gastos del concejo lorquino para el Corpus de 1472." *Estudios Románicos* 6 (1987–1989): 1687–96.

———. *La industria del vestido en Murcia: Siglos XIII–XV.* Murcia, 1988.

Maza Romero, Fernando. "Tensiones sociales en el municipio cordobés en la primera mitad del siglo XV." In *Actas del I Congreso de Historia de Andalucía*, 2:85–112. Córdoba, 1978.

McCrank, Lawrence. "The Cistercians of Poblet as Medieval Frontiersmen." In *Estudios en homenaje a don Claudio Sánchez Albornez en sus 90 años: Anexos de Cuadernos de historia de España.* 3 vols. 2: 313–60. Buenos Aires, 1983.

Menéndez y Pelayo, Marcelino. *Edición nacional de las obras completas de Menéndez Pelayo*, 65 vols. Madrid, 1940–1959.

Menjot, Denis. *Murcie castillane: Une ville au temps de la frontière (1243–milieu du XVe s.).* 2 vols. Madrid, 2002.

Meyerson, Mark. *A Jewish Renaissance in Fifteenth-Century Spain.* Princeton, N.J., 2004.

Miller, Townsend. *Henry IV of Castile, 1425–1474.* Philadelphia, 1972.

Miranda García, Fermín. "La ciudad medieval hispana: Una aproximación bibliográfica." In *Las sociedades urbanas en la España medieval: XXIX Semana de Estudios Medievales, Estella, 15 a 19 de julio de 2002*, 591–626. Pamplona, 2003.

Mitre Fernández, Emilio. "Córdoba y su campiña: Una comarca fronteriza al comenzar el siglo XV." *Cuadernos de Estudios Medievales* 1 (1973): 9–32.

Molina, Ricardo. *Córdoba en sus plazas.* Córdoba, 1962.

Molina Molina, Ángel Luis. *El campo de Murcia en el siglo XV.* Murcia, 1989.

———. "Datos sobre sociodemografía murciana a fines de la Edad Media (1475–1515)." In *Anales de la Universidad de Murcia: Filosofía y letras* 36 (1977–1978): 169–83.

———. "Estampas medievales murcianas: Desde la romántica caballeresca, caza y fiesta, a la predicación, procesión y romería." In *Fiestas, juegos y espectáculos en la España medieval: Actas del VII Curso de Cultura Medieval, celebrado en Aguilar de Campoo (Palencia) del 18 al 21 de septiembre de 1995*, 33–64. Aguilar de Campoo, 1999.

———. *Estudios sobre la vida cotidiana (ss. XIII–XVI).* Murcia, 2003.

———. "Mercaderes genoveses en Murcia durante la época de los Reyes Católicos (1475–1516)." *MMM* 2 (1976): 277–312.

———. "Sermones, procesiones y romerías en la Murcia bajomedieval." *MMM* 19–20 (1995–1996): 229–32.

———. *La sociedad murciana en el tránsito de la edad media a la moderna.* Murcia, 1996.

———. *Urbanismo medieval: La región de Murcia.* Murcia, 1992.

Moyano Martínez, Juan Manuel. "Familia y poder político en la Murcia bajomedieval (siglos XIV y XV)." *MMM* 17 (1992): 9–41.

Navarro, Andrea Mariana. "Pasado y antigüedad clásica en los discursos sobre ciudades: Las *Laudes* en la historiografía andaluza." *Temas Medievales* 16 (2008).

Netanyahu, Benzion. *The Origins of the Inquisition in Fifteenth-Century Spain.* New York, 1995.

Nieto Cumplido, Manuel. *Córdoba 1492: Ambiente artístico y cultural.* Córdoba, 1992.

———. *Historia de Córdoba: Islam y cristianismo.* Córdoba, 1984.

———. "Luchas nobiliarias y movimientos populares en Córdoba a fines del siglo XIV." In *Tres estudios de historia medieval andaluza,* ed. Manuel Riu Riu, Cristóbal Torres, and Manuel Nieto Cumplido, 11–65. Córdoba, 1977.

———. "Religiosidad popular andaluza: La regla medieval de la Cofradía de Animas de Castro del Río (Córdoba)." *Revista del Centro de Estudios Históricos de Granada y su Reino* 16 (2004): 257–82.

———. "La revuelta contra los conversos de Córdoba en 1473." In *Homenaje de Antón de Montoro en el V centenario de su muerte,* 29–49. Montoro, 1977.

Nirenberg, David. *Communities of Violence: Persecution of Minorities in the Middle Ages.* Princeton, N.J., 1996.

———. "Conversion, Sex, and Segregation: Jews and Christians in Medieval Spain." *American Historical Review* 107 (2002): 1065–93.

———. "Was There Race Before Modernity? The Example of 'Jewish' Blood in Late Medieval Spain." In *The Origins of Racism in the West,* ed. Miriam Eliav-Feldon, Benjamin Isaac, and Joseph Ziegler, 232–64. Cambridge, 2009.

O'Callaghan, Joseph F. *Alfonso X and the Cantigas de Santa Maria: A Poetic Biography.* Leiden, 1998.

———. *Reconquest and Crusade in Medieval Spain.* Philadelphia, 2003.

Ortí Belmonte, Miguel Ángel. *Córdoba monumental, artística e histórica.* Córdoba, 1980.

Padilla González, Jesús, and José Manuel Escobar Camacho. "La mancebía de Córdoba en la Baja Edad Media." In *Actas del III Coloquio de Historia Medieval Andaluza: La sociedad medieval andaluza; Grupos no privilegiados,* ed. Manuel González Jiménez and José Rodríguez Molina, 279–92. Jaén, 1984.

Paéz García, Mateo Antonio. "El condestable Iranzo y la frontera con Granada: Un itinerario de sus actividades militares." In *Andalucía entre Oriente y Occidente (1236–1492): Actas del V Coloquio Internacional de Historia Medieval de Andalucía,* ed. Emilio Cabrera, 385–98. Córdoba, 1988.

Palomo Fernández, Gema, and José Luis Senra Gabriel y Galán. "La ciudad y la fiesta en la historiografía castellana de la baja edad media: Escenografía lúdico-festiva." *Hispania* 54, 1 (1994): 5–36.

Parma, Mariana Valeria. "Fiesta y revuelta: La teatralidad política en Valencia a principios de la modernidad." *CHE* 77 (2001–2002): 145–64.

Pascual Martínez, Lope. "Las hermandades en Murcia durante la baja Edad Media." *MMM* 3 (1977): 163–209.

Payen, Jean-Charles. "Théâtre médiéval et culture urbaine." *Revue d'Histoire du Théâtre* 35 (1983): 233–50.

Penna, Mario. "Estudio preliminar," in *Prosistas castellanos del siglo XV*, ed. Penna. BAE 116. Madrid, 1959.

Pérez, Joseph. *The Spanish Inquisition: A History*. Trans. Janet Lloyd. New Haven, Conn., 2005.

Peters, Edward. "Jewish History and Gentile Memory: The Expulsion of 1492." *Jewish History* 9 (1995): 9–34.

———. "*Omnia permixta sunt*: Where's the Border?" *MHJ* 4 (2001): 109–27.

Phillips, William D., Jr. *Enrique IV and the Crisis of Fifteenth-Century Castile, 1425–1480*. Cambridge, Mass., 1978.

Pino García, José Luis del. "El concejo de Córdoba a finales de la Edad Media: Estructura interna y política municipal." *HID* 20 (1993): 355–402.

Piqueras García, María Belén. "Funcionamiento del concejo murciano (1462–1474)." *MMM* 14 (1987–1988): 9–47.

Porras Arboledas, Pedro A. "El comercio entre Jaén y Granada en 1480." *Al-Qantara: Revista de Estudios Árabes* 9, fasc. 2 (1988): 519–24.

———. "La frontera del Reino de Granada a través del Libro de Actas del Cabildo de Jaén de 1476." *Al-Qantara: Revista de Estudios Árabes* 14, fasc. 1 (1993): 127–62.

———. "Las relaciones entre la ciudad de Jaén y el reino de Granada: La paz y la guerra según el libros de Actas de 1480 y 1488." *Al-Qantara: Revista de Estudios Árabes* 9, fasc. 1 (1988): 29–46.

Quesada, Santiago. *La idea de ciudad en la cultura hispana de la edad moderna*. Barcelona, 1992.

Quintanilla Raso, María Concepción. "La caballería cordobesa a finales de la Edad Media: Análisis de un conflicto social urbano." In *Villes et sociétés urbaines au Moyen Âge*, ed. Pierre Desportes, 121–32. Paris, 1994.

———. "El dominio de las ciudades por la nobleza: El caso de Córdoba en la segunda mitad del siglo XV." *En la España Medieval* 10 (1987): 109–24.

———. "Estructura y función de los bandos nobiliarios en Córdoba a fines de la Edad Media." In *Bandos y querellas dinásticas en España al final de la Edad Media*, 135–55. Paris, 1991.

———. "Estructuras sociales y familiares y papel político de la nobleza cordobesa (siglos XIV y XV)." *En la España Medieval* 3 (1982): 331–52.

———. *Nobleza y señoríos en el reino de Córdoba: La casa de Aguilar (siglos XIV–XV)*. Córdoba, 1979.

Ramírez de Arellano y Gutiérrez, Teodomiro. *Paseos por Córdoba, o sea Apuntes para su historia*. León, 1973.

Rawlings, Helen. *The Spanish Inquisition*. Malden, Mass., 2006.

Remensnyder, Amy G. "Marian Monarchy in Thirteenth-Century Castile." In *The Experience of Power in Medieval Europe, 950–1350*, ed. Robert F. Berkhoper III, Alan Cooper, and Adam Kosto, 253–70. Aldershot, 2005.

Richardson, Amanda. "Corridors of Power: A Case Study in Access Analysis from Medieval England." *Antiquities* 77 (2003): 373–84.

Rico, Francisco. "Unas coplas de Jorge Manrique y las fiestas de Valladolid en 1428." *Anuario de Estudios Medievales* 2 (1965): 517–24.

Riquer, Martín de. *Caballeros andantes españoles*. Madrid, 1967.

Rodríguez Molina, José. "Banda territorial común entre Granada y Jaén: Siglo XV." In *Estudios sobre Málaga y el Reino de Granada en el V Centenario de la Conquista*, 113–30. Málaga, 1987.

———. "La frontera entre Granada y Jaén: Fuente de engrandecimiento para la nobleza." In *Relaciones exteriores del Reino de Granada: IV Coloquio de historia medieval andaluza*, ed. Cristina Segura Graíño, 237–50. Almería, 1988.

———. "Jaén: Organización de sus tierras y hombres (siglos XIII–XVI). In *Historia de Jaén*, 201–63. Jaén, 1982.

———. *El reino de Jaén en la baja Edad Media: Aspectos demográficos y económicos*. Granada, 1978.

———. *La vida de la ciudad de Jaén en tiempos del condestable Iranzo*. Jaén, 1996.

———. *La vida de moros y cristianos en la frontera*. Jaén, 2007.

Rodríguez Velasco, Jesús. *El debate sobre la caballería en el siglo XV: La tratadística caballeresca castellana en su marco europeo*. Valladolid, 1996.

Romero Abao, Antonio. "La fiesta del Corpus Christi en Sevilla en el siglo XV." In *La religiosidad popular*, ed. María Jesús Buxó i Rey, Salvador Rodríguez Becerra, and León Carlos Álvarez y Santaló, 3:19–30. Seville, 1989.

Rubin, Miri. *Corpus Christi: The Eucharist in Late Medieval Culture*. Cambridge, 1991.

———. "The Eucharist and the Construction of Christian Identities." In *Culture and History, 1350–1600*, ed. David Aers, 43–63. Detroit, 1992.

———. *Gentile Tales: The Narrative Assault on Late Medieval Jews*. Philadelphia, 2004.

Rubio García, Luis. *La procesión de Corpus en el siglo XV en Murcia*. Murcia, 1987.

Ruiz, Teofilo. *Crisis and Continuity: Land and Town in Late Medieval Castile*. Philadelphia, 1994.

———. "Elite and Popular Culture in Late Fifteenth-Century Castilian Festivals: The Case of Jaén." In *City and Spectacle in Medieval Europe*, ed. Barbara Hanawalt and Kathryn Reyerson, 296–318. Minneapolis, 1994.

———. "Festivités, couleurs, et symboles du pouvoir en Castille au XVe siècle." *Annales: Économies, sociétés, civilisations* 3 (1991): 521–46.

———. *A King Travels: Festive Traditions in Late Medieval and Early Modern Spain*. Princeton, N.J., 2012.

———. *Spain's Centuries of Crisis, 1300–1474*. Oxford, 2007.

———. "The Symbolic Meaning of Sword and Palio in Late Medieval and Early Modern Ritual Entries: The Case of Seville." In *Memoria y Civilización* 12 (2009): 13–48.

Rutherford, Jonathan. "The Third Space: Interview with Homi Bhabha." In *Identity, Community, Culture, Difference*, ed. Rutherford, 207–21. London, 1990.

Sagarra Gamazo, Adelaida. *Juan Rodríguez de Fonseca, un toresano en dos mundos*. Zamora, 2006.

Sampedro Vizcaya, Benita, and Simon Doubleday, eds. *Border Interrogations: Questioning Spanish Frontiers*. New York, 2008.

Sánchez-Albornoz, Claudio. "The Frontier and Castilian Liberties." In *The New World Looks at Its History: Proceedings of the Second International Congress of Historians of the United States and Mexico*, ed. Archibald R. Lewis and Thomas McGann, 27–46. Austin, Tex., 1963.

Sánchez León, Pablo. "Changing Patterns of Urban Conflict in Late Medieval Castile." *Past and Present* 195 supp. 2 (2007): 217–32.

———. "Town and Country in Castile, 1400–1650." In *Town and Country in Europe, 1300–1800*, ed. S. R. Epstein, 272–91. Cambridge, 2001.

Sanz Sancho, Iluminado. "El poder episcopal en Córdoba en la Baja Edad Media." *En la España Medieval* 13 (1990): 163–206.

Schwartz, Stuart. *All Can Be Saved: Religious Tolerance and Salvation in the Iberian Atlantic World*. New Haven, Conn., 2008.

Serrano, Luciano. *Los conversos D. Pablo de Santa María y D. Alfonso de Cartagena, obispos de Burgos, gobernantes, diplomáticos y escritores*. Madrid, 1942.

Sirera Turo, Josep Lluís. "La construcción del *Auto de la Pasión* y el teatro medieval castellano." In *Actas del III Congreso de la Asociación Hispánica de Literatura Medieval*, ed. María Isabel Toro Pascua, 2:1011–20. Salamanca, 1994.

Sponsler, Claire. "The Culture of the Spectator: Conformity and Resistance to Medieval Performances." *Theatre Journal* 44 (1992): 15–29.

———. *Drama and Resistance: Bodies, Goods, and Theatricality in Late Medieval England*. Minneapolis, 1997.

Starr-LeBeau, Gretchen D. *In the Shadow of the Virgin: Inquisitors, Friars, and Conversos in Guadalupe, Spain*. Princeton, N.J., 2003.

Stern, Charlotte. "Christmas Performances in Jaén in the 1460s." In *Studies in Honor of Bruce W. Wardropper*, ed. Dian Fox, Harry Sieber, and Robert Ter Horst, 323–34. Newark, Del., 1989.

———. *The Medieval Theater in Castile*. Binghamton, N.Y., 1996.

Suárez Fernández, Luis. *Los Reyes Católicos: El tiempo de la guerra de Granada*. Madrid, 1989.

Surtz, Ronald. *The Birth of a Theater: Dramatic Convention in the Spanish Theater from Juan del Encina to Lope de Vega*. Madrid, 1979.

Tate, Robert Brian. "The Civic Humanism of Alfonso de Palencia." *Renaissance and Modern Studies* 23 (1979): 25–44.

———. "*Laus Urbium*: Praise of Two Andalusian Cities in the Mid-Fifteenth Century." In *Medieval Spain: Culture, Conflict, and Coexistence*, ed. Roger Collins and Anthony Goodman, 148–59. Basingstoke, 2002.

———. "Rodrigo Sánchez de Arévalo (1404–1470) and His *Compendiosa Historia Hispanica*." *Nottingham Medieval Studies* 4 (1960): 58–80.

Tate, Robert Brian, and Anscari Mundó. "The *Compendiolum* of Alfonso de Palencia: A Humanist Treatise on the Geography of the Iberian Peninsula." *Journal of Medieval and Renaissance Studies* 5 (1975): 253–78.

Toni, Teodoro. "Don Rodrigo Sánchez de Arévalo: Su personalidad y actividades." *Anuario de historia del derecho español* 12 (1935): 97–360.

Toral Peñaranda, Enrique. *Jaén y el condestable Miguel Lucas de Iranzo.* Jaén, 1987.

Torres Fontes, Juan. "El alcalde entre moros y cristianos del reino de Murcia." *Hispania* 20 (1960): 55–80.

———. "El concepto concejil murciano de limosna en el siglo XV." In *A pobreza e a assistência aos pobres na Peni'nsula Ibe'rica durante a Idade Me'dia: Actas das 1as Jornadas Luso-Espanholas de Histo'ria Medieval, 25–30 de setembro de 1972,* 2:839–72. Lisbon, 1973.

———. "Los condestables de Castilla en la Edad Media." *Anuario de historia del derecho español* 41 (1971): 57–112.

———. "Los cultivos murcianos en el siglo XV." *Murgetana* 37 (1971): 89–96.

———. "Don Fernando de Antequera y la romántica caballeresco." *MMM* 5 (1980): 83–120.

———. *Don Pedro Fajardo: adelantado mayor del reino de Navarra.* Murcia. 1953.

———. "Estampas de la vida murciana en la época de los reyes católicos: El pendón de la ciudad." *Murgetana* 13 (1960): 47–72.

———. *Fajardo el Bravo.* Murcia, 2001.

———. "Los Fajardo en los siglos XIV y XV." *MMM* 4 (1978): 108–76.

———. "La guerra de Granada: La documentación de los archivos murcianos." In Torres Fontes, *La frontera murciano-granadina,* 489–502. Murcia, 2003.

———. "La incorporación a la caballería de los judíos murcianos en el s. XV." *Murgetana* 27 (1967): 5–14.

———. *Instituciones y sociedad en la frontera murciano-granadina.* Murcia, 2004.

———. "La judería murciana en la época de los Reyes Católicos." *Espacio, Tiempo y Forma* ser. 3, *Historia Medieval* 6 (1993): 177–228.

———. "Los judíos murcianos a fines del siglo XIV y comienzos del XV." *MMM* 8 (1981): 55–117.

———. "Los judíos murcianos en el siglo XIII." *Murgetana* 16 (1962): 5–20.

———. "Moros, judíos y conversos en la regencia de don Fernando de Antequera." *CHE* 31–32 (1960): 60–97.

———. "Los mudéjares murcianos: Economía y sociedad." In *Actas del IV Simposio Internacional de Mudejarismo: Economía,* 365–94. Teruel, 1993.

———. "Los mudéjares murcianos en la Edad Media." In *Actas del III Simposio Internacional de Mudejarismo,* 55–66. Teruel, 1986.

———. "Murcia y Don Juan Manuel: Tensiones y conflictos." In *Don Juan Manuel: VII centenario,* 353–83. Murcia, 1982.

———. "La puerta de la traición." *Murgetana* 37 (1971): 83–88.

———. *El Regadío murciano en la primera mitad del siglo XIV.* Murcia, 1975.

———. "Relaciones comerciales entre los reinos de Mallorca y Murcia en el siglo XIV." *Murgetana* 36 (1971): 5–20.

———. *Xiquena, castillo de la frontera.* Murcia, 1960.

Torroja Menéndez, Carmen, and María Rivas Palá. *Teatro en Toledo en el siglo XV: 'Auto de la Pasión' de Alonso del Campo.* Madrid, 1977.

Trame, Richard H. *Rodrigo Sánchez de Arévalo, 1404–1470: Spanish Diplomat and Champion of the Papacy.* Washington, D.C., 1958.

Turner, Frederick Jackson. "The Significance of the Frontier in American History." In Turner, *The Frontier in American History*, 1–38. New York, 1920.

Valdeón, Julio. *Los conflictos sociales en el reino de Castilla en los siglos XIV y XV.* Madrid, 1975.

Vauchez, André, *The Laity in the Middle Ages: Religious Beliefs and Devotional Practices.* South Bend, Ind., 1993.

Veas Arteseros, Francisco. "Dinámica del concejo de Murcia (1420–1440): Los regidores." *MMM* 9 (1982): 87–117.

———. *Los judíos de Lorca en la Baja Edad Media.* Murcia, 1992.

———. "Lorca, base militar murciana frente a Granada en el reinado de Juan II (1406–1454)." *MMM* 5 (1980): 159–88.

Veas Arteseros, María del Carmen. *Mudéjares murcianos: Un modelo de crisis social (s. XIII–XV).* Cartagena, 1992.

Velázquez Campo, Lorenzo. "Rodrigo Sánchez de Arévalo." In *La filosofía española en Castilla y León: De los orígenes al Siglo de Oro*, ed. Maximiliano Fartos Martínez, 121–36. Valladolid, 1997.

Very, Francis. "A Fifteenth-Century Spanish Easter Egg Combat and Some Parallels." *Romance Notes* 4 (1962): 66–69.

Vincent, Catherine. *Les confréries médiévales dans le Royaume de France, XIII–XVe siècle.* Paris, 1994.

Walters, Barbara R., Vincent Corrigan, and Peter T. Ricketts. *The Feast of Corpus Christi.* University Park, Pa., 2006.

Webster, Susan Verdi. *Art and Ritual in Golden-Age Spain: Sevillian Confraternities and the Processional Sculpture of Holy Week.* Princeton, N.J., 1998.

Weissberger, Barbara. "'¡A tierra, puto!' Alfonso de Palencia's Discourse of Effeminacy." In *Queer Iberia: Sexualities, Cultures, and Crossings from the Middle Ages to the Renaissance*, ed. Josiah Blackmore and Gregory S. Hutcheson, 291–324. Durham, N.C., 1999.

———. *Isabel Rules: Constructing Queenship, Wielding Power.* Minneapolis, 2004.

Wolff, Philippe. "The 1391 Pogrom in Spain: Social Crisis or Not?" *Past and Present* 50 (1971): 4–18.

Yarza Luazes, Joaquín. *Los Reyes Católicos: Paisaje artístico de una monarquía.* Madrid, 1993.

Yovel, Yirmiyahu. "Converso Dualities in the First Generation: The 'Cancioneros'." *Jewish Social Studies* n.s. 4 (1998): 1–28.

accommodation. *See* coexistence, religious

Acuña, Alfonso Vázquez de, 100

Aguayo, Ferrán Ruiz de, 123

Aguayo, Pedro de, 108

Aguilar, Alonso de: capture of Alhama, 138; Christians, Old and, 124; converts and, 123–26, 132, 133, 170; Enrique IV and, 125; Iranzo, Miguel Lucas de and, 89; Montoro, Antón de and, 110, 135; political influence of, 113–14; religious violence and, 108–9, 127, 128; Rodríguez, Alonso and, 108, 128, 203n56

Alcalá la Real, 19, 64

Alcázar Viejo (castle in Córdoba), 108, 115, 119

Alexandria Crusade, 171–72

Alfahar, David Aben, 142

Alfonso X, 13–14, 15f2, 36, 160

Alfonso XI, 3, 32, 36

Alfonso XII, 27, 38. *See also* Farce of Ávila

'Ali, Abū al-Hasan, 18, 19, 104, 138

ambivalence. *See* amiable enmity; religious coexistence

amiable enmity: audiences and, 34; Christians, Old and, 111; cities and, 55–56; civic spaces and, 78; conquest of Granada and, 138, 168; Corpus Christi and, 140, 167; defined, 9, 13, 21, 180n23; Iranzo, Miguel Lucas de and, 74, 81, 92, 96; Mediterranean, 172; stability and, 169; tournaments and, 43; visiting preachers and, 48. *See also* coexistence, religious

Antequera, Fernando de. *See* Fernando I (de Antequera)

Apocalypse, 128–29, 143

architects, 71, 72

architecture: Christian, 71–72; ephemeral, 22–23, 55, 71, 75–78, 95f3, 101, 109; Iranzo, Miguel Lucas de and, 72–74; Jaén, 82, 90;

meanings and, 22, 71, 72–73; Muslim, 60–61, 72, 119; social divides and, 115. *See also* civic spaces

Arévalo, Rodrigo Sánchez de: church spectacles and, 49; military forces and, 55–56; Muslim architecture and, 60–61; nature of cities and, 55–57; Palencia, Alfonso de and, 59; readership of, 61; tournaments and, 46–47; virtues and, 39–40, 41, 43, 81

associations, communal: civic spaces and, 112, 134; creation of, 28, 36, 69–71, 166; ephemeral architecture and, 78; violence, religious and, 110. *See also* civic spaces; commoners

audiences: amiable enmity and, 34; complexity of, 30, 36–37; ephemeral architecture and, 22, 75–78, 95f3; experiences of, 29–31; Farce of Ávila and, 27–28, 29, 32–37; Fernando I (de Antequera) and, 51; influence of, 37; Iranzo, Miguel Lucas de and, 81; organization of, 75–78, 95f3; overview, 22; participation by, 27–29, 31–32; prompts to aid, 31–32; responses of, 29, 32–37, 37–38, 50–51, 169; social divides and, 74–78; tournaments and, 30, 50–51; violence, religious and, 111

Baeza, Francisco Sánchez de, 20

banners, 3, 32

banquets: Corpus Christi, 145–46, 155, 158; Easter, 91; Iranzo, Miguel Lucas de and, 52, 53; tournaments and, 50, 93, 94

Barcelona, 59, 60

barricades, 22, 55, 77–78, 95f3

Benavides, Juan de, 147

Bernáldez, Andrés, 129

Bhabha, Homi, 12, 13

Black Legend, 7–8. *See also* Edict of Expulsion; Inquisition

Bobadilla, Francisco de, 19
borderlands: defined, 4, 7, 12, 13; overview,
    10–11; use of term, 180n22. *See also* amiable
    enmity; civic spaces; coexistence, religious
Bouillon, Godfrey de, 16
boundaries: anxieties over, 169, 172, 173; civic
    spaces and, 66–71; Jews and, 143; religious
    communities and, 7, 10, 14, 36, 51, 105;
    sexual, 130
bullfights, 49, 52, 65, 77, 145, 159

caballeros de cuantía: charity of, 118; Córdoba
    and, 113, 114; elites and, 38–39, 113, 114; Jaén
    and, 19; obligations of, 45, 56, 140, 140–41;
    political power of, 112, 114, 132; romances
    and, 41, 183n30; tournaments and, 38–39,
    43; use of term, 182n19. *See also* knights;
    tournaments
Cabra. *See* Córdoba, Diego Fernández de
Caliphate of Córdoba, 10
Cambil, 18, 19, 20, 100
Cantar de los Comendadores de Córdoba,
    65–66
Cantar de mio Cid, 87
Cantigas de Santa Maria, 13–14, 15f2, 160,
    162f5
Carnival, 37, 49, 100–101, 110, 159
Carrasco, Rafael, 122
Carriazo, Juan de Mata, 20, 21
Cartagena, Alfonso de, 44–48, 49, 59, 81, 129
castles. *See specific names of castles*
Castro, Américo, 13, 175
cathedrals. *See specific names of cathedrals*
Charlemagne, 16
Chincoya, 13–14, 15f2
Christians, New. *See* converts
Christians, Old: architecture and, 71–72;
    Iberia and, 10–11; political alliances of, 125;
    profit from violence by, 132. *See also*
    amiable enmity; coexistence, religious;
    Cofradía de la Caridad; converts; war, holy
churches: converts and, 130; Córdoba and, 71;
    Cyprus, 171; Iranzo, Miguel Lucas de and,
    91; Murcia, 149; processions and, 68, 125;
    styles of, 71. *See also specific names of*
    churches
Cid, the: ideal of, 16, 43; Iranzo, Miguel Lucas
    de and, 34, 87, 89
cities, 53–60, 61. *See also* civic spaces; *specific*
    names of cities

civic spaces, 52–78; access to, 67–68, 74–78,
    116; ancient versus modern, 59–60; associa-
    tions, communal and, 112, 134; associations
    and, 69–71; audience responses and, 54–55;
    biased views of, 65–67; boundaries in,
    66–71; Córdoba and, 115–20; ephemeral
    architecture and, 55; inverted use of, 53;
    Jaén, 52–53; marketplaces, 65, 67–69, 74;
    meanings and, 22, 54–55, 69–78, 78;
    natural environments and, 55–58; neigh-
    borhoods and, 54–55, 62–65, 63m2, 67, 68,
    115–16; overview, 22, 78; *Retrato de la*
    Lozana andaluza (Delicado) and, 62–67,
    75; social divides and, 74–78, 115; transfor-
    mation of, 72; violence, religious and, 112.
    See also architecture; cities
clergy: converted, 123; Córdoba and, 116, 118;
    Corpus Christi and, 149; elites and, 113;
    Jewish processions and, 4–5; overview, 22;
    restrictions on, 49, 143; secular festivals
    and, 48–50; segregation of, 66–67, 118
coexistence, religious: anxieties over, 4–6,
    13–15; breakdown of, 6–8, 167, 169–70;
    Cyprus, 170–72; frontier, concept of, 173;
    Iranzo, Miguel Lucas de and, 70–71,
    82–83, 96–97; irrelevance of, 138, 167;
    Mediterranean, 170, 172; overview, 5–7,
    12–14, 17–18, 21, 24, 169; pageantry and,
    173; persistence of, 168–69. *See also* amiable
    enmity; converts; violence, religious
Cofradía de la Caridad: overview, 124–26;
    status of, 118; violence, religious and, 107,
    110, 124–27, 132–33
Colónia, Simon de, 72
commoners: access to civic spaces, 74–78;
    civic corporations of, 117–18; elites and,
    6–7, 28, 66–67, 83; meanings of spectacles
    and, 34, 50–51; military obligations of, 140;
    overview, 22; raiding and, 20–21; social
    divides and, 74–78; tournaments and, 93;
    violence, religious and, 23. *See also* associa-
    tions, communal; audiences; *caballeros de*
    cuantía; Cofradía de la Caridad; Iranzo,
    Miguel Lucas de
concejos (municipal councils): church spec-
    tacles and, 47–48; Córdoba and, 116, 119;
    Corpus Christi and, 145–48, 149, 150,
    157–58; legislation of morality, 143–44;
    Murcia, 76–77, 139, 140, 142; war with
    Granada and, 138–39
conversion: as compromise, 83, 96–97, 98, 99,
    102–3, 106; to Islam, 4, 100; of Jews, 120;

legal approaches to, 144; of Muslims, 6, 82, 93, 119

converts: Aguilar, Alonso de and, 123–26; Apocalypse and, 128–29; churches of, 130; Córdoba and, 64–65; criminalization of, 122, 123; discrimination against, 123, 132; distrust of, 120–22, 124–25, 127, 133–36; Easter and, 127–29; Edict of Expulsion and, 165; emigration by, 109, 132; Ferrer, Vincent and, 143–44; Inquisition and, 122, 122–23, 168; integration of, 120; Iranzo, Miguel Lucas de and, 82, 103–4; Jaén, 103; looting of, 104, 105, 132; Murcia and, 142; neighborhoods and, 64–65, 133; overview, 6–7, 23; plays about, 93; racial pride of, 129–30, 131–32; Segovia and, 134–35; segregation of, 129, 130; self-defense by, 108; spying by, 17–18; support for, 104–5; Toledo and, 122, 135, 136; violence against, 104–5, 107–12, 122, 123, 127, 130–31; war with Granada and, 139. *See also* Christians, Old; coexistence, religious; violence, religious

convivencia. *See* coexistence, religious

Córdoba, 107–36; Alcázar Viejo (castle in Córdoba), 108, 115, 119; boundaries in, 66–71; Caliphate of, 10; Calle de la Feria, 62–64, 65, 67, 68; church of San Francisco, 107–8; civic spaces of, 60, 115, 115–20; clergy of, 116, 118; Cofradía de la Caridad, 124–26; *concejos* (municipal councils), 116, 119; converts in, 64–65; Great Mosque of, 60, 120; guilds and cofraternities of, 117–18; *hidalgos* in, 114, 116–17; Inquisition in, 122–23; Jews of, 60, 64, 118, 119, 120, 135–36; markets of, 65; Monastery of San Pedro el Real, 107–8, 124; Muslims of, 118–20, 136; neighborhoods of, 62–65, 67, 68, 109, 115–16; overview, 6, 23, 111–12; political structure of, 112–15; politics of, 114–15; *Retrato de la Lozana andaluza* (Delicado) and, 62–67; social divides of, 66–67, 115–20, 134; violence, religious, 107–12; virtues of, 60. *See also* converts; violence, religious; *specific names of populations*

Córdoba, Diego Fernández de, 18, 114, 124, 126

Córdoba, Gonzalo Fernández de, 132

Córdoba, Jerónimo of, 57

Córdoba, Luis de, 132

Córdoba y Solier, Fernando Alonso, 65–66, 124

Corpus Christi: Christian society and, 145, 148; conquest and, 139; conquest of Málaga and, 158–59; control of, 28; elites and, 150; *entremeses* (skits), 76; expenses of, 145–48, 158, 163; fall of Granada and, 159–60; Jews and, 146, 152–58, 159, 160, 170; *juegos de Corpus*, 139, 157–58; Murcia and, 6, 76–77; Muslims and, 154–58, 159, 160, 166–67, 170; overview, 24, 38, 145–46; plays, 148, 149–54, 158–59, 163, 165–67; processions, 145, 146, 148–49; significance of, 148–49; taxes and, 146, 158, 163; violence portrayed in, 152–53; war, holy and, 157–58. *See also* festivals

Corte, Juan de la, 95f3

Crónica anónima, 87

Cyprus, 170–72

De perfectione militaris triumphi (Palencia), 58, 59

Delicado, Francisco, 62, 64, 65, 66–67

Descriptio cordubae (Jerónimo of Córdoba), 57

Doctrinal de los caballeros (Cartagena), 44, 45

Easter, 91, 110, 127–29

Edict of Expulsion, 4–5, 6, 109, 164–65

Edwards, John, 135

elites: access to civic spaces, 74–78; *caballeros de cuantía* and, 38–39, 113, 114; central authority and, 137; civic spaces and, 69, 115; commoners and, 6–7, 28, 66–67, 83; control of spectacles, 22, 28, 34–35, 54–55, 75, 169; Córdoba and, 111–12; Corpus Christi and, 150; legitimacy of, 39–40, 71, 75; Muslims and, 119; political power of, 114–15; reconquest and, 174; social divides and, 74–78; social structures and, 51; violence, religious and, 132; virtues, knightly and, 39–41; war with Granada, 138–39

England, 38, 45, 151–52, 154

Enrique II, 39

Enrique IV: Acuña, Alfonso Vázquez de and, 100; Córdoba, Jerónimo of and, 57; Farce of Ávila and, 22, 27, 32–33; favoritism of, 85, 87–88, 194n6; funeral rites of, 33; Iranzo, Miguel Lucas de and, 83–86, 125; legitimacy of, 33; misrule of, 170; Moorish tastes of, 73, 105, 174; Muslims and, 136;

Enrique IV (*continued*)
overview, 8–9; Pacheco, Juan, Marquis of
Villena and, 194–95n16; religious violence
and, 122; social anxieties and, 9; succession
concerns, 124–25; truces and, 83, 89, 92,
92–93, 137; visit to Jaén, 102; war, holy and,
137. *See also* Farce of Ávila
entremeses (skits), 41–42, 44, 49, 50, 73, 76.
See also theater
Escavias, Pedro de, 104

Fajardo, Pedro, 8, 125, 140, 150, 157
Farce of Ávila: archetypes in, 43; audiences
and, 27–28, 29, 32–37, 50–51; overview, 22,
27; political significance of, 38; violence,
religious and, 103
Fernando I (de Antequera), 1–4, 5, 21, 27, 51
Fernando II, 9, 23–24, 72, 125, 137, 138, 164
Fernando III, 1, 2, 10, 15
Ferrari, Antonio, 4–5
Ferrer, Vincent, 47–48, 143–44, 165
festivals: civic spaces and, 68, 69; clergy and,
48–50; diversity within, 28, 35–37; elites
and, 75; enjoyment of, 51; expenses of, 94;
Iranzo, Miguel Lucas de and, 5, 94, 97–99;
Luna, Alvaro de, 42; sixteenth century, 174;
three kinds of, 36; wars and, 138–39. *See
also* Corpus Christi
Fiesta in the Plaza Mayor (Corte), 95f3
Florence, 58, 60, 61
Fonseca, Juan Rodríguez de, 66–67
frontier, concept of, 9–13, 173

game of canes (*juegos de cañas*), 93, 94, 95f3,
96, 101
games of Corpus Christi (*juegos de Corpus*),
139
games of ridicule (*juegos de escarnio*), 49–50
García, Michel, 104
Girón, Pedro, 89
González, Fernán, 16, 43
Granada: ambivalence toward, 5–6; conquests
of, 8, 139, 167, 168; fall of, 174; Fernando I
(de Antequera) and, 1, 2–3; Fernando III
and, 10; incitement of war against, 137;
overview, 10–13, 24; wars with, 3, 9,
138–40, 146. *See also* amiable enmity; coexistence, religious; Iranzo, Miguel Lucas de;
Muslims; war, holy
Great Mosque of Córdoba, 60, 120
Guadix, 19

Guas, Juan, 72
Guzmán, Fernán Pérez de, 1

Hacén, Mulay. *See* 'Ali, Abū al-Hasan
Harris, Max, 174
Hechos del condestable (chronicle): audiences
in, 34, 35; authorship of, 195n20; Iranzo,
Miguel Lucas de, 34, 87, 90, 103–4, 195n20;
Magi play, 98–99; military ideals in, 93;
Muslim emissaries in, 100–102
hidalgos, 41, 84, 113–14, 116–17, 118. *See also*
elites; knights; tournaments
holy war. *See* war, holy
Huelma, 18–19
Huizinga, Johan, 40, 43
humanism, 55, 61–62, 75
Hurtado, Alonso, 147, 159
Hurtado, Antonio, 77

Image of the City (Lynch), 68
Inquisition: Córdoba and, 122–23; effectiveness of, 138; establishment of, 106, 122,
138; overview, 6, 24, 109; protests against,
122, 202n40; significance of, 8. *See also*
Black Legend
Iranzo, Miguel Lucas de, 81–106; Aguilar,
Alonso de and, 89; amiable enmity and, 74,
81, 92, 96; architecture and, 72–74; assassination plot against, 103–4; atrocities and,
17; audiences and, 51, 81; birth of his son,
52–53, 75, 78; boundary marking by, 69–71;
building by, 90; campaigns by, 84–85, 92,
94, 99–100, 137; Christmas tournament,
93–94, 96–99; Cid, the and, 34, 87, 89;
coexistence, religious and, 70–71, 82–83,
92, 96–97, 98, 102–3, 105–6; converts and,
82, 103–4; death of, 105; departure from
court, 86–88, 195n24; Enrique IV and,
83–86, 125; *Hechos del condestable* and, 34,
87, 90, 103–4, 195n20; intentions of, 34–35,
54; legitimacy of, 75, 85, 90–91; military
skill of, 89–90; Moorish tastes of, 82, 92,
96, 97, 102, 106; Muslims and, 82,
100–102; overview, 5–6, 8, 16–17, 81–83,
105–6, 170; Pacheco, Juan, Marquis of
Villena and, 84, 86, 103–4; palace of,
72–74, 88; popular opinion and, 75, 83, 90,
102, 106; public appearances by, 69–71,
75–76, 92; public ceremony and, 85, 90,
106; taxes and, 94, 99; theater and, 81; tournaments and, 43–44, 91, 93–94, 96–99;

trade and, 93, 99; truces and, 83, 89, 92–93, 99–100; virtues, knightly and, 81, 82; war, holy and, 82, 83, 85, 88–89, 91, 106, 196n32; wedding of, 73. *See also* Jaén

Isabel I: Jews and, 142, 164; Muslims and, 119; overview, 9, 23–24; San Juan de los Reyes (church), 72; support for, 125, 134; war, holy and, 137

Islam, conversions to, 4, 100

Israel, Gabriel, 142

Italy, 57, 58, 59–67, 109

Jaén: administration of, 90; architecture, 82, 90; boundary marking, 69–71; Chincoya and, 13–14; civic spaces and, 52–53; elites of, 34–35; Jews of, 103; loyalty to crown, 125; military forces of, 19–20, 82, 89, 100; neighborhoods of, 54–55; overview, 23, 105–6; tensions in, 94; tournaments in, 43; trade, 82; truces and, 18–19; wars and, 82, 89–90. *See also* Iranzo, Miguel Lucas de

Jerónimo of Córdoba, 60–62, 64–65, 66, 75, 119

Jews: conversion of, 120; as converts, 109–10, 120–22; Córdoba and, 60, 64, 118, 119, 120, 135–36; Corpus Christi and, 152–58, 166–67; decline of, 144–45; Easter and, 127–29; Edict of Expulsion, 164–65, 168; Inquisition and, 122–23; Jaén, 103; military obligations of, 140; Murcia and, 139–40, 141, 142–43, 157; overview, 6–7, 8, 23–24; participation by, 139; processions and, 4–5; racial pride of, 129–30; restrictions on, 142–43, 144, 154–56; scapegoating of, 109; segregation of, 118, 130, 142–43, 144, 145; taxes and, 163–64; violence against, 4, 5, 109, 120. *See also* coexistence, religious; converts; Muslims

Juan II, 8, 41–42, 43, 66, 84, 112, 114

juegos de cañas (game of canes), 77, 93, 94, 95f3, 96, 101

juegos de Corpus, 139

juegos de escarnio (games of ridicule), 49–50

knights: chivalry, ideals of, 44; civic politics and, 114; costumed, 93, 97–98, 102; *hidalgos*, 41, 84, 113–14, 116–17, 118; virtues, 39–41, 42–43, 81, 82. See also *caballeros de cuantía*; elites; tournaments

leisure, 48, 54, 56, 59

letrados, 38–39

Linehan, Peter, 13

Loarre, 71–72

Lorca, 142

Lorca, Lope Alonso de, 147–48

Lucero, Diego Rodríguez, 123

Luna, Alvaro de, 41–42, 86

Lynch, Kevin, 68, 69

Mackay, Angus, 32, 33, 35, 94, 127

Magi plays, 93, 97–98, 197n53

Málaga, 17, 24, 72, 139, 158, 167

Mata Carriazo, Juan de, 20

memory, communal. *See* associations, communal

Mendoza, Pedro González de, 122

merchants. *See* commoners; trade

Merlo, Diego de, 138

Mexía, Fernán, 103–4

Miguel Lucas. *See* Iranzo, Miguel Lucas de

military forces: Arévala, Rodrigo Sánchez de and, 55–56; Córdoba, 113; Jaén, 19–20, 82, 89, 100; legitimacy of elites and, 75; participation in, 140–41; tournaments and, 38–39

minorities, religious: Murcia, 139–40, 141–45, 152–58, 165–67; overview, 8, 9; popular opinion and, 6–7, 9, 173–74; processions and, 159, 160, 162, 166–67; taxes and, 163–64. *See also* converts; Jews; Muslims

Mirabilis urbis Romae, 55

Monastery of San Pedro el Real, 107–8, 124

Montoro, Antón de, 110–11, 121–22, 129, 130–31, 135, 202n35

Moorish, use of term, 192n67

Moorish tastes: of Enrique IV, 73, 105, 174; of Iranzo, Miguel Lucas de, 82, 92, 96, 97, 102, 106

Moors. *See* Muslims

Muhammad, Prophet, 93, 96, 160

municipal councils. See *concejos* (municipal councils)

Murcia, 137–67; access to civic spaces, 76–78; Aragón and, 141; Arrixaca, 141, 160, 162, 163; Calle de la Trapería, 76–77, 146, 149–50; commemorative galas in, 139; *concejos* (municipal councils), 76–77, 139, 140, 142; demographics of, 141; Edict of Expulsion and, 165; festive culture of, 49–50; Granada and, 165; loyalty to crown, 125; map of, 76m3; military forces and, 147; overview, 23, 24, 139; religious minorities in, 6, 139–40, 141–45, 152–58, 165–67; trade

Murcia (*continued*)
    and, 141. *See also* Corpus Christi; *specific
    names of populations*
Muslims: architecture of, 60–61, 72, 119;
    conversion of, 6, 82, 93, 119; converts to
    Islam, 4, 100; Córdoba and, 118–20, 136;
    Corpus Christi and, 154–58, 159, 160,
    166–67, 170; decline of, 144–45; economic
    relevance of, 24; emigration by, 164; emis-
    saries, 100–102; expulsion of, 21, 118,
    119–20; influence of, 96, 174–75; intol-
    erance of, 127, 136; Iranzo, Miguel Lucas de
    and, 82, 92–94; Málaga and, 158; military
    obligations of, 140; Murcia and, 139–40,
    141–45, 160–65; musicians, 155, 162–63;
    overview, 6–7, 8, 23–24; participation by,
    139; persistence of, 168–69; restrictions on,
    143, 144, 154–56, 168; segregation of, 119,
    143, 144, 145; taxes and, 163–64; tourna-
    ments and, 93–94; Virgin Mary and, 160.
    See also amiable enmity; coexistence, reli-
    gious; converts; Granada; war, holy

Native Americans, 8, 24
Nicholas V (pope), 4–5
Nirenberg, David, 8

Osorio, García Enriquez, 4
Ottoman Turks, 45

Pacheco, Juan, Marquis of Villena: converts
    and, 125, 129; Enrique IV and, 88, 194–
    95n16; Iranzo, Miguel Lucas de and, 84, 86,
    103–4; master of Santiago, 125, 197n53;
    overview, 170; violence, religious and,
    134–35
pageantry, 3, 6, 7, 9, 21, 55, 173. *See also specific
    names of events; specific types of pageantry*
Palazol, Alfonso de, 163
Palencia, Alfonso de: audiences and, 35; civic
    spaces and, 69; converts and, 124, 125–26,
    128–29; Enrique IV and, 194n6; environ-
    ments of cities, 57–58, 61; Farce of Ávila
    account, 32–33; humanism of, 61, 75;
    Iranzo, Miguel Lucas de, 89–91; Iranzo,
    Miguel Lucas de and, 88, 104; Italy and, 61;
    looting and, 132; military discipline and, 58;
    Pacheco, Juan, Marquis of Villena and, 86,
    134–35; readership of, 61; violence, reli-
    gious, 108, 110, 127; violence, sexual, 131;
    war, holy and, 137

participants. *See* audiences
Partidas, 48, 55
Payen, Jean-Charles, 54
peasants. *See* commoners
Peter I of Cyprus, 171
physical insecurity: amiable enmity and, 34,
    43; influence of, 170; Murcia and, 140;
    overview, 4, 5, 15, 18
plague, 90, 109, 141, 171
politics, 38, 112–15, 125, 132, 173–74
Ponce de León, Rodrigo, 2, 16–18, 137, 138
popular opinion: Iranzo, Miguel Lucas de
    and, 75, 83, 90, 102, 106; minorities, reli-
    gious and, 6–7, 9, 173–74
Portugal, 9, 18, 72, 128, 137
preaching, public, 47–48
Primera crónica general, 59
processions: boundaries and, 68; churches
    and, 68, 125; civic spaces and, 69; Cofradía
    de la Caridad, 125, 126; Corpus Christi, 145,
    146, 147, 148–49; egalitarian, 53; Jewish,
    4–5; Magi plays, 97–98; neighborhoods
    and, 53; plague and, 4–5, 171–72; religious
    minorities in, 159, 160, 162, 166–67; tour-
    naments, 93–94; violence incited by, 6,
    107–8, 110, 134
Pulgar, Hernando del, 122, 202n40

Ramiro I, 45
reconquest: Cartagena, Alfonso de and, 45;
    elites and, 174; Fernando III and, 1;
    overview, 10; *reconquista* ideology, 78, 94,
    111, 160, 162; use of term, 178n16. *See also*
    war, holy
religious coexistence. *See* coexistence,
    religious
Retrato de la Lozana andaluza (Delicado),
    62–67, 69, 75
Rivas, Lope de, 148
Rodríguez, Alonso, 107–8, 110, 124, 126–27,
    127, 128, 132
Rome, 46, 58, 59–60, 61, 62–67, 90
Ronda, 138, 158, 166, 167

San Francisco, church of, 107–8
San Juan de los Reyes (church), 72, 73
San Pedro at Loarre (church), 71–72
Sánchez-Albornoz, Claudio, 174
Sancho Ramírez (king), 71, 72
Santa María, Pablo de, 47–48, 143
Santiago, 45, 102

Santiago, Master of the Order of, 86–87, 98, 101, 103, 125

Segovia, 134–35

Seville: loyalty to crown, 125; overview, 1, 3, 4, 5; religious violence in, 122; trade and, 3, 59; virtues of, 60

sexual issues, 109, 130–31

Sixtus IV, 16

spectacles. *See specific components of spectacles; specific names of spectacles; specific types of spectacle*

spectators. *See* audiences

Stern, Charlotte, 167

structures. *See* architecture

Suma de la política (Arévalo), 39, 61

sword of Fernando III, 1–2, f1, 3

Tate, Robert Brian, 61

taxes: Corpus Christi, 146, 158, 163; Iranzo, Miguel Lucas de and, 94, 99; religious minorities and, 163–64; trade and, 141

theater: architecture and, 73–74; cities and, 54; Corpus Christi plays, 148, 149–54, 158–59, 163; *entremeses* (skits), 41–42, 44, 49, 50, 73, 76; Iranzo, Miguel Lucas de and, 81; Magi plays, 93, 97–98, 197n53; political power of, 173–74. *See also* architecture, ephemeral; Corpus Christi; tournaments

Thomas, Peter, 171–72

Toledo, 72, 120, 122, 135–36, 138, 143, 151

Torreblanca, Pedro de, 107–8, 127

Torres, Teresa de, 73, 88, 97, 100

Torres Fontes, Juan, 88

tournaments: amiable enmity and, 43; Arévalo, Rodrigo Sánchez de and, 46–47, 56; audiences and, 30, 50–51; burlesque, 101, 102; clergy and, 48–50; competing groups and, 38–39; contexts for, 37–47; demilitarized, 41–42; Easter, 91; Iranzo, Miguel Lucas de and, 43–44, 91, 93–94, 96–99; *juegos de cañas* (game of canes), 77, 93, 94, 95f3, 96, 101; justifications for, 44, 46–47; literary debates and, 38; mock battles, 91, 98, 101, 102; opposition to, 44–46; overview, 30; physical insecurity and, 43; responses to, 37; romances and, 41; sixteenth century, 174; status and, 42–43; theater and, 41, 41–42, 97–98, 183n31; virtues and, 39–41, 42–43. *See also caballeros de cuantía*; knights

trade: amiable enmity and, 5, 74; fall of Granada and, 159; guilds and cofraternities, 117–18; Iranzo, Miguel Lucas de, 93, 99; Jaén and, 19, 82, 94, 103, 105, 106; markets, 67–69; Murcia and, 139, 141; *Retrato de la Lozana andaluza* (Delicado) and, 65; Seville and, 3, 59; taxes and, 141; truces and, 3, 19; wars and, 20, 83

trade guilds, 111, 115, 117–18

Trastámara dynasty, 39

truces: effectiveness of, 180n38; Enrique IV and, 89, 137; Iranzo, Miguel Lucas de and, 83, 89, 92–93, 99–100; motivations for, 20; overview, 15–16, 18–20. *See also* war, holy

Turner, Frederick Jackson, 10, 11–12

Valdés, Francisco de, 87–88

Valera, Diego de, 39–40, 43, 81, 124, 125–26, 129

Vergel de los príncipes (Arévalo), 46, 61

Viedma, Diego de, 19

Villena, Juan Pacheco. *See* Pacheco, Juan, Marquis of Villena

violence, religious: civic spaces and, 112; Cofradía de la Caridad and, 107, 110, 124–27, 132–33; converts and, 104–5, 107–12, 122, 123, 127, 130–31; Córdoba, 107–12; Corpus Christi plays and, 152–53; motivations for, 8, 21, 109–12, 123–36; against peers, 107–8; processions and, 6, 107–8, 110, 134; as public performance, 111; sexual, 109, 130–31; Virgin Mary and, 6, 23, 107, 127, 133

Virgin Mary: Corpus Christi and, 160; Fernando I (de Antequera) and, 1, 2; Magi play, 97; Muslims and, 160; Ponce de León, Rodrigo and, 16–17; processions, 107, 160; statues, 14, 15f2; violence and, 6, 23, 107, 127, 133; Virgin of the Arrixaca, 160, 161f4, 162f5; visions of, 16–17

virtues, knightly, 39–41, 42–43, 81, 82

war, holy: Apocalypse and, 128; architecture and, 71–72; constraints on, 20–21; fear of, 18–20; identity and, 21; Málaga and, 158; overview, 16–17; promotion of, 72. *See also* truces

wars: Corpus Christi and, 146; Granada, 138–140, 146; Portugal, 137. *See also* Granada

Yehuda, 157

ACKNOWLEDGMENTS

This book, like many, began modestly enough, with questions about how spectators understood and experienced Miguel Lucas de Iranzo's grand pageants in 1460s Jaén. But it subsequently went through several iterations, a process that has depended in large part on the generous contributions of a number of people. It is my pleasure to have the opportunity to thank at least some of them here.

In particular, Amy Remensnyder gave freely of her time while providing the inspiration, advice, and criticism that helped transform an inchoate set of ideas into an intelligible argument. Sheila Bonde encouraged me to expand my methodological approach and to ask new kinds of questions of my sources, always keeping in mind the material and spatial aspects of the past that do not come across in written documents. Tara Nummedal's insightful comments on my drafts have helped me to clarify my arguments and to ensure that I never lose sight of the forest for the trees.

Several other scholars have read excerpts, offered ideas, and suggested sources. I would like to thank, among others, James Green, Moshe Sluhovsky, Teofilo Ruiz, Patrick Geary, Nora Berend, Katherine Allen Smith, Julio Hernando, and Alexandra Cuffel. I owe a particular debt of gratitude to the late Olivia Remie Constable. Her careful and perceptive comments on a draft of the entire manuscript allowed me to improve it in innumerable ways. Participants and spectators at a workshop at the University of Bergen's Nordic Center for Medieval Studies, an AHA panel sponsored by the University of California Mediterranean Seminar, and at the Spain-North Africa Project's conference on "Power Relations in the Western Mediterranean" provided further insights and suggestions, while reminding me that there was indeed an audience for this work.

All historians depend on the assistance of librarians and archivists at various institutions. In the United States, Bill Monroe at Brown University's

Rockefeller Library was there as I first began to explore the sources while Alan Unsworth and Alan Lupack at the University of Rochester's Rush Rhees and Robbins Libraries and David Coppen at the Eastman School of Music's Sibley Library all assisted with materials needed for the finishing touches. In Spain, I had the good fortune to meet several knowledgeable archivists who took the time to discuss the project with me. Elena Fontecha at the Archivo Municipal de Jaén provided helpful advice about working with the *Actas capitulares* while introducing me to the work of several local historians. In Córdoba, Alicia Córdoba Deorador and Pilar Sáenz-López introduced me to several collections that proved to be of immense utility. In Murcia, María José Hernández Almela at the Archivo Municipal de Murcia showed me how to navigate the collections while Pepe Vigueras at the Church of San Andrés generously helped me to find illustrations.

None of this would have been possible without the generous financial support provided by Brown University's Department of History, the Cogut Center for the Humanities, Indiana University South Bend, and the University of Rochester. Several other organizations also provided funds that enabled me to travel to Spanish archives. These include the Council for European Studies at Columbia University, the Medieval Academy of America, and the Program for Cultural Cooperation between Spain's Ministry of Culture and United States Universities.

At the University of Pennsylvania Press, I owe sincere thanks to Jerry Singerman, whose patience and thoughtful advice has made the publication process a pleasant and rewarding one. The two anonymous reviewers read my manuscript with great care; their suggestions played no small role in shaping the final version of this book. Needless to say, any errors that remain are my own.

Finally, I would like to thank my family for their support during this long process. My wife Elizabeth and my children Ella, Julia, and Eoin exhibited remarkable patience with my extended research trips and many hours of writing. More important, they served as a constant reminder that this project is but one step on a larger path and that I need to step away from the manuscript from time to time to laugh and love. This work is dedicated to them.